MY WILD LIFE

Jimmy Chipperfield

MY WILD LIFE

FOUNDED 1838

GPPS

G. P. PUTNAM'S SONS   NEW YORK

For
RICHARD
4.6.41–18.4.75

FIRST AMERICAN EDITION 1976

SBN: 399–11616–8

Library of Congress Catalog Card Number: 75–23497

PRINTED IN THE UNITED STATES OF AMERICA

Contents

	LIST OF ILLUSTRATIONS	7
1	Circus Family	9
2	On the Road Again	25
3	Wild Animals	48
4	One-Day Tenting	62
5	Building Up	74
6	Fighter Pilot	82
7	The Big Show	100
8	Casting About	123
9	Animal Catching	148
10	The Idea of the Parks	157
11	The Parks in Action	172
12	Branching Out	185
13	Animal Facts and Figures	195
14	A Family Business	207
	INDEX	213

List of Illustrations

(*between pages* 112 *and* 113)

1   The original James William Chipperfield.
2   My great-great-grandfather James William Chipperfield.
3   My great-grandfather James Chipperfield.
4   My grandfather James Francis Chipperfield.
5   An early poster for the show.
6   Rosie's parents, Captain and Mrs Purchase.
7   My father Richard.
8   The show after the comeback, between the wars.
9   Myself working tigers in the early days.
10 More tiger training.
11 I wrestle Bruni the bear at the London Palladium, 1936.
12 Fighter pilot: Edward Seago's portrait.
13 The Big Show: myself with my brother Dick and comedian Arthur English.
14 The Raluys' human cannonball act.
15 The big wagon where we entertained visitors to the Big Show.
16 A worm's-eye view of the Big Show.
17 The Big Show from the air.
18 In Africa with my son Richard.
19 Among the Tuareg.
20 This was my life – with Eamonn Andrews.
21 The monkey jungle at Longleat.

22 With James the chimpanzee and my daughter Mary.

23 With Suki the tiger.

24 Catching an elephant.

25 A warning to the public: a lion leaps on to a car.

26 Princess Anne visits Blair Drummond.

27 With Lord Bath and the Duke of Bedford.

28 With giraffes at Woburn.

29 A baboon hitches a lift at Blair Drummond.

30 At Woburn, I teach young African elephants 'trunks up'.

31 Richard on safari.

32 Esme, a baby hippo at Longleat.

33 With my grand-daughter Suzanne, and Dandy Lion, a cub.

CHAPTER ONE

Circus Family

I was born in the top bunk of a mahogany wagon during the early hours of 17 July 1912. Our show was pitched in a field outside the Wiltshire village of Corsham, and as it was a lovely summer's night, it was no hardship for my father to sleep out under one of the tent-flaps while the local nurse helped my mother with the birth. Nor was it any novelty for a child to be delivered in the caravan: generations of my ancestors had been born in just these circumstances. Even so, the arrival of a boy provoked a great celebration the next day, and in due course I was christened James Seaton (my mother's maiden name) Methuen, after Lord Methuen, on whose estate our show had been pitched at the time. Soon afterwards another travelling family, who were not blessed with any sons, offered one hundred pounds for me. My father was showing me off to them, and the man said suddenly: 'I could do with that boy.' My parents always joked about it afterwards, but the offer was a serious one – in those days one hundred pounds was a lot of money – and I have often wondered what sort of a life I would have had if my father had given in to temptation.

That, however, was the last thing that he was likely to do, for to him the family was the most important asset in the world. Like his father, grandfather and great-grandfather before him, he had been brought up in a travelling circus that was essentially a family show. Not only did members of the family own the show and run it: they themselves were the clowns, the acrobats and the animal trainers; they built up the tent and pulled it down; they made and painted the ornate façade and even played enough instruments – atrociously, I expect – to form a band. Within the family there were no such words as 'yours' and 'mine'; everything was 'ours', and for a child brought up in this tightly knit circle it was impossible to imagine the existence of another bigger world outside.

Gradually, as I grew older, I became aware of our long history as a circus family stretching back nearly two hundred and fifty years into the dimly remembered past. The first Chipperfield recorded as a showman took a performing bear on to the ice when the Thames froze over in the bitter winter of 1684, and from his time Chipperfields travelled all over the country, at first with little menageries of perhaps a bear and a couple of baboons, sometimes as conjurers or jugglers, but later as compact little circuses with a considerable variety of acts. My great-grandfather, James, who was born in 1824, must have assembled quite a collection of animals, for he established permanent winter quarters in Norwich as a base for his menagerie. Like all the Chipperfields, he was born with excellent balance, and it is said that at the age of sixteen he could simultaneously balance a cartwheel on his chin and a saucer on his nose.

My grandfather – James Francis – further embellished the menagerie with wire-walkers, tumblers and clowns, and by siring a family of nine children ensured that the family circus would flourish in the next generation. It was in the 1890s, when his four sons and five daughters were old enough to take part, but he himself was still in charge, that the show probably reached its zenith.

We, as children, always heard about this as 'the big show', but by the standards we attained later it was still tiny, and relied heavily on domestic animals such as dogs, horses, donkeys and pigs, all of which were cheap to look after. The dogs were the family pets, trained to do simple tricks like walking on their hind legs; the horses and donkeys, besides performing, would walk from one place to the next, or even pull the wagons; and the pigs, as well as making the most of all the scraps, could do apparently quite complicated acts.

Pigs are much more intelligent than most people suppose and can easily be trained. One of the oldest tricks was for a clown to bring a rolled-up carpet into the ring and tell the pig to unroll it: this the animal would proceed to do, pushing along with its snout – and then, having been given a start by its human partner, it would roll the carpet up again. What the audience almost always failed to spot was that the pig had succulent incentives in the form of pieces of food, one in the middle of the roll, and another slipped under the end for the return journey: the animal would snap these up so quickly that they usually disappeared unnoticed.

The pig would also walk round the ring, stop, sit down, lie down and tell fortunes or the time by halting opposite one of the huge cards laid out in the pattern of a clock. The trainer achieved all this by giving the animal cues – and the better the pig, the finer the cues could be. Often a slight movement of the hand would be enough to stop and start it, and my grandfather had one pig whose wits were so acute that it reacted to the clicking of his finger-nails – a noise imperceptible to the audience. Only once did it let him down, when he was invited to demonstrate its prowess in somebody's house, and the ticking of a clock made it impossible for either of them to work.

Another favourite, trained in much the same way, was the fortune-telling pony. Here again the aim of the handler was to make his signals so minute that the horse apparently reacted of its own accord: the best ponies would respond to a fractional inclination of the man's body, a tiny shift of his hand or elbow, or even a sniff – cues so slight that even the most suspicious spectators never picked them up. Thus primed, the pony could easily answer questions or tell the time. 'Is So-and-So here today?' the handler would ask, and in response to an all-but-invisible signal the horse would shake its head. 'Oh,' the man would say. 'Where is he, then? Has he gone to the seaside?' and the horse would nod. For counting or telling the time, the pony would bang its forefoot on a board, stopping at the signal, and it could pick out the girl who was going to get married by stopping opposite her as it galloped round the ring.

Half the fun of the performance was the patter of the handler. If the act was going well he would invite the audience to watch him to see if he gave the pony any cue: of course they saw nothing, and by the end half of them believed that the horse really could understand human speech. No doubt it was an animal of this kind, trained so finely that it would respond to a sniff or a quick intake of breath, that delighted Queen Victoria and her family at Buckingham Palace some time in the 1860s (see the poster reproduced as plate 5). Of course, a pony conditioned to this degree by hundreds of hours of patient instruction was a very valuable creature, and it was looked after with the greatest care; but even so it was a cheap animal to feed, and it obligingly transported itself from one pitch to the next.

Clowning was another field in which the family specialised. All my immediate ancestors were first-class clowns: they had inherited the mantle of the medieval jesters, and some of the entrées, or sketches, that they handed down from one generation to the next were centuries old. A typical example was the egg entrée, a mixture of slapstick and conjuring in which the Auguste, or coloured clown, was assisted by his partner the White Clown, thin, silent and lugubrious. The act itself was very simple: all the clowns did was to hand each other eggs, breaking one or two on the way, put them into a pan, pour on some petrol, light it, clap on the lid, and from the lid (which had a hidden compartment) produce a live duck or a dove. It was as simple as that. But, as in many other acts, everything depended on the build-up. A good Auguste would have all the children in the audience squealing with anticipation long before anything happened. 'Go on,' he would say to the White Clown. 'Hold it *tighter*. I'm sure you're going to drop it.' And the White Clown would clench the egg in his fist, right in front of his nose, so that when it did eventually break, it would burst all over his face.

In those days the contact between the circus and its audiences was far closer and more physical than anything that survives today. For one thing, there was almost no entertainment available in the country villages, so that the annual visit of the circus was an event tremendously looked forward to. A second reason was that the tent and the audience were relatively small, so that the ringmaster or the clown could easily be heard without a microphone. But perhaps the most important difference was that the members of the circus deliberately involved the audience in the show.

The most spectacular form of audience-participation was the tug-of-war with the elephant. 'Twenty men to pull the elephant!' the ringmaster would announce, and a score of the heaviest locals would line up on the rope, little realising that the elephant would not have the slightest trouble in pulling them flat on their faces. When given the signal, the creature leant back and did just this – but then, outside the tent, someone would rattle a bucket full of apples, and the elephant would trundle out towards the noise, knowing that it signified a snack. The men, not having the wit to let go of the rope, would be dragged head-first out of the arena and covered in mud and cinders – to general confusion and delight. Today, any show that treated its spectators as roughly as that would be inundated by claims for compensation; but in those days no one dreamed of complaining.

Another rough act was wrestling the bear. The bear was well trained and knew the form exactly: even though he wore a muzzle, and so could not bite, he could easily have demolished his human opponents by brute force alone. But generally he was happy enough to play the game, knowing that good performances would bring rewards of sugar. Normally a member of the family wrestled with him as a gladiatorial stunt; but in the villages through which they passed the circus men made a practice of inviting members of the audience to take on the monster as well. First they would find some hulking lout and offer him a small amount of money to have a go. 'You're a big fellow,' they would say, deliberately giving him the wrong advice. '*You* can manage him. *Grab* him hard and *really* throw him about.' The bear, accustomed to meeting only token resistance, would be maddened by the man's clumsy attacks and would hurl him round the ring like a pillow. When he had been thoroughly knocked about, a much smaller local man would come in to take his place – a poor, weedy, little runt of a fellow who (everybody thought) would be butchered in a matter of seconds. He, however, had been armed with lumps of sugar and told what to do. As soon as he grappled with the bear, the animal smelt the sugar and rolled over on his back on the floor, knowing that this manoeuvre would get him a lump – which the man then covertly slipped him.

Another rough act was the Man-Eating Donkey – a jack donkey corned up to make him full of mischief, who was trained to chase the clown and seize hold of him with his teeth. The clown would scream and pretend to run away, and even though he wore specially padded clothes, he some-times got quite badly hurt, for a stallion donkey has a vicious bite. The same donkey would be trained to do one or two simple tricks – for instance, the clown would bet the ringmaster that he couldn't make the donkey go over a jump. The ringmaster would put a little pony over the pole first, and then send the donkey at it, but the donkey did what he was taught to do – to bend his back and slip underneath, making a ridiculous spectacle besides winning the clown his bet.

Another traditional method of involving the audience in the show was the Duck Race, in which one of the clowns conducted a form of Blind Man's Buff. Having found two volunteers, he would blindfold them securely and arm each with a small sack of sawdust. Their task, he told them, was to hit him, and the first one who did so would win the duck, which he carried about under his arm. Besides the bird, the clown had a bell, and by giving it quick tinkles in different parts of the ring, and by making the duck quack every now and then, he could keep the fight going as long as he wanted, causing the two adversaries to rush about, belabouring the air, or each other, and occasionally leading them up the king pole of the tent, to which they would administer a tremendous thrashing, believing from the solid impacts that it was their human target. By holding several heats, and then a final, the clown could create twelve or fifteen minutes of riotous entertainment, all for the couple of shillings that the duck had cost to buy.

This, then, was the kind of circus in which my father grew up – a show, as he himself put it, given by a family for other families, which toured all over the south of England, stopping for one day in each place. This one-day tenting was an immensely hard and energetic existence (as I myself was to discover later), and it coloured my father's whole attitude to life. Work, he believed, was the proper occupation for a man: if you worked, you ate; if you didn't work, you went hungry. In due course he instilled this maxim into his children, and, no matter how much we hated it when we were young, we came to appreciate it later.

My father was born at Sileby in 1874, and grew up one of the most versatile members of the family show. He was tall and powerfully built, with the terrific arms and shoulders of an acrobat: he could walk on his hands almost as well as on his feet, and he remained astonishingly fit throughout his life: when he was seventy he could still do upstarts – that is, lie flat on his back and come to his feet in one movement. He was also an excellent clown, with a great gift for improvisation. Sometimes, when a hitch occurred in the show and a stop-gap act was needed, he would go into the ring alone with a peacock feather and play for time so skilfully that he would set the audience in a roar. He would blow the feather into the air, wait as it came slowly down, and then catch it on his nose, his foot or his chin. That was all he did – but I have seen him tear the people up by doing it. I've seen them crying with laughter, just at this feather. All on his own he made the tent sound like a football ground at the climax of a match.

He had many other accomplishments, not least that of being able to command an audience when he was talking. His grammar was by no means perfect, for he had had little formal education, but he spoke with such charm and natural authority that he easily held people's attention, and he made a wonderful ringmaster or parader out on the front of the show. He also taught himself to paint, and through his extraordinary persistence made himself a highly competent artist: he painted all the wagons and the elaborate show-fronts, and was outstandingly good at animal heads. He believed that a man could do *anything*, provided he tried hard enough; and in a way he proved this by his painting, for it was only after long and bitter struggles that he became proficient at it. One thing he could *not* do was sing – and he had to admit that singing was an accomplishment which no amount of effort could perfect if a person was tone-deaf. Another blind spot – oddly enough – was animals. The gift of handling animals has run in our family for generations, but for some reason it missed my father. 'Nothing that growls,' he would say, for he was nervous of wild animals and had no touch with them at all.

It was through the circus that he met my mother, Maud Seaton – although the first occasion on which he came across her could scarcely be called romantic. She too came from a family with circus and fun-fair connections. Her father, George Seaton, was the son of a schoolmaster in Peterborough, but, being passionately fond of horses, he left home and worked with circus people. Such was his skill that he became one of the best-known horse-trainers of his generation. In those days circus people generally trained their own animals, but if someone bought or bred a horse which he thought would make something special, he would send for George Seaton to take it on. Seaton, in turn, was very choosy: he would not bother with a horse unless he thought it had exceptional potential. He was also highly independent, and would never stay with any one show for long: he did not consider that to travel with a circus for a while meant that he was working *for* it. He worked always for himself, and as soon as one animal was finished, he would move on to his next booking.

In due course he came to train an animal for my grandfather's show, and one day my father – then a boy of ten – was left to look after little Maud Seaton, who was only two. Later, when her father died, Maud went to live with her great uncle and aunt, the Clarks, who were fun-fair people, but well off. There too she landed among horses, for Tom Clark was famous for his trotters, which he bred and drove as a hobby, much as young men drive sports cars today. Although my mother had no special way with animals, she did have exceptional nerve, and she delighted her great uncle by driving his trotters fearlessly, like the wind. If any other horses ever overtook her, he used to say, he wanted to know why, and whose they were.

The Clarks spent the summers travelling round the fairs, and from time to time, at big fairs like the one in Oxford, they met up with our family, for the circus sometimes would pitch on the same ground. My father and mother thus must have seen each other from time to time as they grew up, but it was not until 1901, when he was twenty-seven and she nineteen, that they fell in love and decided to get married. By then she was a small, slender young woman, with brown hair and very fine features, and no less fine a determination. It was just as well that she had such resolution, for her family was strongly opposed to the idea of marrying a wild young man in the circus, especially as he did not seem to have much money. There was opposition from my grandfather, too (although on what grounds, I have never been sure), and in the end my parents got married secretly in Bristol.

For a whole year they lived on in their own homes, apart, not daring to tell their families what they had done. During this time my father organised the building of the wagon which was to be their first home. This, too, he did in secret, ordering the caravan in a roundabout way; but the firm who made it realised more or less what was up and kept joking with their other customers that the building of an anonymous wagon must mean that someone was getting married. Eventually the caravan was delivered to Bristol by rail, and my parents rushed to the station to inspect it, only to find that it had not yet been unloaded. Unable to wait to see it, they walked along the line until they found it, and climbed in to explore their new home.

At last my mother nerved herself to break the news of her marriage to her family. She told her mother first, and went with her to tell her uncle. To her great relief, no one made any fuss, and she and my father settled into their wagon together. Their first child – my eldest brother Dicky – was born in 1904. Two years later came Tom, who died in infancy, then

Maud, then myself, with Marjorie and John bringing up the rear at four-year intervals.

In those first years of my parents' marriage big changes overtook the circus world, the most sudden and drastic being the invention of moving pictures. The first films – or 'flickers', as they were aptly known – were extremely primitive by modern standards, yet in their day they were a sensation as big as television became fifty years later. All at once, everybody wanted to see films, and the craze hit the circus hard; at first there were no proper cinemas, and shows were given in tents, with the projectionist encased in a fire-proof steel box, turning the film by hand past a flaring gas lamp. For circus men who owned tents already it was tempting – and easy – to switch to the new form of entertainment, and several members of our family decided to try their luck at it. The first to go was our Uncle Jim, who acquired a film show of his own and toured the villages successfully; but my father had already begun to branch out himself, and gradually the family split up.

Part of the reason, no doubt, was that my father and his brothers realised there was not room for all of them and their children in the same show; but a contributing factor was certainly my father's character. Although he set himself the highest standards of conduct, he was not in the least ambitious, and had no desire to own or be part of a big show: he much preferred something small and individual – a compact, personal unit which he could run as he liked, and with which he could tour the villages, rather than the larger towns. The instinct to travel was bred deeply into him: 'As soon as you can tread on two daisies, it's time to be off,' he would say every spring. He absolutely loved the English countryside, and rejoiced when he heard the cuckoo heralding another summer.

He was the most straightforward man you could hope to meet: if he said he would do something, he did it, and no one ever had to worry that he might default. As a result, he was greeted with tremendous affection and respect wherever he went, and he enormously enjoyed his ability to move freely about the country being received as a visitor of some consequence.

He first left the immediate family circle when Tom Clark asked him to go for a winter's work, painting shields and show fronts. Then he went winter-painting for his Uncle Jim, who had bought one of the first film shows, and after that he began to travel with the Clarks and their fun-fair. They had a hoop-la stall, and some birds, and my father was always looking for novelties. One year, hearing that somebody had given away goldfishes as prizes, and thinking that this was a splendid new idea, he made a special journey to London to buy up a stock for himself. He smuggled them under wraps into Bristol Fair, and took – by the standards of those days – a small fortune. Later he bought a pair of little bear cubs and exhibited them as Teddy Bears in a pit. Whatever he did he brought to it some original touch of his own, and he developed a real old show-man's line of patter, telling the tale (as we call it) out in front of the booth in his wonderfully natural and easy manner.

Yet soon he found that fun-fair work did not satisfy him. He wanted more variety, and so formed a parading show which featured girls who danced and sang, as well as comedians and jugglers, in a square canvas booth with a little stage. This did well for a while, but then the variety shows also began to feel the impact of the craze for films, and my father himself went into the new medium, at first in partnership with his brother-in-law, but then on his own. In 1911 – the year before I was born – he bought a complete cinema outfit from a man named Thompson, a rich businessman who had had a quick fancy for films but soon got tired of them. Besides the projection equipment, my father acquired a large steam-driven traction engine, and a fine mahogany living wagon – the wagon in which I was born.

The switch from horses to steam must have been a great jolt to people whose life had been geared, as long as anyone could remember, to four-legged transport. Until then horses had been used for everything – for shopping, for visiting friends, for moving the show from one place to the next. Now, suddenly, the family had a huge and complicated steel monster to deal with; my father, being hopelessly un-mechanical, refused to have anything to do with it, so a man had to be hired to drive it. But he had to admit that, besides pulling the wagon, the engine did have the merit of producing – from its auxiliary dynamo – enough electric current for some feeble lights.

My father built and painted an ornate façade for the new show, with 'ELECTROGRAPH' emblazoned over the entrance, and a surviving photograph shows him telling the tale out in front, while a pretty girl walks the rolling globe beside him. This and other little variety acts helped pad out the films themselves, and my mother, besides being the projectionist, would sing songs like 'Come Into the Garden, Maud' to accompany the still lantern-slides that filled out the programme. My father never dared enter the claustrophobic projectionist's box, and my mother did not like being in it either, but at least she mastered her nerves sufficiently to do the job. Once she had started a film (turning it by hand), she never dared stop, for she knew that if she did the celluloid was liable to catch fire.

The main glory of the cinema outfit was the living wagon – an old-fashioned mahogany caravan, with high and low wheels that had iron tyres and wooden spokes. My father painted the spokes yellow, and picked out every one of them with a fine red line down the centre. The wagon had what in those days was called a mollycroft, or lantern, roof and on the inside of it my father painted a riot of cherubs and roses. The inside of the wagon was all one room. There was a small stove, with a tiny oven, that burned wood and coal; on either side seats and cupboards with mirror fronts, and at one end two hinged beds, top and bottom, with sliding doors to close them off from the rest of the living-space. Our parents slept in the top bunk and the children below: one of the compensations of being ill was that you were allowed into the top bunk to cuddle up with your mother – a privilege so delicious that by itself it made you well again. Outside, the wagon had a cool back-box, where food was kept, and belly-boxes for extra storage space. Across the front was a footboard, on which you rode while on the move, and on which the water-can and coal-scuttle stood when the caravan was parked. At the back was a harness-rack – for although we used a traction engine to pull it, the wagon had really been built for the horse age.

This, then, was the home in which I spent the first two years of my life, travelling round the south of England. Then, in 1914, the outbreak of war found the family in Amesbury, a village nestling in a hollow of the Wiltshire downs; and my father, not knowing what unpleasant consequences the war might bring, thought he had better put down roots there. He must have done quite well with the films and the parading show, for he had enough money to buy a strip of land and two bunga-lows, one big and one small. He also discovered a large building which had been designed as a garage, but which was left empty when war was declared. This he rented, and by building a gallery inside it he converted it into a passable cinema. Later, at the army camp at Bulford, about three miles away, he found another empty building, made of wood, which he bought, dismantled and rebuilt into a permanent cinema in Amesbury.

He himself, at forty, was already on the old side for active service, and in any case a motoring accident soon put paid to any remaining chance he might have had of being called up. Considering the speed that cars went at in those days, it seems absurd that he could have had so serious a crash; but, being too nervous to drive himself, he had a chauffeur, and the man had been drinking to deaden the pain of toothache. My father and my Uncle Tom (my mother's brother-in-law) came out of a lawyer's office in Salisbury, went down a hill too fast and turned over. My uncle died in hospital, and my father split one leg open from top to bottom – an injury from which he took several months to recover.

The accident was a disaster for the family, but it did have one compensation, in that it enabled my father to stay at home and supervise the cinema. At first we did reasonably well, since Bulford Camp, on Salisbury Plain, provided us with a steady supply of troops for audiences; my own earliest memories are of soldiers picking me up and dandling me and giving me little toys and sweets. I also remember the war songs, like 'Keep the Home Fires Burning', and 'Where Are the Lads of the Village Tonight?' Those tunes have never left me. There was once a big family row when, with the best intentions, I went round during a performance selling copies of our handbill for a penny each. The bills were the ones we gave out as advertising, but the soldiers, thinking in the dark that they were programmes, seemed happy to pay for them. When I took the money back to my father he exploded, for absolute, one-hundred-per-cent honesty was one of his fundamental characteristics.

As long as the troops were in town, we made a reasonable living, occupying one of the bungalows and letting the other. But then, at Easter 1916, the Irish Rebellion suddenly drained Bulford dry of troops, and there was hardly anyone left to patronise our shows. Although my parents struggled on with the cinema, they gradually went through the money that they had saved, and we became very poor. Even I, young as I was, noticed a change. In the days of our prosperity important local people like the chief of police had frequently called on us, in the wagon or the bungalow: my father had always been entertaining – modestly enough, no doubt – and we always seemed to have visitors. Then suddenly the people stopped coming, and instead of pleasant conversation I would hear my parents anxiously discussing money.

Yet still I could not accept that we were poor, for we had in the bungalow a lovely silver stand in the form of an oak tree, with three cut-glass dishes hanging in its branches, and two stags, also made of silver, standing on either side of its trunk. Ever since I could remember I had looked on the oak tree as a symbol. In my simple, childish way I used to think, as a kind of slogan, 'The Oak Tree Must Be Right,' and for as long as we still had it, I could hardly believe that we were destitute. Every time I came home I used to look quickly to make sure it was still in place, and while it was, I felt sure that all must be well. But then one day I came home and it was gone – and then I knew that we really were hard-up. Many times I have tried to find that stand again, for it repre- sented far more to me than the value of the silver it contained.

The strange thing was that my father seemed positively to *enjoy* being poor. I think the attitude had been bred in him by his background of circus life: he used to say that he enjoyed being as free as the birds, which woke up every morning with nothing and had to go out and find what they needed. He liked the challenge, and revelled in the fact that he could meet it: he knew that he had the ability to work hard and earn enough to feed us. To me, this hand-to-mouth existence seemed dreadfully pre- carious, but to him it was a delight. He was never interested in money for its own sake, or in material possessions, and as long as he could provide for the family he was content.

In some ways the period of poverty brought out the best in him. Even though we had no money, he never lowered his own standards of dress and appearance: his breeches and boots, which he always bought from the same firm in Marlborough, were always immaculate. Nor did he change his standards of honesty: even in his most difficult moments he would never consider doing anything the least bit illegal. He never dreamed of poaching, for instance – and that, for a man with a big family to feed, must have been quite a temptation. As a cautionary tale he used to tell us the story of how, in the days of the travelling circus, one of the men had suddenly produced a new headcollar for a horse. When my father asked him where he had got it, the fellow told him slyly how he had found it in the stable where they had stayed the previous night, and how he had 'accidentally' changed it for the old one that he had been using before. At this my father was furious, and he made the man walk all the way back to the stable – ten miles – to return the stolen collar to its owner.

It was this kind of rigid discipline that had held the family together for generations and given it an enviable reputation; and now it served all us children well, for without it I am sure that I would have become a terrible poacher, or even a burglar. The hunting instinct is strong in me, and if my father had been less strict, I would surely have indulged it. I believe that my mother would have cooked any game that I had brought home, but my father would never have eaten it — and in any case, the mere idea of poaching was so far out of court in my father's code of behaviour that I did not even consider it.

As it was, we managed to survive, largely through my father's skill as a painter, carpenter and wood-carver. I remember looking at his hands and thinking how clever they were. I used to say to myself: those are the hands that can do it all – paint a picture, mend a gate, carve a scroll, earn a living. With those hands we're safe. And safe we were, for my father never had the slightest false pride, and there was no job, however menial, that he would not undertake. One winter soon after the war he painted all the road signs between Amesbury and Salisbury: for day after day he went off with his bicycle and ladder, and I have never forgotten how outraged I felt when I looked at his hands – those hands that could do so many things – and thought how awful it was that they were reduced to that — painting signposts and milestones in the freezing winter weather. But he, typically, did not resent it in the least, and when, many years later, I once said to him: 'Just think of it – you could *buy* the road from Amesbury to Salisbury now, never mind paint the signs on it,' he just said how surprised he was that I had nursed that grievance for so long. Having money and being able to buy things, he said, meant nothing: but having the guts and the stamina to go out and paint the signs in winter was all part of a man's character.

His painting was really what kept us going. He could always get the price of a meal by going up to the owner of a house, pointing out that the gate was broken, and offering to mend it – something which he did with such charm that no one was ever offended. But it was his pictures, and in particular his animal paintings, that earned most of our meagre income. He could not paint if anyone was watching: he would have to go off on his own, and back he would come with a beautiful animal head, often on a shield, whose elaborate scrolled edges he had carved himself.

The nadir of our fortunes came when, for about a week, we were left without a proper home. We had sold both bungalows and moved back into our old wagon, which was parked beside the cinema; but then we sold the caravan too, and we had to move out before another caravan that we had ordered was ready. So there was one short period when we had nowhere to live except the cinema.

It so happened that a repertory company had taken a lease of the building, and that the set for their play was a kitchen. Luckily it was a thoroughly realistic set, fully equipped with furniture and cutlery, and for a few days it became our home. In the evenings, during the performances, we would sit nodding in the audience, unable to go to bed until everyone else had gone away. Then, as soon as the place was empty, we would swarm on to the stage and take possession of the actors' props, using them for real. We had to sleep on the floor, but in the morning we would use the furniture and cutlery for breakfast, and after it we would wash up and tidy it all away, taking immense care not to break anything and to put every piece back exactly where we had found it, so that no one should realise what was going on. As a child of ten I soon came to believe that all these things were *ours*, and it seemed odd to me, sitting in the audience, to watch the actors using *our* cups and plates, sitting at *our* table. No one discovered what we were doing – or, if they did, they were too kind to ask embarrassing questions.

As far as I remember, we never suffered physically from having so little money. We were never cold or seriously short of food, and afterwards my father often used to say that he was glad to have been through that bad period, because it showed him what being poor really was like and made him more tolerant of the problems of other people who found themselves in the same sort of difficulties.

Yet, even though our family came through unscathed, we gradually realised that we could not linger on in Amesbury. The instinct to travel was in our blood: by breeding we were itinerant showmen, not static cinema operators, and we felt more and more that we must go back on the road. My brother Dicky – eight years older than me – was the prime mover – and it was largely his energy and enthusiasm that persuaded my father to set off again. Dicky's main ally was my mother: more ambitious than my father, younger, and full of energy, she was never one to sit down anywhere, and she saw that, with the war over, there was no future for us in a place as quiet and cut-off as Amesbury. I think my father – who was nearly fifty by the time we began travelling again – would have been content to stay where he was: he had spent all his youth on the road, and probably felt he had had enough. But, urged on by his wife and eldest son, and also by the lack of money, he at last agreed to have another go.

Obviously, having practically no capital, we could not at first mount a very ambitious show, and we started out with little more than our transport and our wits. But our over-riding ambition was to get moving again – and so it was that in the autumn of 1923, when I was eleven and Dicky nineteen, we took to the road once more.

CHAPTER TWO

On the Road Again

CRAZY as it seems in retrospect, we set out again in November, right at the end of the travelling season. Why we started then, I cannot now imagine – except, I suppose, that if you have spent years planning a major upheaval, you plunge into it as soon as you are ready. In any case, we went off at the worst possible moment, for in another week or so the fun-fairs would close for the rest of the year, and we would have to settle into winter quarters again.

No such considerations, however, worried a boy of eleven: for me it was a thrilling moment, and I can still remember vividly how we got the traction engine out into the lane, and all the neighbours came out to wave us goodbye. Needless to say, a sharp anti-climax followed, for before we had gone a yard one of the tubes in the engine blew out, and we had to suspend operations for the day, letting the fire go out before we could tackle repairs.

But at last we really were off. Leaving an uncle in charge of the ailing cinema, the rest of us piled aboard, with a hired man driving, and away we went, chugging up the long hill out of Amesbury in the direction of Weyhill. Not only was it November: it was also nearly dark, and sparks poured up out of the chimney into the wintry dusk. To me, that was terrific: I thought we were going to set fire to half the countryside. All we had in the world was the traction engine and the living wagon behind, with a dart stall which my father had made built on to the side; but I felt tremendously excited. All that mattered was that we were on the road, and free.

We took part in the fair at Weyhill, and then one at Burbage, but that was the last of the season, and after it we went to Newbury, where we spent that winter, all five children living with our parents in the wagon. To feed us, my father painted signs and pictures, and for the first time in my life I went to school – an experience which I quite enjoyed. In the spring of 1924 we set off again and travelled to several fun-fairs: with our dart-boards reinforced by a hoop-la stall, we scraped a living, but only just, and during our second winter – at Woolston, outside Southampton – my father had to sell his dress suit, which he had kept since our prosperous days before the war. I remember how annoyed he was when he tried to sell the clothes to a pawn shop, and the man there told him snootily to take them down the street to a shop near the theatre, where they bought stuff like that for the comedians. My father was maddened by the suggestion that his fine dress suit should be worn by a second-rate actor – yet he had no option but to sell it.

Another object which – it seemed to me – we could well do without was a rather fancy perambulator, again a relic of our better times. My sister and I decided to take it down to the pawnbroker, our agreement being that I would push her there in it, and, if we failed to sell it, that she would give me a ride back. Unfortunately the shopkeeper showed no interest at all, so back the pram came, with me in it – but the details of our innocent and practical little plan were later distorted by frequent re-telling, until the story came to be that I had tried to sell not only the pram but my sister too.

That second winter at Woolston I went to school again. In those days the children of travelling families could just walk into a local school; but although it was useful for parents to be able to enter a child at short notice, they often paid the penalty, for the teachers had little interest in a boy or a girl who, they knew, would not be with them for long. Perhaps it was the temporary nature of the arrangement that unsettled me. At my first school I had done well, showing talent at arithmetic and winning a prize for handwriting; but now, after a long summer on the road, I seemed to have lost the touch, and I could not get on. After that I never went to school any more, so that my entire formal education amounted to no more than three or four months, but it was not until the Second World War, nearly twenty years later, that I felt the lack of a proper school career.

Looking back, I now feel sorry for my parents, who must have found life very tough just then. My mother, who was a bit of a snob, cannot have enjoyed being poor – although, being immensely energetic and practical, she must have realised that the family's best chance of restoring its fortunes lay in returning to the form of showmanship that it knew best; she did not at all mind giving up the relative spaciousness of a bungalow for a circus caravan, in which everyone lived on top of each other at extremely close quarters, for this, she felt instinctively, was the way for the family to get on.

For my father, the irritations were greater: there he was, overrun by all these hungry children, who had no idea how to manage the stalls and could not be relied on to do the simplest jobs. Most men of his age and position could sit back and watch their families build the show up and take it down – but not he. Idling about in Amesbury, we had grown up soft and useless: we had no idea how to book a ground in the fair, how to run the stalls, how to earn our living.

Young as I was, I soon began to realise how backward we were compared with all the other children in the business. They amazed me by their precocity: they knew every wrinkle. They had their own money. They could change money. They could take money for the stalls and answer customers' questions. They seemed absolutely brilliant, and beside them I felt an idiot. I have never been able to forget how funny they thought it was that my sister Maud wore gloves when minding the stalls: that was the sort of life we had been used to, and it was a bit of a shock to find ourselves surrounded by people so much sharper.

Yet there were several factors in our favour which helped us to survive. One was the friendliness of the other fair-ground people, who were always ready to help or give us advice, and to share the secrets of their trade: they had a tradition of looking after lame ducks, and as we children obviously needed instruction, they gave it to us unstintingly.

Another asset was that my father was a born showman, and a master at telling the tale. He could stand up in front of our meagre stalls and spin such a yarn that people would be almost hypnotised. He could talk, tell jokes and generally chat to anyone, and the people who gathered round his stall would always be laughing. But perhaps our greatest asset was his rock-like character. No matter how bad things were, he never changed in the least. Whatever the circumstances, he remained himself, and he taught us all wonderfully well by his example – the most vital lesson being the essential importance of work. One of the first and most hateful jobs I remember was being made to clean the traction engine. It had brass bands round the boiler, and every time the engine got up steam they went dull and dirty. My father made us polish them every day, partly out of pride in the appearance of the machine, but mainly because it was his policy to make us work, and teach us to enjoy work, or at least to realise that hardly anyone can be happy without it.

Life in the wagon was very strict. We were never allowed to drink, smoke or gamble, and we never even had playing cards. If we boys did anything wrong, we were liable to be beaten, and an equally rigid code of behaviour governed the girls as they grew up: if any of them went out with a young man, she had to be back by a certain time, and my parents never went to bed until she was safely in place in the bottom bunk. Yet although my father was tough in many ways, he was very soft in others: if you were ill, for instance, he would be really concerned and put his arm round you, as if he thought that close physical contact could restore you. He had a horror of violence, and hated to see anyone hurt, although I did once see him knock a man down for swearing in front of the children. He never went to church – having no very high opinion of most clerics – but he was intensely religious and said his prayers every night. He would never allow anyone to tell funny stories involving God, or to take the name of the Lord in vain, for he feared that any such irreverence might later be repaid by some form of divine retribution.

Poor though he might be, he would never dream of asking anyone to lend him money. But once, I remember, he did accept an unsolicited loan. We were in a post office, and the woman behind the counter suddenly handed him an envelope saying: 'Oh, Mr Chipperfield – there's your change.' We had bought nothing, and were not owed any change: it was a measure of my father's reputation that the woman gave him the money spontaneously. Years later, he was delighted that an opportunity arose of returning the favour: we had already repaid the money long ago, but a member of the same family ran into trouble and needed a loan, and my father exclaimed: 'There's luck for you – luck that they should ask me just at a time when I can help them.'

In spite of all the difficulties, travelling round the fairs seemed to me a lovely existence. Every day there would be a new place and new children to play with, and life went gently on at a pace that is almost inconceivable today. The measured gait of the traction engine itself was an indication of the rate at which we moved from one place to another: it went at a walking pace, and going up hills we always had time to get off and pick blackberries before trotting on to catch up with it again. When we stopped for lunch, we stopped right in the middle of the road and had a picnic there, for the chance of any other vehicle coming along was negligible.

Soon, however, we began to feel that we were still in the wrong business. Fun-fair work was too static for us: it did not involve us enough, and above all it had no place for animals. My brother Dicky had inherited the family's traditional flair for handling animals more strongly than any of the rest of us; for years he had bred rabbits, chickens, bantams, guineafowl and game-cocks, and now he began to urge my father more and more strongly to go back into a line of business that would both involve animals and give us a chance to perform. Thus it was that we bought some big Indian rock pythons and two miniature crocodiles, and a second wagon (also pulled by the traction engine) in which the creatures lived in tanks of warm water. There was, in fact, very little that we could do with the reptiles, but we built a snake-pit and stood up in front of it and told the tale about how deadly its inmates were. My sister Maud was best at this, and she handled the pythons as though she had done it all her life.

Even with the added attraction of the sideshow, we were still very short of money, and in the winter of 1926, to earn us some out-of-season income, I was sent to work in the Armstrong car factory in Coventry. I cannot have earned very much, because one day my father sent me – with hardly any money – to get some meat for our lunch. 'Go and tell the tale for it,' he told me: in other words, I was to use my initiative and imagination, and get the meat for as little as possible, but without telling any lies.

After pondering for a while, I had an inspiration. I found a butcher's shop and told the man behind the counter that we had some crocodiles, which ate a tremendous amount of meat. 'Crocodiles!' he said. 'Oh. What sort of meat do they need?' That took me aback, because I hadn't thought of an answer, but I recovered quickly and said: 'Well – mince-meat.' So he gave me an enormous parcel of mincemeat, for which he charged me about threepence, and I took it home in triumph to my mother, who was amazed: there was enough to feed the whole family for several meals. Everyone was delighted, and said that whenever we needed meat I would have to go back to this splendid butcher – and so I did.

All through that winter I told the tale, and day after day I brought those parcels of mincemeat back like bags of gold. My mother made it into every kind of dish – shepherd's pies, Cornish pasties, sausages. Halfway through the winter one of the crocodiles died, and there was only one little creature left (eating hardly an ounce of meat a day) about which I could spin my yarns. This made things rather awkward, and I had to pick my words carefully so as not to tell any outright lies; but luckily the butcher, besides being generous, had a good sense of humour, and he soon divined what was going on.

At first he thought that we really *had* got some big crocodiles, and although he must have realised that humans were eating the meat, he was happy enough to maintain the pretence, for it became a joke much enjoyed by the other customers in his shop. 'Crocodile meat again!' he would exclaim as I came in. 'We'll have to see what we can find them today,' and all the other people in there would laugh. He used to tease me dreadfully by saying: 'Those crocodiles must be as big as me by now – I must come and see them one day' – and that really made me sweat. But he never forced the issue, and in the end we stopped talking about crocodiles altogether. The game must have cost him the earth, but he and his customers enjoyed it so much that he was happy to go on playing it.

Every season we looked for new ways of extending our repertoire, and gradually we worked out a series of little acts. Dicky bought a few cheap conjuring tricks from Gamages, and soon turned himself into a passable magician, giving his show out in front of our booth, or on the stage, dressed in a dinner jacket. Then he had the idea of getting a long narrow box, shutting someone into it, and passing swords through him. I, of course, was the person who had to go into the box, and together with a girl who was working with us I used to crouch inside. By sitting very tight we could guide the swords down between us, but as we did so we would utter the most bloodcurdling screams, as though we were being sliced to pieces.

Another cheap and simple but effective trick was the funnel – a utensil that looked empty and harmless when displayed to the audience, but which in fact had double sides filled with water. There were two small holes, top and bottom, and the flow was controlled by covering or uncovering the top hole, which was hidden by the handle. If the operator kept his finger over it, no air could get in, and so no water could escape from the bottom; but if he moved his finger off (which he could easily do without anyone seeing) water would start running out.

With this ingenious device any number of jokes could be conjured out of the audience: for instance a boy would be summoned, and the funnel would be held under his ear; after his arm had been pumped up and down for a bit, water would apparently start trickling out of the side of his head. Generally the trick was infallible, but once we had a disaster when the stage collapsed just as we were going to do it. I was standing in the wings with a whole bath full of water, from which I filled the funnel, and was about to hand the funnel to Dicky, who had already got a boy lined up. Suddenly the stage gave way, and there we were, both of us and the bath on the ground in a flood of water, but with the funnel empty. Although Dicky ad-libbed like a master, the trick was off the bill for that day.

Then my father taught my younger sister Marjorie an old-fashioned turn that he had known in his own youth – the ladder act. To do it, she had to become a contortionist, and he began teaching her when she was about ten. The key to this is to make your spine supple – to make it bend backwards as well as forwards – and you start learning by bending further and further backwards. You stand with your back to a wall and walk your hands down it until you can put your head between your knees. In about six months Marjorie had become supple enough to slip in and out of the rungs of a ladder. She started off hanging on the top rung by her legs, and would go down through the other rungs, backwards and forwards. Before she started each performance, no one would believe that it was possible, so that my father had a fine chance to play up the rarity and difficulty of the act that was about to take place; but in fact the ladder was a specially-built one, with rungs slightly further apart than usual, and she could go through them easily.

I myself put the traditional Chipperfield sense of balance to good use by learning to walk the wire. No one could really teach me this: it was just a question of practice and patience, and it needed a terrible amount of both. I had no pole, but merely used to extend my arms, and at first I fell off continuously. For months I felt I would never get the knack. My father encouraged me all the time, and ceaselessly urged me to practise, but I think he made a mistake in also using practice as a punishment. If I had done something wrong he would tell me to go and do an hour's practice, and from his point of view it was useful, because it kept me out of mischief for that time. But it also made me resent the whole idea of practising, and so, I think, did more harm than good.

At any rate, I persevered, and in the end began to make progress. The wire we used was a semi-slack wire, about five feet off the ground, and in order to balance on it you have to move your feet as the wire gives (the technique for a tight wire is quite different, but we did not have the equipment for that). I found that if I kept my eyes on the same line, looking at a fixed point at the end of the wire, it was much easier, and at last I was able to stay upright for a few seconds at a time. In the end I found it was like riding a bicycle: once you have mastered the trick of it, you can always do it, and it is no harder to lie down on the wire, or to juggle with balls and hoops, than it is to stand up.

With Dicky's conjuring, Marjorie's ladder act and my walking the wire, we had the beginnings of a family show. But our return to a proper circus really began when we bought our first horse – a little stallion which we called Black Spangle. We saw him in a field during the horse fair at Shrewton, and we paid five pounds for him. He seemed enormous to me, but I think he was about fourteen and a half hands, and three years old: certainly he was old enough to attract mares, and we had some hair-raising journeys with him, since at first we had to ride him from one fair-ground to the next, and every time we went through a town we would involuntarily pick up an escort of mares. By the time we reached the outskirts we would have half a dozen milk-carts and other tradesmen's carts following along behind, and we had frightful difficulty getting rid of them.

Black Spangle was the first four-legged animal we trained. When we got him he was not even broken for riding, and we ourselves hardly knew how to ride, so we had some lively times just scrambling on to him bareback and trying to stay there. Our Uncle John, who was exceptionally good with animals, suggested that we should revive the old act of the Fortune-Telling Pony, so we taught Black Spangle to nod and shake his head, and to scrape with his front foot, for counting. At first we made exaggerated movements to give him his cues, and stood close in front of him; then gradually we moved further and further back, and refined the cues until they were almost imperceptible. Thus he became a genuine, old-fashioned Talking Horse, and a considerable attraction: one year at Oxford Fair people queued from eight-thirty in the morning until ten at night to see him perform. His only real defect was that he was almost too intelligent, and some days he just decided that he wasn't going to work. By then we had a square booth with a front painted by my father and a little stage, on to which we brought the pony. The audience had to stand in the open, out in front.

At the same time as Black Spangle we bought a fiery jack donkey whom we christened Barney. He was a devil. We trained him to chase and bite the clown, and he would put on a terrific display, giving a loud roaring bray as he came into the ring and really going for his victim. As long as he bit on the padding, the clown was all right, but sometimes the donkey managed to get his long yellow teeth under the padding, and to this day I have scars that bear witness to the strength of his jaws.

As soon as Barney had done his man-chasing act, he would quieten down, and we developed another trick which was so old that most people had forgotten it. We found that by putting a little patch of fresh sawdust in the middle of the ring, we could always make the donkey lie down for a roll; but once he had gone down, we taught him to stay down, while the clown lay beside him and started talking to him about how his breath smelt of onions, and someone else spread a coverlet over the pair of them.

In this – as in all our acts – we had to be very careful that the humour did not become bawdy. The circus, then, was very much a family entertainment, and we could not risk offending all the people who brought their children along. By today's standards we were tremendously prudish. When we were working the Fortune-Telling Pony, for instance, we would single out a pretty girl in the audience and ask the horse to predict when she would get married. 'In three years' time?' we would ask Black Spangle, but we would stop him counting after only one scrape of the foot, 'Oh – next year, then, is it?' we would say. 'And how many little ... ?' at which we would go off counting furiously. Only when the laughter had died down would we finish the question: '... bridesmaids will she have?' That was the nearest we ever came to any kind of a blue joke.

Another big step forward was the acquisition of a lorry, which replaced the old traction engine. The episode was typical of my father, who loved showing people just what he could do, and when he saw this wreck of a lorry abandoned in the middle of a field, he bought it more because it looked such a challenge than for any practical reason. 'Wait till you see what I'll do with that,' he said – and so we acquired the rusting remains of an ex-army F.W.D., or four-wheel drive lorry, up to its axles in mud. For the mechanical side of the rescue operation he had to enlist the help of a garage, for he knew nothing about engines; but he tackled all the rest himself, taking the whole thing apart and scrubbing and polishing every part until it was like new again. He built a new back for the truck, fitted it out as a living wagon, and painted it from top to bottom, and eventually the vehicle was delivered to Nuneaton, where the fair had just been held on a large car-park.

My brother's driving experience had been limited to the traction engine, which had no clutch or any similar refinement, and simply went backwards or forwards. So he was hardly prepared for the response he got from this petrol-engined giant, and when he first tried it he shot forwards at an alarming speed. Then he went into reverse and roared backwards even faster, straight towards a line of stationary cars, and everyone rushed after him shouting 'Whoa!' as if he had been a horse. But he soon mastered the new machine and became its regular driver, with me as driver's mate.

It was a very high vehicle, with spoke wheels and solid tyres, and the driver's cab was perched up above the bull-nosed engine. As there was no built-in means of communication between there and the back of the lorry, we had to use various improvised methods of keeping in touch with the people travelling behind. One was a piece of string, which I was supposed to keep tied to my arm and which anyone could pull if they wanted to attract our attention; but often I forgot to connect the string up, and as a stand-by system my father carried a stack of turfs which he would hurl past our windows. Often we would be merrily trundling along, and suddenly we would see clods coming past the cab, and we'd say to each other: 'Hullo – the Old Man's going mad in the back,' and we would stop, to find that something had fallen off, or that the wagon we were towing had come adrift. Sometimes, though, we found it was my father himself who had been cast off, for he, accustomed by the habits of a lifetime to proceeding at a walking pace, would often step off the lorry for a moment, forgetting that it could go about five times the speed of a horse or the traction engine, and so would be left behind. When that happened there was no question of going back for him, since the truck and its wagon were far too cumbersome to turn round in the road: all we could do was to sit and wait for him to catch up. We'd see him coming – a speck on the horizon – and sometimes it took him an hour to reach us again. When he arrived he would be purple with rage, not least because he knew that what had happened was entirely his own fault.

The lorry was a devil to start in the mornings, and our efforts to get it going became an absolute ritual, lasting nearly an hour. Our first move was always to boil a kettle of water and to fill the radiator with it, so that the engine was warmed all through; then we would start pulling on the rope – a half snatcher – to turn the heavy flywheel and magneto. Usually that produced no result, and someone would suggest we should heat the plugs. So we would do that – but still no result. Then somebody would say: 'Black-lead the plugs,' so we would do that, too, and perhaps she would fire, only for us to discover that hay-seeds had got into the petrol tank and come up into the jets in the carburettor, cutting off the fuel supply. Dealing with all these problems morning after morning seemed an awful chore at the time, but the experience served us well, for it made us quite skilled mechanics, and before long I could undertake major jobs like putting in new big ends and clutch plates.

When the lorry *was* going, it ran beautifully, and I suppose it could do about twenty miles per hour. Dicky and I slept in the back of it, and we cut a hole in the back door so that Black Spangle could come in and travel in a kind of makeshift stall between our bunks. It was typical of my father that, as he rode along in the back or in the living wagon, which we towed, he thought he was still in full control of the family pantech-nicon, even though it was obviously Dicky and I, up front, who were physically in charge.

By today's standards its brakes and steering were highly dangerous, and once it ran away with us completely, going down Portsdown Hill on the way to Petersfield. Dicky was driving, as usual, when it jumped out of gear, and a second later he shouted out that the brakes had failed. I leaped out, hoping that I could slow both the lorry and the trailer down a bit by putting on the trailer's brake. For a few yards I ran alongside, but it was an awkward job to apply the brake even when the trailer was at a standstill, as one had to reach in between the wheels, and at that speed it was impossible.

Away went both the vehicles, faster and faster, and as their pace increased the trailer began to whip backwards and forwards across the road. My father was spreadeagled on the tail-board, arms out, leaping from side to side in an effort to counter-balance the violent swings. I suddenly felt convinced that everyone on board was going to be killed, and that I would be left an orphan. I walked on in a daze, wondering what would happen to me. Meanwhile, aboard the runaway, lively scenes were taking place. Up front Dicky was steering for his life, in and out of the other traffic, and beside him Black Harold – the African whom we called our snake charmer, although in fact he knew nothing whatever about snakes – was feverishly rubbing himself with the rabbit's foot that he always carried as a charm. In the wagon somebody announced: 'We're away!' and when my five-year-old brother John innocently asked: 'What does that mean?' they told him he would find out soon enough. A few seconds later, as the speed and swaying increased still more, one of my cousins was seized by his mother in the panic and had an ear half torn off.

Luckily for everyone the road was fairly straight, and Dicky's nerve held. When at last he saw an up-hill stretch ahead, he shouted to Black Harold to jump out and shove a block behind the wheel, to stop them running backwards and repeating the manoeuvre in reverse. If I drive down that hill today, more than forty years later, I go through every second of the nightmare again.

In 1928, when I was sixteen, we bought a second lorry – another substantial step towards our re-establishment. Later that year, when we had gone into winter hibernation near Basingstoke, we bought six Shetland ponies which we had seen advertised in Scotland. They were so small that they were sent all the way down in sheep crates, and Dicky at once began to train them. He has always been a much better trainer than me, because he has marvellous patience: he can sit with an animal all day, and even if at the end of it he seems to have made no noticeable progress, he may still be delighted by some minute extra degree of understanding that he has achieved.

That winter of 1928–9 was bitterly cold; we were parked in a field, and had no indoor place in which to practise, so that we had to train the horses in the open. My job was to get up very early in the morning, when it was still dark, and light a bonfire in the middle of the practice-ring, to thaw out the ground. While I did this Dicky groomed the ponies, and then he would run them on lunges for hours. By the time spring came he had trained them to canter, waltz, lie down, sit up, and stand with their forefeet on tubs – only simple routines, but enough for our little show. The best thing about them was that they cost nothing to feed: farmers allowed us to graze them free in their fields, and even gave us hay in the winter.

In those days people were extraordinarily generous. Almost everywhere we stopped to do a show someone would come up to us and offer us eggs or butter or cream. They knew we hadn't got much money, but it wasn't because they thought we were poor that they were so kind to us: it was because they enjoyed the circus's visit, and liked talking to the people in the show, and above all because they wanted to offer tokens of friendship to the travelling strangers. The farmers would come along and watch us practising, and they loved chatting to my father, for he could talk to them on their own terms – and, by always arriving from some other part of the country, he acted as a primitive kind of news service. I still cherish that feeling of warmth and security which we got from being welcomed into so many small country communities.

To show the Shetland ponies we needed a bigger booth, and we got one about thirty feet across, almost filled by a twenty-five-foot ring. Round the sides of the ring were a few low seats, and a full house would have been about a hundred people, with most of them standing.

By then we had started to revive another of the family's traditional skills – clowning. My father still did a bit – for instance with the peacock feather – but his real role was as a teacher, for we children were at last old enough and sensible enough to appreciate the value of his experience, and in any case I found that I had a natural aptitude for clowning. It was a strange fact that although I had a great fear of appearing in the circus as myself, I felt completely at ease as soon as I was wearing clown's make-up. Dicky, by contrast, was hopeless as a clown, but he had inherited our father's gift of being able to address audiences naturally: he could act as a parader on the front of the show, or ringmaster inside it, with almost as much panache as the Old Man. The idea of having to do either of those things terrified me – I had a real physical dread of them, and I felt I would rather die than have to announce an act. I never liked to admit this to my father, and for years I was afraid that one day he would order me to go out and introduce the show. But perhaps he sensed how deep my embarrassment was, and he never brought the matter to a head: either he or Dicky was always there to do the job instead.

Safe behind the exaggerated make-up of the clown, however, I felt perfectly relaxed: it was not me, but the Auguste, that the audience could see. My father had already taught me the rudiments of being an acrobat – I could walk on my hands, and do handsprings and upstarts, and I used these movements in various combinations to make silly little turns for the clown. I would trip, fall down, and instead of getting up normally, shoot up into a handspring. Everything about the clown was supposed to be ridiculous, not least his clothes, and I was always dressed exactly the same. I would come in wearing big boots, with long toes, and a hat and a huge fur coat, to which was attached a long cord. Before doing any tricks I would strip off, starting with the coat. I would take it off, and say to it: 'Out!' and away it would go, apparently of its own accord, pulled by the string. Then I'd take off my shirt-front, which looked like a dinner-jacket with a big white collar and black tie, but in fact was made of iron, with a sharp spike at the bottom, so that when I dropped the whole thing on to a board it would stand there upright, on its own. Under it I would be wearing a long jersey, knitted by my mother: when I came in I had it rolled up, but then I'd let it unroll, right down to the ground. In the seat was a pillow, to make my behind stick out. Each of these moves, done right, produced a good laugh, and the audience would have warmed to the clown before he had even tried to do a trick.

As we gained confidence, Dicky and I began to revive some of the old-fashioned entrées which my father remembered from his father's show, among them the egg entrée and the duck race. My father would produce the ideas, and Dicky would work out a scenario: although we never had a written script, we always stuck precisely to the prearranged pattern, and our timing had to be absolutely spot-on. The entrées themselves were very slight, and depended a great deal on the build-up of patter that we exchanged before them: the egg entrée, for instance, was always preceded by a lot of argument about what we could and could not do. I and my partner the White Clown – who was always thin, dumb, and dressed in black, with three-quarter-length trousers and artificial hairy legs – would wander in, sometimes coming opposite ways through the audience as though we were looking for each other.

'Who are you?' the ringmaster would demand.

'We want a job with the circus,' I'd reply. 'We can do anything you want.'

'That's fine,' he would go on. 'I need a wild-animal trainer. Can you train lions?'

'Lions! Well . . . no. Anything but that.'

'All right, then: I need an acrobat. Can you do a somersault?'

'A somersault! That's easy. . . .' and I would take a run and square up for a somersault, only to pull up at the last moment and say: 'Oh – a *somersault*. Oh no. I don't think I'll do *that*.'

At last we would agree on something that we *could* do. 'We're *magicians*,' I would tell him. 'We'll do you a trick.' And so we would lead off into the egg entrée, eventually hatching a live bird from our omelette.

Another favourite slapstick routine was that of the horse and cart on their way to market. The horse consisted of two men under a skin, pulling the rickety cart, which was driven by the Auguste with a great load of belongings on the back and the White Clown dressed up as his wife sitting beside him. After a couple of circuits of the ring the horse would stop and refuse to go on, so the wife would climb down and start to heave on the reins – whereupon the horse would suddenly jump forward, knock her down, trample over her and stop with one wheel of the cart resting on her chest. From above, I would peer down (on the wrong side first, of course) and then, when at last I had sighted her, descend to her assistance, lifting up the wheel and dropping it again on her chest. Each time I dropped it, she would scream, and her legs would go up in the air (although in fact the cart was very light, and she wasn't being hurt at all). Eventually I would get her out and throw her back up on to the cart – only at the first attempt I would throw her clean over and down the other side. When we were both on board again, the horse would bolt, upsetting the cart and scattering bloomers, brassières, cabbages, onions and a mass of other belongings about the ring. Eventually we would pile everything back on top and canter out.

In their mixture of comedy and pathos, in their grotesque appearance with its medieval echoes of Harlequin and the jesters, the clowns were the very essence of the old-fashioned circus, and although people laughed at them, I think they were sometimes a little scared of them too. When we were clowning our aim was always to enlist the audience's sympathy, by appealing to them for justice in our arguments with the tyrannical ringmaster, or for help in our struggles with recalcitrant animals or machines. Often we used to involve the crowd directly in the show by jumping in among them: I always made for the prettiest girl in sight, and sat on her lap and chatted to her, amid shrieks of excitement and laughter. The ringmaster would order me to come back, but I would say: 'No, no – it's much nicer here.' Then the ringmaster would offer me money – say five shillings, and I would still say I was staying, because the girl was worth a great deal more than that. By the end the girl would have laughed herself silly, and afterwards she would go on talking for weeks about how the clown had sat on her lap. I had to watch out while doing that, though, for in many places it was a traditional joke to drive a hat-pin into the clown's backside when his attention was engaged elsewhere. But anyone who did that was in for a nasty shock, for he, imagining that he was jabbing a decrepit old bundle of skin and bone, suddenly found himself gripped by an exceedingly fit young man with the muscles of an acrobat.

Thus our show gradually increased in size and variety. But by far our biggest single purchase (in every sense of the phrase) was a young elephant called Rosie.

We bought her from a dealer in the Tottenham Court Road for four hundred pounds. To us that seemed a fortune, and my father was disgusted by the fact that we could raise only part of the money, and so had to borrow the rest on a form of hire-purchase; but Dicky and I were determined to have her, since in those days even a single elephant was a tremendous attraction for a small country circus to possess, and we fondly imagined that Rosie was going to make us rich.

Had we been less clueless, we might have noticed sooner that she had a long scar on her back (the result, we learned later, of her bolting through the plate-glass window of a shop in Oxford Street), and if we had seen that, we might have hesitated longer before buying her. As it was, we took delivery of her more or less unseen. She was in Nottingham at the time, and we had her sent by train to Coventry, where we saw at once that we were in for trouble.

A good elephant (we gradually learnt by painful experience) is one that will stay with its human partner under even the most trying circumstances: no matter how nervous it may be, it trusts the human to protect it. If you see an elephant walking quietly down a busy street with its handler, you can be sure it has a lot of confidence in him, built up over years of training. The most striking illustration of this kind of trust I have ever come across was that of a German trainer who saved ten or twelve elephants during the bombing of Hamburg in the Second World War: he led them out into the open, and they stood round him all night, facing inwards, believing that he would protect them.

A bad elephant, by contrast, is one that is either mischievous and evil-tempered, or never masters its nerves properly, and so is constantly liable to bolt. Such an animal we call a runner. Rosie was a runner: although she was never positively malicious, her tendency to bolt caused us endless anxiety, and many a stable up and down the country was left perforated by her dainty silhouette.

The moment we first unloaded her from the train, we were in trouble, for she instantly took off. We had to move her about a mile and a half to the yard in which we were staying, and the only way of getting her there was to walk her. But no sooner had we started than she took off along the street. Once an elephant goes, it goes, and there is very little you can do about it except run alongside and try to keep with it until it slows down from exhaustion. This Dicky did: he had hold of the chain that was linked to the fetter round Rosie's ankle, and away he went, running in front of her, heading her off and trying to point her in the right direction. My poor father was horrified: he was nervous of having the elephant anyway, and now he saw most of our money disappearing, out of control, away down the street in front of him. Fortunately Rosie ran out of steam before too long, and we were able to settle her in to her new quarters.

Never having owned an elephant before, we were dangerously inexperienced at first; but luckily we got some expert help right at the start, when we needed it most. A cousin of ours who was an actress happened to be playing in Coventry that very week, and her husband was one of the best animal trainers in the country, so that for the whole of the first week we got his close attention and support. Thereafter we handled Rosie ourselves, and she was certainly worth the money we paid for her, for she proved a tremendous novelty. We taught her to sit down, lie down, and walk on wooden bottles, but she hardly needed to do any tricks, for she was rare enough to be an attraction in herself. My father never got on with her at all – especially after she had nearly squashed him by suddenly backing out of a horsebox just as he was lifting up the tail-board – and it was left mainly to Dicky and myself to look after her.

Yet my most vivid memories are not of her success as a circus attraction: more freshly and painfully I remember the various hair-raising escapades in which she landed us. Even at home, so to speak, she was a considerable nuisance. Having used the trailer for a while, Dicky and I adapted one of our lorries as a loosebox for her, installing a partition to separate her from our bunks up at the front, so that we could look over from time to time and keep an eye on her. Often in the night her trunk would come waving over the top of the partition, feeling about for something to play with, and once she excelled herself by stealing and eating my trousers, whose pockets contained, among other things, my driving licence. At the last moment I realised what was happening, but I was too late, and I just had one glimpse of my trousers disappearing into her mouth.

Outside, in public, we lived in constant fear that she would seriously injure someone – or herself – by bolting – and a typical incident occurred one summer in Monmouth, where we were staying for the May Fair. We had stabled her in the yard of a pub, and one morning as we were walking her to the fair-ground, about half a mile away, we met a herd of cattle being driven in to market. One look at the cows was enough to set Rosie off: away she went, screaming and trumpeting, back in the direction we had come, seeking the safety of her stable in the pub yard. It so happened that at that moment a man with a terrible hangover was picking his way unsteadily across the bridge over the river. Looking blearily up, he saw an elephant coming at him with ears and trunk erect, and without waiting to decide whether the animal was real or some apparition surviving from the excesses of the previous night, he sprang over the parapet into the shallow water, hurting his leg quite badly.

Further up the street a man was at the top of a ladder, painting a house. He too saw the elephant coming and, thinking that his ladder was going to be skittled, let go of his brush, crooked his arms round the sides of the ladder, dropped like a stone the whole way to the ground and vanished – all in a couple of seconds. He need hardly have bothered, for Rosie missed the ladder and charged on up the street, scattering people in every direction, until she reached the pub. There, however, she made a mistake: in her haste she rushed into the first open doorway that she saw, and this unfortunately belonged not to her stable but to the gents' outside lavatory. The doorway was a narrow one, and she had to elongate her whole body to get through it: but she forced her way in, and there she stuck, jammed so tight that the brick walls of the building bulged in and out when she breathed.

People began to gather, and the landlord rushed out, going mad with rage and shouting: 'Get that elephant out of there!' All right, we said: *we* wanted her out as much as anyone, but it was obvious that until she settled, she wasn't going to move, so that the only thing to do was for everyone to calm down and wait. Rosie herself did nothing to hasten that process by pulling the cistern off the wall and starting to blow water backwards over her head: the building had no roof, and we could all look over the wall and watch her ripping out the plumbing. Eventually she got fed up with being in there and backed out, with one of us pulling her tail and the other urging her from in front. I am not sure who paid for the damage she had done, but we never went to that pub again.

An even more embarrassing scene took place in North Wales one autumn when we were overtaken by an early snowstorm and forced to stop for the night in the village of Coed Porth, near Wrexham. There

we were, stuck on a mountain in a blizzard, with this elephant, so our
first concern was to find her somewhere to spend the night. We went to
an inn, and sure enough the place had a stable. Half of it was stacked
full of all the furniture and fittings from the church, which was being
rebuilt at the time: pulpit, lectern and pews were all piled up there, a mass
of old wood, much of it beautifully carved. But the other half was empty,
and the landlord said we could use that. So we chained Rosie up there,
gave her a feed, and bedded her down with Black Spangle, the pony, who
had become her constant companion. When she was comfortable we
withdrew to our wagon for a cup of tea and a snack, and later we went to
bed.

Then, in the middle of the night, there came a knock on the door – the
local policeman. 'Your elephant,' he said. 'It's got out. It's carried away
the front of the stable.' We ran out, and there she was, standing in the
snow, and the whole front of the stable had gone. That was bad enough,
because we thought our most valuable asset would surely catch pneumonia
and die. But what was much worse was that she had dragged all the
church furniture out into the snow with her and smashed it to pieces.
All round her lay the remains of the pews and pulpit, trampled into
splinters, and she was standing in the middle of the wreckage, hurling
bits into the air with her trunk. The policeman was so angry he could
hardly speak: he just couldn't put into words the things he was going to do
to us, and as he stood there spluttering the elephant kept going *whoosh*,
and up went another piece of shattered pew into the air. Why she did it,
I shall never know, and I am sorry to say that once again we failed to
pay for the damage. Nor, as far as I can remember, did anyone try to sue
us: they must have seen that we had no money, and decided that it was
simply not worth harassing a small travelling show like ours.

The climax of Rosie's career came at the turn of 1930 and 1931, when
she performed a star turn at the Piccadilly Hotel in London. By then we
had a man who acted as our agent, and somehow the manager of the
hotel heard that he had access to a tame elephant. The manager, it
appeared, had conceived a novel idea for entertaining his guests in the
evening of 31 December and for bringing the New Year in with a
flourish: as the bells rang the Old Year out, all the lights would go out,
and when they went up again, there would be an elephant standing on

a tub in the middle of the ballroom, with a little Indian boy on its back. To follow the idea through, each of the guests would be given a model elephant as a souvenir.

Could we, the manager asked, provide the elephant? And we – whose policy it was never to refuse any reasonable offer or request – immediately said that we could. We knew that, Rosie's nerves being what they were, we faced formidable problems; but the man was offering us the princely fee of ten pounds, and for that nothing seemed too much trouble.

Had I known what we were in for, I would never have taken the job on. Nor would I do it now if someone offered me a thousand pounds. It was a miracle that we got through it without any serious mishap, and that we did not cause damage or an accident for which we could not possibly pay.

We were wintering in Shepherd's Bush, and we drove into central London easily enough, with Rosie in her trailer, and parked in some stables in a yard off Jermyn Street. All through that day we gave her very little to eat or drink, in case she should make a mess on the dance floor at the critical moment. As soon as she had settled, I went back to Shepherd's Bush, hoping to leave the whole business to Dicky. But suddenly I got an urgent message: the page-boy from the hotel who was going to play the little Indian rider had fallen off during a rehearsal and lost his nerve, so that I – still quite small at eighteen – was going to have to take his place as mahout.

I rushed back into town. The journey to the hotel passed off without incident: we led the elephant along Piccadilly with her chains on, praying that she would not take fright at the traffic and bolt, and as soon as we reached the hotel I changed into Indian robes and a turban, making up my face and hands brown, and was given a huge basketful of beautifully made velvet elephants. Then we waited in a back room for our cue. At last midnight came. The lights went down, we trundled through into the ballroom and took up our position. A moment later the lights blazed up again, and we realised belatedly what we had taken on.

Everybody in that place was drunk. There was one great shriek of enthusiasm, and people surged forward at us from every side. I was convinced that Rosie would take off with the noise, but for once she was rock steady – perhaps because she was hungry and had seen and smelt all the food on the tables round the floor. Far from bolting, she just strolled forwards and began to filch things from the tables: rolls, fruit and sweetmeats disappeared by the plateful. Then she took hold of one of the tablecloths and with a twitch of her trunk sent everything on it crashing to the floor. Nobody seemed to mind losing the remains of their dinner: on the contrary, they were wild with excitement and began feeding her more and more delicacies. A few of them tried to climb on her back and she was knocking them down like ninepins with her trunk between mouthfuls. I sat tight on her shoulders, handing out the baby elephants as fast as I could. Soon someone began to shout: 'Fetch her a drink! Fetch her a drink!' and while a tub was being brought she turned her attention to the potted palms, eating a few of them and throwing the others up in the air. Then a large tub appeared – a bath, almost – and into it went a stunning variety of drinks: champagne, wine, brandy, beer, whisky – anything that people could lay their hands on. The tub was filled to the brim, and Rosie (who was of course thirsty by then) drained the mixture off at one draught.

On her almost-empty stomach the brew produced an immediate effect, and although she kept on eating anything offered her, in a few moments she began to sway about. That was enough, Dicky and I decided: we had better get her home.

There cannot be many people who have had the task of leading a drunk elephant along Piccadilly in the first few minutes of a New Year; but those who have tried it will know what a terrifying experience it is. I don't suppose it took us more than a quarter of an hour to get her back to the stable, but the journey seemed to last half the night. The street was packed with cars and people, all of them merry, to say the least. They were happy enough already, and when they saw an elephant coming at them, that was all they needed: they all yelled and charged towards her. We hardly knew what to do: if we tried to go down the road, the drivers came at us blowing their horns; if we kept to the pavement, the drunks came at us on foot, blowing whistles and hurling streamers. And all the time Rosie just kept bowling forward, with Dicky and me each hanging on a chain, running with her, unable to stop her. Any moment, I was certain, we must run somebody down and trample them: any moment somebody was going to be killed. But somehow the elephant just kept clearing the bodies out of her way. Plenty of people were *knocked* down, but none of them seemed to resent it, and nobody was badly hurt. At last we were through the maelstrom and back in the calm of the stable, all three of us severely shaken. We got our ten pounds all right, but we agreed that it was the hardest-earned money we had ever come by.

Never again did Rosie hit such a high spot. In purely financial terms she proved a good investment, for she attracted hundreds of people to our show; but the cost to our nerves was prodigious, and we eventually sold her to a zoo, together with Black Spangle, who had become her inseparable companion. The best thing about her was that she taught us a great deal about keeping animals, and about elephants in particular – an experience which later served Dicky especially well, when he acquired a whole troupe of elephants after the war.

CHAPTER THREE

Wild Animals

JUST as in my father's generation one branch of our family had allied itself with the Clarks, so in my generation, we joined forces with another well-known show-business family, the Purchases. In those days there were many celebrated clans in the circus world, among them the Sangers, the Fossetts, and the Rosaires, and breeding counted far more than wealth in a person's standing. If a boy of seven or eight said 'I'm a Sanger,' or 'I'm a Fossett,' it really meant something, and a man who had been in the circus for twenty-five years was considered an amateur if he hadn't been born in the business.

In due course my sister Maud married a Fossett, and many were the strange stories we heard about that family – not least the fact that one of the men (a contemporary of my father) used to carry all his money in the form of diamonds, wrapped up in his handkerchief, or sometimes gold sovereigns, which he would throw down in challenging fashion on to the counter whenever he went into a pub. The Fossetts were famous for being ultra-cautious: one of them had a set of false teeth made, but he was so afraid of swallowing them that he fastened a cord to them and anchored the other end in his buttonhole. Later, we heard that the family became so nervous before the Second World War broke out that they buried a great deal of petrol, and a lot of their money, in various fields in Ireland, only to be unable to find the places again when the war was over.

The Fossetts were notoriously careful with money, and although they eventually agreed to install a telephone, they deliberately put it in an out-of-the-way shed so that it should be used as little as possible. Finding that they could not hear it ring, they trained a dog to bark whenever someone called, and for as long as it lived, the dog answered the telephone satisfactorily. But when the animal died, no one answered at all, and it was useless to try to ring the Fossetts up. And yet, tight though they were among themselves, they were marvellous about helping other circus families who were in trouble. They would seldom refuse an appeal, and dozens of small shows owed their existence to the Fossetts' generosity.

Although we came across the Fossetts and Sangers from time to time, our immediate concern was with the Purchases, who had been in the menagerie business for seven generations. When we got to know them, the head of the family was Tom Purchase, a fine-looking man of about forty-five, whose artificial leg (got as a result of a mechanical accident) in no way hampered him in the ring. He was known as 'Captain' Purchase, although he was no more a captain than I was, but merely used the title to enhance his status as a lion-trainer – the common practice of the day, when all wild-animal trainers assumed arbitrary ranks and wore comic-opera uniforms.

For me, the main interest of the Purchase family lay in the fact that the Captain had a daughter called Rosie whose beauty was renowned throughout the circus world. Her looks were such that people would ask you if you had seen her, rather as if she had been a film star, and her reputation was made the more striking by the fact that she danced in the lions' cage, between two huge males sitting on pedestals, before her father put them through their paces.

The first time I saw her was at Mitcham Fair, where both our families were pitched, and although I was only sixteen I plucked up the courage to ask her out – correctly addressing my invitation to her father. There was no question of my taking her out alone – the social rules of the day precluded that absolutely – but fortunately I had my sister Maud to act as a chaperone.

First I got Maud to introduce both of us to Rosie, and then I produced my pre-arranged plan: flying was a great novelty, and I had discovered that down the road at Croydon aerodrome someone was offering five-shilling trips in the air, so I proposed that we should all go for a quick flip. This we did, and the flight proved to be the beginning of a lifelong association. (The fact that Rosie the elephant had the same name was pure coincidence, and later it often happened that animals were given the same name as members of the family. But we never deliberately named any animal after any person, and no one took it as an affront that an elephant, for example, or a chimpanzee had been christened after them: rather than seeing in such an event some ribald reference to their shape or appearance, people just hoped that the animal in question would become a good character.)

Two years after my first meeting with Rosie, our families joined together. The initial union, I think, was an accident: it happened at Oxford Fair (which took place then, as now, on the broad, level expanse of St Giles), where our show and the Purchases' were pitched next to each other. My father, being well respected, always got excellent grounds, and that year at Oxford we had the best of the lot, right at the end of the fair, across the middle of the street. The Purchase menagerie was next to us, and we realised that if the families joined forces they would make a very strong combination; we with our horses and variety acts, they with their wild animals. So for the rest of that season – the back end, as it is known in the trade – we travelled together, and at Stratford, Barnstaple and other places in the west we did tremendously well together. Dicky at once began to work with the lions and showed great promise with them. My father and Tom Purchase got on splendidly together: both strong characters, they went easily into harness, and never even looked like having an argument.

That winter our evenings were full of ambitious plans: we talked and dreamed endlessly about the big show we were going to create, full of excitement at the new possibilities open to us. But then, in Manchester, during the first stop of our new season's tour, disaster struck.

Altogether the day was a traumatic one for me, since in the morning I worked a wild animal for the first time. The stress of going into the cage would have been enough on its own, but on top of that I had a family row to deal with. I was mad keen to work the lions and tigers, but my father did not want me to. Being afraid of them himself, he thought it was quite enough to have one of his sons – Dicky – putting his life at risk, and said he did not want me to go in as well. Tom Purchase, who was a gentle and perceptive man, saw that it was very important to me to go in, and said that he would put me in, and stand by to keep an eye on me. By then I was in a temper and stupidly said: 'Oh, don't bother,' but he insisted that I should do it and told me to get ready. So suddenly I found myself, rather ruffled, about to try my hand with a tigress.

We set up the usual drill of three safeties, or people on hand to help in case of trouble. We always had one person on the door, who never left it, no matter what happened; a second helper was armed with a pole, to fend off the animal if it attacked the man working it, and the third person was standing by to go in and drag the man out if he was injured. For me, Rosie was on the door, her father had the pole, and Dicky was standing by.

These preparations, simple as they were, of course increased my anxiety – for no matter how many times you have seen a wild animal perform, it is a different matter when you yourself are about to go into the cage. Apart from anything else, the animal seems to double its size. I had a whip, but the cage was such a small one that there was no room to wield it, so that I would not be able to use it except to hold it in front of me, and in any case the tigress I was going to work was so highly strung that there was no question of hitting her anyway. If anyone so much as touched her, she would just lie down and sulk, watching to see if she was going to be hit again.

Even though she was on the whole a reliable animal, there was still a chance that she might come for me, as I was somebody she did not know particularly well.

At last Rosie's father said: 'Right – we're ready,' and in I went. Having watched the act dozens of times, I knew exactly what to do, and I put the tigress through part of her routine. I made her do two or three jumps, and then she went back on her pedestal – not much, but enough for me. By that time I was sweating all over, and glad enough to get out. But at least I had made a start, and afterwards I felt terrific.

That afternoon, during the show, there occurred one of those accidents that circus people always dread. Rosie had done her turn, dancing in the lions' cage, and her father had just finished his own act with them. He was putting them in their places before he came out, when one walked slowly towards him. He backed into it accidentally, and the animal bit his artificial leg. Whether the lion started off meaning to give him a playful nip, and was disconcerted by striking its teeth on this curious limb of wood and metal, we never knew. But whatever its motives, it completely lost its head, striking out and pulling him to the floor, where it ripped his ears, bit him in the neck, and drove its claws right through his back into his lungs.

With a big lion like that, it takes only a second for a man to be in real trouble, because the injuries it can deal are immediately serious. For a moment the animal had Rosie's father in its mouth. Then, in a flash, Dicky was inside the cage and driving a short feeding-fork down the lion's throat to make it let go. As soon as it opened its jaws, Tom Purchase got up and walked out, pouring with blood, but Dicky was still in the cage, stuck between the two lions, in such a position that he was going to have to move one of them before he could escape. I shouted 'Get out!' in a panic, and wanted him to leap for the door, because I knew that if the lion got him too, I was the next one who would have to go in.

Luckily Dicky ignored me – for if he had moved fast, he would almost certainly have been bitten as well. In that kind of situation he goes absolutely ice cold, and on this occasion he kept still and just said in a flat voice: 'Everyone keep quiet, and I'll drive him round.' A few seconds later, he gave the lion an order, and it moved round like a lamb, so that he could walk steadily out.

We stopped the show and rushed Rosie's father to hospital, and there he showed how deeply the old-fashioned standards of modesty were ingrained in him, for although he was bleeding profusely and badly hurt, he refused to undress until the nurse had withdrawn from the room. Several times she told him to get a move on, as his life was clearly in danger, but he would have none of it until she had gone away.

Today, with penicillin and other modern drugs, I am sure he would have survived. But the lion's claws had punctured his lungs, and he developed septic pneumonia, from which he grew gradually weaker. As he fought for life I had my first taste of the malevolence which poisons animal cranks, for one of them wrote to him saying he deserved everything that happened to him, and expressing the hope that his death would be protracted and agonising. The sister in charge snatched the letter away in a fury, threatening damnation on the person who had sent it, and I kept reflecting on the difference between him – whoever he was – and this devoted woman. In the end the crank's wishes were at least partly fulfilled, for after three weeks Tom Purchase died.

The calamity drove our two families even closer together, and my father became head of the joint clan. Dicky at once took over the lions and tigers, and in due course became one of the best trainers in the country.

At first he had been determined to work the lion which had run amok: it had always been a good animal, though inbred, and we did not want to part with it. In the end, however, caution prevailed, and we sold the animal to a zoo, obtaining a guarantee that the new owners would not sell it on to anyone who might try to work it in a circus.

The accident taught me many things, chief among them the fact that one must never relax one's vigilance with a wild animal or take its good behaviour for granted, no matter how many times it has performed satisfactorily. In that year and the ones that followed I laid the foundations of a lifetime's work with lions. You learn very fast if your life is literally dependent on your knowledge and skill, and I quickly acquired a basic understanding of wild animals.

One of the first things I appreciated was the nonsense of the common view that circus lions are beaten or drugged into submission – an idea so utterly wrong that it can only be held by someone who knows nothing whatever about the animals involved. In one way a lion is very like a human: he does not like anyone to come too close to him. Just as most people prefer to keep a slight distance between themselves and their fellows, and feel pressured if bores at cocktail parties lean closer and closer, thrusting right into their faces to talk, so lions need a certain minimum distance between themselves and their handler – and this built-in repulsion factor is the corner-stone of most training.

A circus lion's education generally begins when he is a cub. But he must not be too small: he must be big enough and have enough courage to challenge his handler. His natural instinct is to try the man out by rushing him and seeing if he runs away; if the man stands his ground, the lion is confused and does not press home his attack. I have seen some trainers so cool that they just sit in the cage reading a book and let the lions run about snarling and growling but not daring actually to attack. A very bad lion may come right at you at first, but if he does you push him off with a chair or some other solid barrier; that shows him you are the boss, and that you are not going to move out, no matter what he does. Once he understands that, the basis of training is established.

As with people, the distance to which you can approach varies from one lion to another. But whatever it is, once you go beyond the critical point the lion will strike out at you with his paw. If you press him closer still, there are only two courses open to him: either he must retreat, or, if he has not the room to do that, he must come for you. Half the art of training is to provoke the lion to a show of temperament that will excite the public, so that he roars and lashes out, but not to press him so that he feels really uncomfortable.

An expert trainer will go so near that he *does* make the lion come for him: he goes in really close, then as the lion starts to move he eases back, drawing the lion on, then stops again, and the lion stops with him. As he does this a few times he can see the lion thinking: 'Right – in a minute I'm going to run him.' And sure enough, in a moment the animal does try to run him, but after a couple of paces backwards he stands his ground and repels the animal again. In the ring the effect is terrific, but it can be achieved only after hundreds of hours of practice by a real expert. My nephew Richard is just such an expert: he can bring a lion bounding and snarling at him and at the last second turn his back on it – whereupon the animal drops its charge and lies down.

A critic might say that in this kind of training you are teasing the lion. In a way this is true. But to claim that it is cruel is entirely to misunderstand the lion's temperament. A lion is essentially an extrovert character, and loves a rough-and-tumble. If he comes snarling at you, and you push him off with a chair, the odds are that he'll rush at you again, because he enjoys a bit of a battle. In making him swipe at you, you *are* teasing him, but in a way that he understands and enjoys. Far from being cruel, you're having a game with him, and he is with you. A snarly lion is a good one: the more noise he makes, the better, and a good trainer will talk to him all the time, going *aargh* and *aaao* and making other lion noises. You can tell in a second from the sound a lion makes what sort of mood he is in, and even if your answers are not in very convincing lionese, the animal realises that you are talking back to him and knows that you are a friend.

After a while the lion sees his trainer not as a human, but as another animal – and the boss animal at that. When the lion rushes the man, he is not thinking of killing and eating him, but merely of challenging him, to see if he can make him run. A lion who is *really* after you comes in a quite different way. He walks slowly. His head goes down, his jowl drops, and his face changes altogether. Far from running, he just keeps steadily walking. He is a different animal. An expert can spot the change in an instant, and many a trainer has been saved by his assistant, on standby outside the cage, noticing this change come over an animal and warning him in time. Yet, even if a lion does charge you only for fun, he is still dangerous enough, for he may well claw you and – if he draws blood – he may lose his head and really bite, as did the one who killed Tom Purchase.

Another common misconception about lions is that they are all the same. Obviously their characters do not differ as subtly as those of humans, but all the same they show a considerable variation. Some are much cleverer than others, some more playful, and so on. They, in turn, see humans as individuals, just as much as we do, and it is always dangerous for someone to approach a lion – or for that matter, any wild animal – if he does not already know it. Once, after the performance of a winter circus, a man who worked with a tame tiger had the animal loose in his dressing room, and invited us in to see it. I refused to go anywhere near it, and the man was openly contemptuous, thinking I was frightened. I just told him that if he put the tiger in its cage, I would come and look at it, but not otherwise. How did he know the animal would like me? I asked him. What if it took exception to my clothes? What if my clothes didn't happen to smell right for it? How did the owner know that some small movement I might make would not set the tiger off? A really good trainer would never have issued such an invitation, but would have put the animal away first.

Another fact I soon learned about lions is that their perception is extraordinarily keen. Not only can they instantly spot a hole or a weak point in a cage: they can also sense a person's frame of mind from his physical movements alone. If their trainer walks into the cage firmly and slams the door in a determined way, they know they have met their match; but if a man comes in nervously, with a hesitant or faltering tread, they do not hesitate to try to mess him about. Even if the trainer only has a cold, or is a bit under the weather, it is risky for him to work, because the animals sense that he is somehow slightly different from normal, and therefore are upset. This is the reason I have never drunk alcohol in any quantity, and never drink spirits at all: to go into the cage after a couple of drinks is the act of a madman: the trainer may think his voice and movements are perfectly normal, but the lions know better. Their sense of smell is acute, and they detect the difference at once – often with lethal results.

Dominating a lion is one thing: to train him to move about the ring and do what you want is infinitely more time-consuming, and requires enormous patience. To make him go and sit on a pedestal, for instance, you can either push him, by coming close, or lure him, by holding pieces of meat up in front of him on the end of a stick. Either way, it may take weeks before he will put even his front feet up on the pedestal, and few people outside the circus realise how dreadfully boring training can be. A really good trainer is one who has worked all day, perhaps without much success, but then after tea gets up and goes back for another hour with his difficult animal. His patience must be inexhaustible.

What is certain is that you cannot beat a lion into doing what you want: you cannot possibly beat him so that he goes and sits on a pedestal or jumps from one place to the next. If you hit him at all hard, he may well go berserk: he may not recognise you any longer, or know you from Adam. His relationship with you is ruined, and he is just as likely to bolt headlong into the bars of the cage as he is to go in the required direction. To drug a lion would be equally dangerous: even supposing you could work out exactly the right dose (which even with modern tranquillisers is difficult), the main effect would be to alter the animal's perception, and the odds are that he would not recognise you, so that the chances of his attacking you would be greater, rather than less.

Another snag would be that the other lions would almost certainly attack *him*: our experience of tranquillising animals in the safari parks has been, first, that a partially-drugged animal is much more dangerous than a sound one, as he does not know what he is doing, and second, that an animal recovering from the effects of a drug cannot be let out with other lions, as they immediately sense something odd about his gait or behaviour and rush in to try to kill him. So the drugging of circus lions is out of the question.

Tigers are even more highly-strung, and therefore even more dangerous. Except for the big Siberian tigers, which are relatively calm, they are difficult to handle, and you have to be tremendously careful not to hit them, even accidentally. If you so much as touch a tiger, he will usually lie down and refuse to work – and if he lies flat on his side, that is the worst possible sign. Anyone who did not know might think he had been knocked into submission and was lying there passively. In fact he is just about to come. His ears go flat down to his head, and the end of his tail flicks. As he lies there on his side, or even on his back, he is just a ball of muscle coiled and ready to spring: and when he comes, he uncoils and springs all in one movement, up to eighteen feet in a single bound. So if ever a tiger goes on the floor, you don't go anywhere near him.

A good tiger, by contrast, makes a lovely sound – a kind of fluttering purr. You know at once if he's in a good mood, because he blows at you, and the trainer always talks back to him in the same language, blowing and letting his lips flutter. Some tigers never do this at all, being too nervous, but whenever one does do it, you can be certain he is all right. Even a good one, however, has to be treated quite differently from a lion, for no tiger enjoys the kind of rough-house on which a lion thrives: he needs altogether more delicate handling. If the lion is the carthorse of the big cats, the tiger is very much the thoroughbred.

The idea that the training of wild animals involves cruelty is thus absurd – and equally absurd is the theory that to make lions and tigers jump through hoops is somehow an insult to them, and undignified. To the animal, the hoop means nothing whatever: he probably does not even notice it, for all he is doing is jumping (a perfectly natural activity) from one point to the next, and his attention is concentrated on his landing-point. The important feature is not the hoop, but that the landing-place should be solid and steady: otherwise the animal's confidence may be wrecked, and his whole training programme set back by weeks or months.

The relationships which trainers establish with their lions and tigers are very much like those between other people and domestic pets. Just as you get to know your own dog, and gradually find out what it will do and what it will not, so the trainer knows just what each lion is capable of, and treats him accordingly. Equally, just as most people respect their dogs' likes and dislikes, so a trainer knows a lion's preferences and takes care not to abuse them. If lions, for instance, are brought up in someone's house, they often lose their dislike of coming really close to humans and are happy to lie on top of their trainer or to eat pieces of meat off his throat. But it is useless to expect a normally-trained lion to accept this degree of proximity.

Another trait common to both wild animals and domestic ones is the desire to please: before long lions and tigers know perfectly well that they are part of an act, and they become desperately keen to do their job well.

All right, a critic may still object. Perhaps the animals do enjoy their work. But is it not cruel to keep them behind bars? Are they not pining away, in their cages, for open spaces on which they can run and hunt?

Having seen lions running wild in Africa, I naturally prefer to see them at large in a park, rather than in cages. Yet I believe that if a lion is well housed, well fed and well exercised, he can be perfectly happy in a small area. He is a lazy animal in any case, and even in the wild does not exert himself more than he has to. So long as he gets good exercise in the circus ring, I do not believe that he feels any sense of confinement in his cage. Since nobody knows what a lion is thinking, one can only go by how he is *looking*, and if he is looking well, it strongly suggests that he is content, for no animal has the intelligence to disguise anxiety, and if one is worried, the strain must show in its physical condition.

All this I learnt in due course by working with the animals which we had taken on from Tom Purchase. But one of our most urgent problems after his death was to decide what to do with Vixen, or Vic, the lioness he had used for perhaps the most thrilling of all the old-fashioned circus acts: the Untameable Lion. This had always been a great favourite with the audience – or, at least, with as many of them as saw it, for about half the women present generally never saw it at all, having fainted from fright before the climax took place.

As the finale of his performance the trainer would produce the Untameable Lion – in fact a lioness – roaring and snarling and striking out at the bars of her small travelling cage. Then he would tell the tale about her to great effect: how, of all the animals he had tried to train, this was the most dangerous; how he could do nothing with her, and could not even go near her. The lioness would back up his every word by producing a crescendo of noise and fury whenever he approached the cage, charging the door with terrific crashes and gnashing at the bars. 'I guarantee that no man here can go in there and come out alive,' he would announce, and no one in the audience doubted him. But, he added, as a special favour to those who had come to see the show, he himself would go in for a moment. That was all he could promise: he could not work the lion, but at least he would go inside the cage.

So a few seconds of intense excitement were set up; and when the act at last took place, everything happened so fast that the audience could scarcely distinguish what was going on. First someone manoeuvred the animal to the far end of the cage with a long pole. The door of the cage was flung open. The trainer stepped inside. The door clanged shut behind him. The lion charged with a roar. Inside the bars there was a blur of lion, man, lion as the animal hurtled round. A few seconds later the door opened again, the man backed out, and the lion hit the inside of the door with a tremendous crash. By then the audience were absolutely terrified, and some of them, as I say, were unconscious.

What nobody outside the show realised was that the lioness, far from being the savage which she appeared to be, was a very complex character and played to the gallery as faithfully as any prima donna. Tom Purchase had bought her as an imported cub, and even as a baby she had proved very lively, rushing everybody who came near her. So he had started going quietly into her cage and letting her charge before he stepped out again. At first she rushed round at floor level, but as she grew bigger, the impetus of her charge began to carry her up the wall, and by the time she was full grown she was going round at roof level. The trainer's secret was to step inside her charge, so that as she sprang down the door-side of the cage, she passed behind him, brushing the back of his neck. Then, as she turned right-handed round the end of the cage and came back along the far wall, he stepped back again, so that on her return journey she passed in front of him. His timing had to be perfect because the cage measured only eight feet by six feet, and the lioness was round it in a flash. But provided he kept to the usual rhythm, he was perfectly safe, and he did it hundreds of times without getting a scratch.

Even inside the family opinions differed about why the lioness behaved as she did. Some of us thought that her movements were entirely governed by the laws of kinetic energy, and that once she had launched herself into a charge, she needed all four feet to take the shock of her impact on the end of the wagon and to get her round the corners, so that it was physically impossible for her to take a swipe at the man as she went past, even if she wanted to. But most of us believed that she positively enjoyed the whole performance, and was doing it for fun: had she really wanted to get the man, she could surely have varied her charge enough, or even not charged at all, but come for him steadily. If she had once knocked him down on to the floor, that would have been the end of him.

This second theory was certainly confirmed by her behaviour between performances, for the extraordinary thing was that she laid on her displays of ferocity only when an audience was present. With people whom she knew, she was perfectly quiet, particularly with Tom Purchase's elder brother Andrew, who himself had been a lion-trainer, and was about seventy when we got to know him. He was a sweet, gentle old man, and he and the lioness made a regular couple: when no one else was about he would go up to her cage and call her over, and start talking quietly to her, and she would roll over on to her back and let him stroke her stomach. But as soon as any stranger appeared – even if somebody just peeped at her through the tent-flap – she would fly into a spectacular rage.

After Tom Purchase had been killed, we had a big family debate about what to do with Vic. Dicky, of course, was determined to work her, but my father thought it would be far too dangerous, as no one could be sure how she would react to a different person. For several days no one went into her cage at all. Then Uncle Andrew announced that he was going to sweep out, and the rest of us held our breath while he went steadily in. All the time he kept talking quietly to the lioness as he swept. 'She's wondering: "What's this stupid old sod doing in here?"' he murmured. '"What's he messing about at? He should have packed it in years ago."' And all the time, as he talked and swept, the lioness's eyes followed him, sizing him up. The cage was so small that she had to walk right past him as he worked, so that she was between him and the door; then, as he came on round, she went back past him again – and he just went gently on with his soothing monotone of small-talk, until he was ready to come out.

In a way this reassured us, for her behaviour had been exactly what we had expected. But it also made us apprehensive. What if she behaved like that when someone *else* went in? Or, worse still, what if she half-charged but stopped short of the full-speed attack? Then, for certain, Dicky would be caught.

To test her reactions, we laid on a full-scale dress rehearsal: we assembled an audience of friends, and Dicky gave exactly the sort of preliminary speech that Tom Purchase might have made. We tried to make the circumstances precisely the same as they had been before, and we evidently succeeded, for Vic immediately gave a characteristically alarming display of ferocity, charging the doors and snarling, with her teeth right through the bars. When Dicky eventually went in, she flew round behind him with every bit of her old precision.

Thereafter we worked the act hundreds of times, always with a carefully arranged drill. Uncle Andrew, wielding a long pole through the bars, would manoeuvre the lioness to the far end of the cage, and Rosie would control the door with a rope (had she had her fingers anywhere near it, she would have lost them). Then Dicky would step inside, lean forward, lean backward and step out again. In all the years he did it, he never received so much as a scratch. It was, as he put it, like being inside an explosion, and the only contact the lioness made with him was when the fur on her flank brushed past the back of his neck as she made her first spring. But even though we, with the confidence of experience, knew that the act was safe enough, it never lost its power to terrify the audience: it lasted only a few seconds, but the movement was so violent and the noise so loud that the chances of the man escaping unhurt seemed negligible. We kept Vic for years, until eventually she died of old age, and although I have since seen people try to copy the act, I have never seen another lioness a quarter as good as her. She was an absolutely true character, and she never changed in the slightest.

CHAPTER FOUR

One-Day Tenting

By the summer of 1932 we had sold the elephant and the Shetland ponies, and we concentrated on showing the menagerie. In spite of the disaster of losing Rosie's father, the show went fairly well, and Dicky was delighted to be handling lions and tigers. Yet still we hankered to get back to the circus proper. The menagerie season was too short for us: we wanted to get out and do a longer season, and to develop acts which we could book into winter circuses. So in the winter of 1932–3 we bought a tent and prepared ourselves, and in the spring we started out on full-scale one-day tenting.

Our initiation could hardly have been tougher, for we began in Devon and the weather was appalling, with continuous wind and rain. Until then we had hardly realised what we were letting ourselves in for, but as we struggled round the small villages, we soon found out. That was the most strenuous life I have ever known. We would be up at dawn every morning, and by five o'clock we would be on the move to our next destination. On the way we generally had a stop for breakfast, and always, wherever we were, someone would appear out of a cottage and offer us a cup of tea. In Cornwall people would come out and offer us entire breakfasts of pasties and saffron cakes.

As soon as we arrived on the new ground, we would build up the tent and the seats, starting about eleven and finishing at lunchtime. After lunch we would practise and maybe have time for a short rest before the two shows in the evening. Finally, after each doing five or six different acts twice over, we would pull down and pack up, so as to be ready to leave again first thing in the morning. If we got to bed by eleven, we were lucky. Bad weather made the whole business even more exhausting, for not only were we ourselves wet through half the time, but the canvas of the tent was about double its weight when dry.

Occasionally some stranger, besotted by the romance of the circus, would ask if he (or she) might travel with us for a while, and we usually agreed, for we knew from our own experience that nobody else would stand the pace of that life for more than a few days. Whenever people joined us, we would joke among ourselves, saying that within a week a telegram would arrive with the message GRANDMOTHER VERY ILL RETURN AT ONCE, or some similar subterfuge. Once in Gloucestershire a young schoolmaster came with us, keen as mustard and fit – as he said – for anything. Having sized him up, we gave him three or four days. He started with us on a Monday; by Tuesday he was on his knees and sure enough, on Thursday came an urgent cable to say that some member of his family was dying. That was the way it took them all.

And yet, hard as this new life was for us, we revelled in it. Once, soon after we had started out, our ground was next to a school. The field was so sodden that the lorries could not cross it, and we had to carry everything from the road. As we were toiling away the schoolmaster brought out all his children and got them to carry the seats for us. He just could not stand by (he told us) and watch people labouring like that. Later that night he passed our caravan and to his amazement heard us all roaring with laughter. What on earth have they got to laugh about, he wondered, in weather as filthy as this? But that was how it was: we just did laugh back at it all.

One reason for our high spirits was that we were tremendously fit. Even though we were constantly getting soaked, we never seemed to catch colds, because we were always in the open air, and I fully believed that headaches were something that only rich people got. If somebody said he had a headache, I thought he was spoofing, because I honestly didn't think that our kind of people could get such a complaint.

Working as hard as we did, we had terrific appetites, and we ate wonderfully well, for both my mother and my elder sister were first-class cooks. They really *did* cook in those days, too, for there were no tins or deep-freezes, and almost all our food was fresh: eggs, milk, butter and cream came from local farmers, often as presents; new bread from the village baker, meat from the local butcher, and vegetables from the neighbourhood as well. Also, we usually had a side of bacon hanging in the wagon, for it was a favourite of my father's.

He it was, more than anyone or anything else, who drove us on to such exertions. To have satisfied him fully, each of us would have to have done the work of ten men, for although, as it was, each of us seemed to be doing the work of five, he was still constantly at us for being lazy. I, particularly, was the one he criticised, and now, looking back, I suppose I *was* a bit lazy, and a bit cheeky too, already becoming headstrong with ideas of my own. At the time it was annoying to be told off so frequently, but later I came to be thankful for the training he had given me, because it forcibly extended my own horizons and made me capable of far more than I would otherwise have achieved.

He deliberately kept us short of sympathy. Once in Devon, the shoes in which I walked the wire got soaking wet, and I asked him what I should do. He just answered: 'What are you making such a fuss about? Take them off.' So I walked the wire barefoot – and dreadfully painful it was. At the end of the act I had a deep groove printed along the middle of each sole.

Later, one night when we were pulling down, a much worse accident befell me. Dicky was on one side of a tall flagpole, with me on the other, and he accidentally let go the guy-rope. The pole fell silently, and the next thing I knew, there seemed to be a terrific flash inside my head. I felt nothing – just saw this flash. I shouted to Dicky that I had been struck by lightning, but he had seen what had happened. The pole had broken in half over my skull. Back in the wagon, my whole head felt red hot, and it seemed to have been driven right down between my shoulders, my neck having been compacted by the blow. My mother dripped butter on to my scalp, and there was no serious surface wound; but the next morning my neck was completely stiff, and I could not turn my head either way. My father was not at all impressed. 'If you're dead, you'd better lie down,' he said. 'But if you're not, get up and drive that lorry.' So I had to get up and drive, even though I could not see behind me unless I screwed my whole body round. We realised afterwards that I had missed death by inches, for on the pole which fell was a T-iron with a ring on it to take the pulley blocks, and if that had hit me, I could hardly have survived.

On the whole, though, my father was very careful about our health, especially if we got wet: he had a great fear that we would be crippled by rheumatism, and he would not even let us sit on grass, in case we got damp. Whenever we were caught in the rain he would insist that we changed as soon as we came in; he didn't care what we put on, as long as it was dry, and that was just as well, for by the time we had gone through two or three lots of clothes in the same day, we would be left in some terrible old rags, perhaps even in part of the clown's wardrobe.

The West Country was my father's favourite beat. In those small villages, with their gentle, easy-going people, he was in his element. As we built up the show we would see him standing talking to the farmers and other local luminaries who came to pass the time of day, always looking perfectly turned out in his well-cut tweeds. In Devon and Cornwall many of the people in the audience knew us individually, and thus enjoyed our performances even more – although once someone came up after the show and remarked on how many different artistes he had seen – not realising that, apart from one extra man, the entire show consisted of four members of the family.

From that damp and exhausting start we gradually developed the show, reviving many old-fashioned acts, not least the Joey Pony, or clown's pony. When other circus people heard we were doing it, they sometimes said: 'Oh, God, you haven't gone back to *that*!' as though the idea was light-years out of date. But that was precisely the point: the act was *so* old that no audience of the day had ever seen it.

The Joey Pony was always a small one, so that the children would fall in love with it, and its act was very simple. The tale we told was that it belonged to the clown, and to prove its allegiance it did everything the clown told it to. An argument would break out between the clown and the ringmaster, each claiming authority over the little horse; and to settle the dispute they would have a bet, the ringmaster wagering that the pony would jump a hurdle three times running, and the clown betting that it wouldn't. On the first two circuits of the ring the pony would jump perfectly and amid mounting excitement the ringmaster would cry: 'There you are – I told you so,' whereupon the pony of course would run out at the third attempt, and all the children would roar because the clown had won.

One great joy of those early days of our come-back was the compactness of the whole operation. With a small tent and a small audience, we were in as intimate contact with the spectators as our grandfather's generation had been. We had no microphones or other mechanical aids, not even any electricity: the lights were flare-lamps, in which paraffin ran down a pipe until it hit the hot burner, whereupon it flared out in a loud, roaring hiss. Before the show the lamps were all set on the ground together, and lit from a single flame: the pipes, sticking up, formed a kind of primitive primus stove, and tea was brewed up on them before they were hung up round the ring for the performance.

By then, besides being a clown, I was quite a proficient acrobat. My father had started to teach me the art, but I had also learnt a lot from other circus people, particularly in the winter. Circus people are wonderful at giving others a hand, and anyone with a moment to spare would always come and offer help or advice. 'Do you want a pat?' they would say when I was learning – a pat being the touch someone else gives you to help teach you a backward somersault. At first they would give me an actual lift, and then just a pat to give me the timing; but even to have someone merely watching and telling me where I went wrong was always a help. Any circus kid learns to walk on his hands and to do handsprings, but you need an expert teacher to show you how to go into some of the more complicated movements – for instance a round-all back, or running back somersault, in which you get up speed by running forwards, turn without losing impetus, and do the somersault backwards. If you set about that kind of thing in the wrong way, you could kill yourself quite easily.

Dicky, with his passion for animals, was always after more, and soon we bought a handsome brown Russian bear cub which we christened Bruni. Although he was small when we got him, he grew into a huge and splendid animal, about six foot six when he stood up on his hind legs, and weighing at least two hundred and fifty pounds. As soon as we acquired him I began teaching him to wrestle, and in due course our bouts became one of the show's best-known acts. Unlike a lion, a bear does not mind a man coming to close quarters and grappling with him; but, at the same time, he does not like to feel pressured, so the man wrestling him has to judge very carefully the amount of resistance he can offer. When Bruni grew up he was so strong that he could throw me – or, worse still, hit me – clean across the ring if he wanted to, and I could not possibly hold him if he really decided to go. So the whole act was a carefully-contrived display of token resistance.

Even so, it made a good impression. After a build-up from the ring-master, I would lead the bear in on a collar and chain – but he didn't need much introduction, because he looked so huge walking in after me. Then I would slip off his collar, leaving him only with a muzzle, so that he could not bite, and we would set to. I was stripped to the waist, for better effect, and after circling each other for a moment, we would grapple like two human wrestlers. Then he'd throw me and sit on me, until I wriggled out and tried to throw him. He was much too powerful for me to put him down properly, but sometimes he would let me kid him down, and we could do that quite realistically. As an assistant I had a man called Frank Turrell, a hulking young fellow whose job was to stand by and engage the bear's attention if he looked like wandering off into the audience, or to help me if I got into trouble, and between us we kept Bruni busy for the five or six minutes that he was in the ring. Even with two of us, it was a lively and exhausting session, for if the bear was enjoying himself – as he usually was – he was looking for action all the time.

The only difficult season was in the autumn, in September and October, when bears go through a peculiar period. In the wild they would be thinking about hibernating, and although they don't hibernate if they are being artificially fed, they still get the feeling that the seasons are changing, and they are liable to be bad-tempered. In this period it was sometimes impossible to wrestle with Bruni, for instead of grappling with me, he would hit out with his paws – a highly dangerous habit, since one swipe could do serious damage, as I was later to discover only too well. Sometimes during the hibernation season I found that I could bluff him into a bit of a fight, without really wrestling, but the act was never so impressive at that time of the year.

Even when he was in good form his sheer strength made him a potential menace. Once in Ireland he was hugging me against his chest; I tried to snatch away, and he put on even more pressure, and one of my ribs broke with a sharp crack. It hurt like anything, and the bone re-set itself slightly overlapping, so that I still have a lump to mark the spot. On another occasion we had taken Bruni out in front of the tent and had paraded him up and down in the open to attract people, before the show began. His handler was leading him back through the ring (with some of the audience already in their seats) on his way to his cage behind, when suddenly he spotted the pantomime horse, with two men under it. For some reason he took against the creature, and made a dash for it, dragging his handler headlong.

With one chop he split the horse clean in half. The man in the back, whose head had suddenly come free from the horse's shattered midriff, saw what had happened and disappeared like smoke. But the one in front (who was Tommy Purchase, Rosie's brother) had his head tangled up in the horse's neck, and in a second Bruni had pinned him among the seats. The first I knew of the accident was that a woman from the audience rushed out screaming that we'd better hurry up, because there was a fellow in there being killed by a bear.

We ran in, and there was Tommy shouting 'Murder!' and 'Help!' The bear had him in the seats, and was gripping and hugging him, and all we could see was his legs kicking about. We rescued him not much the worse, and Bruni settled down quite quickly. But once a bear that size decides to take off, nobody can stop him, any more than they can stop an elephant.

A few years later, in Tottenham, my brother Dicky was dragged head-long from the tent by another bear, just as the show was about to begin. He was wearing his ringmaster's dinner jacket and walking into the ring when the animal took fright: away it went, and when we looked outside for it, there was no sign of man or animal. Obviously they had gone too far for it to be worth us waiting, so we started the show without them. An hour later Dicky came back with the bear sitting beside him in a taxi; it had towed him for nearly two miles through the streets before it recovered from its alarm.

In general, bears are far more dangerous than most people realise. They look cuddly and soft, and are associated with woolly toys, but in fact they tend to be mean-minded, and become increasingly unpleasant with age. A man wrestling with a bear is really at its mercy: he cannot hurt it at all, except by hitting it on the nose, and if he tries to do that the bear simply puts its nose away, so that there is no target left. Wrestling the bear, in short, is not the sort of thing people queue up to do; but it was a good act, and brought us a lot of custom.

Another disadvantage of bears is that they do not make any useful, exciting noise, like lions. Far from roaring or snarling, they just utter a quiet whimper or whine, and so give the public no idea of how potentially lethal they are. Nevertheless, they form a good attraction, and besides Bruni we soon acquired three other bears which I worked free and unmuzzled in a cage. These, too, we got as cubs, and we trained them – mainly by strategic feeding – to do a Teddy Bears' Picnic – one sitting on each end of a see-saw and one walking up and down in the middle to rock the others. They would also walk round drinking milk out of bottles, besides going up some steps and coming down a slide. They gave every appearance of enjoying themselves, and I think they really did like working, but even so they were not to be trusted. Two of them were ring-trained only, but the third was properly tame, having been handled since infancy, and, ironically enough, it was he who hurt me quite badly.

He used to walk around behind me, and I would put lumps of sugar in my teeth and turn round and give them to him over my shoulder. Once, feeling that he was too close to me, I shoved backwards at him without thinking, just as one instinctively shoves backwards if one is jammed in a crowd. It was a stupid thing to do, and I should have known better. His mouth happened to be open at that second: my shoulder went right into it, and he closed his jaws. As soon as he'd done that, he lost his head. He gave me a real crunch and lifted me right off my feet, shaking me as easily as a dog shakes a rabbit. Then, still holding me, he put me on the ground and started trying to bite my neck.

I shall never forget lying there on the ground and looking straight into his mean little eyes as he was trying to crunch me. It was a terrible position to be in, but luckily in those days I had huge shoulder muscles, from wrestling the bear and playing the acrobat, and I think they saved me. In a few seconds my brother Dicky had jumped into the cage, and as soon as the bear saw someone else, he dropped me, to see what was happening. Dicky said: 'Are you all right?' and I got up, not sure how badly I was hurt, but by the time I reached the ringside blood was running down inside the sleeve of my leather jacket into my hand. It so happened that Dicky's fiancée was watching the show, and she passed out with fright. But in fact I was not too badly injured: I just had two large tooth-holes, one in front and one behind, and after the doctor had given me an injection, they healed up quickly. If the bear had succeeded in getting my neck I would have been in big trouble, for although he was not so large as Bruni, he was still a very powerful animal.

To make a real success of bears, I think, a trainer must devote himself to them exclusively: he must live with them, eat with them and sleep with them, so that he gets to know each one really well, and they him. Without this really close attention they never realise their full potential, and one finds that all the best bear trainers give their entire lives to the animals. Only by lifelong study can a man discover what is safe and what is not.

The same applies to the training of any animal: if a man is prepared to live with it, he will get far more out of it. I once knew a circus man who kept half his animals in the wagon with him. In that caravan, besides his wife and a pair of twins, he had several pekingese, a chimpanzee and a horse, and because of his constant attention that horse became almost human, learning the most extraordinary tricks, including the ability to kick in slow motion, and to pretend to bite its owner, but never to exert any real pressure. Only by man and animal living together can such things be attained.

Whenever someone in the show was hurt or fell ill, it was a serious matter, for it meant that several of our acts were put out of commission, and in general, at that stage, I think we must have been living on a shoestring. All available capital went into new animals or equipment, and we never seemed to have any money. By today's standards our takings were ridiculously small: I remember that when we once took ten pounds in a day – the entire proceeds of two shows – we considered it phenomenal, and we began making grandiose plans for expansion, thinking that we were already rich. As far as I know, my father did not use a bank account, but carried what capital he had about with him in the form of gold sovereigns; nor, I think, did we have any insurance. We lived very much from one day to the next, buoyed up by our youthful energy and intoxicated by the excitement of reviving the old traditions that were buried so deeply in our blood.

In retrospect, I realise how much we were favoured by luck: somebody always seemed to be looking after us, and never was our good fortune more consistent than on a journey we made from Somerset to Kent in the early summer of 1934. We had been having a thin time, and were particularly short of cash, when we landed a contract for installing a summer zoo on the pier at Hastings. This entailed loading up some spare animals which we did not need for the circus and driving them across country; our cargo included several lions, a kangaroo, some snakes and an emu, and although we had a big lorry, it turned out that the load was far too heavy for the engine. As a result we growled to a halt on every steep hill and had to wait for a more powerful vehicle to come along and give us a tow to the top. Lorry drivers were quite used to this kind of rescue operation in those days, and we had no difficulty in getting help: the trouble was that we felt obliged to give everybody who towed us a couple of shillings, and well before we reached our destination we were down to our last florin. Again we failed to climb a gradient, and again we had to enlist help, but this time, when I half-heartedly offered the man a tip, he good-naturedly refused it, and I quickly put the money back in my pocket. It was impossible to explain to the man that we were all but penniless, but I have never since ceased to feel ashamed at having been forced to appear so tight-fisted.

The journey was long enough anyway, but our constant halts lengthened it still more, and by nightfall, having driven all day, we were still a few miles short of Brighton. Feeling exhausted, I handed the wheel to Dicky, who was (and is) a terrible driver. By then the light was very bad, so that he had some excuse, but in any case, whatever the reason, he very soon put us in the ditch. One moment we were going along nicely: then suddenly we were off the edge of the road, with the lorry tilted over at a horrible angle. At once I began struggling to get out. 'Keep still!' Dicky told me. 'Don't shake it, or we'll go right over.' I didn't mind about that: I just wanted out, because I was thinking of the animals in the back – two lionesses of known bad character, especially – and I didn't fancy them escaping. So I jumped out, and Frank Turrell, who was with us, leaped out too.

At the back we found that the hinged shutters on the side of the lorry had swung open, but the only passenger who came out was the emu, who had been loose among the crates. Out he came – a great big bird, about five feet high, and away he went down the road. He fairly strode it off, and we went after him.

About a hundred yards along the road were the lights of a house, and as we approached a door was opened – I suppose because the people inside had heard us shouting. Anyway, the emu saw the light, made for it, and flashed straight into the kitchen. It was a farm labourer's cottage, and the family was having supper, when suddenly in rushed this great bird, with us hard behind it. There was no time for polite introductions. 'Don't worry! He's not dangerous. Just let him settle,' I panted. 'Do you mind if he just stands there for an hour or so, because we're in the ditch?'

They – marvellous people that they were – immediately agreed that that would be fine, and that one of them would come out to help us recover the vehicle.

Dicky went on ahead to get help from Brighton, but Frank and I stayed, and the family pressed us to have supper with them. So there we were, being fed like princes by these strangers, while the emu made messes all over their kitchen and knocked cups off the dresser. Far from being annoyed, they seemed thrilled that such an extraordinary event should have befallen them. What was more, Frank – who was a strapping young fellow – made a lightning conquest of the farmer's daughter. She was astonishingly good looking, and into the three hours that passed before we got going again the two of them crammed half a lifetime's romance. Apart from anything else, Frank had a legitimate excuse for taking the girl to see the lions.

Eventually Dicky reappeared with a huge, shiny breakdown truck, and this pulled our lorry back on to the road. Having only two shillings between us, we told the man to send us the bill, and frog-marched the emu back to the wagon, walking one on either side of it, like policemen, with our arms round it, and then hoisting it bodily aboard.

Altogether it was a major slice of luck to ditch ourselves where we did, and to hit on those splendid people. But events took an even more miraculous turn next morning, when we reached Hastings. Having driven on through the night, we came to the town quite early, and at about eight pulled on to the front, right outside a big hotel. Frank and I looked like death: neither had washed or shaved, and we had had no sleep. Dicky looked the best of the bunch, so he straightened himself up and went off to find the man in charge of the pier, to see what time he wanted the animals unloaded.

Frank and I sat there in the front of the lorry, dozing. It was a lovely morning: bright sunshine, and very quiet, with no traffic about. Suddenly I saw a waiter in a white jacket come out of the hotel opposite carrying an enormous tray with a silver cover over it. I knew that Frank hadn't been out of the lorry, so that he could not have ordered it, but I also felt instinctively that the tray was meant for us. 'Frank,' I said quietly, 'I've got a feeling that waiter's heading for *us*. Don't accept anything from him, whatever you do, in case they try to charge us. Say it isn't ours.' So we sat there looking straight ahead, ignoring the man, until he came right beside the cab and knocked on the door.

'This is for you,' he said.

'Oh no,' I told him. 'We haven't ordered anything. It can't be for us.'

'Yes it is,' he answered. 'One of the guests ordered it for you. He said he thought you looked tired. There's no charge.'

So I accepted the tray and took off the cover, and there was the most magnificent breakfast either of us had ever seen – eggs, bacon, sausages, mushrooms, tomatoes, toast, coffee, marmalade. We were staggered, but we recovered ourselves pretty fast and ate the lot. Hardly had we finished when Dicky reappeared, still starving. He saw this huge tray and couldn't believe his eyes. 'What are you *doing*?' he kept asking. 'We can't possibly afford things like that.' It took us some time to convince him that we had been given the whole thing: he felt certain we must have stolen it or done something else dreadful.

We were far too scruffy to go into the hotel, but presently the waiter reappeared to collect the tray. Thus fortified, we went on and deposited the animals on the pier, drawing an advance against our earnings to see us home, and leaving Frank in charge. Who our benefactor was, I shall never know. 'One of the guests,' the waiter had said, and I have often thought how nice that person must have been – how nice to have had the thought in the first place, to have reacted quickly to his impulse, and not least to have phrased his message of greeting so pleasantly. He thought we looked *tired*, he said – not scruffy, or down-and-out, or broke, any of which would have been equally true: just tired. Whoever that man was, he had a great influence on my life, for his single act of kindness made me realise how important it is to translate one's warm feelings into prompt action. It is easy to *think* of doing something pleasant, but far harder actually to do it. What that man taught me was to act quickly. I suppose that since then I have made many similar gestures, and all because of him.

CHAPTER FIVE

Building Up

IN July 1934 Rosie and I eloped. We had known for some time that we wanted to get married, but we found ourselves in circumstances oddly similar to those which had beset my parents in an earlier generation. First, she and I had seen each other on and off for years as chance and the annual pattern of the fairs brought our families together. Then, when the two clans joined, we had seen each other all the time; but the more we became involved with each other, the more it became clear that my father was against the whole idea of our getting married. The trouble was not that he did not admire Rosie: on the contrary, he – the typical old showman – thought she was a girl in a million, and much too good for me. She was the eldest of her family, and I was a no-good, layabout second son who never measured up to his own standards. Besides, he considered that we were both – at twenty-two – much too young.

So clearly was he set against a wedding that we did not even discuss it with him. In fact, we mentioned our plan to no one, but arranged to get married secretly in Plymouth. It was, I suppose, a tribute to the strength of his character that we chose to run away, rather than face him; in any case, when the show was in Dartmouth, we hired a boatman to row us across the river late one night, and a car on the far side to drive us to Plymouth, where I had arranged to stay with a friend. I left a note for my mother, and at the last moment told Dicky what was happening, and off we went.

I knew that, by the time we left, the ferry would have stopped for the night, so I had done a deal with this boatman who made special trips to save people being stranded. But he must have been drinking all evening, because when he came for us, in a tiny boat, he was absolutely lit. The Dart was full of ships, and he rowed without ever once looking behind him, missing them by inches and talking continuously. I kept saying to him: 'Look behind you – or this ship will sink us in a minute,' but he never drew breath. The river seemed miles wide in the darkness, and as Rosie could not swim, it was not a very promising start to our honeymoon. In the end, however, our drunken mariner landed us safely on the far shore, and there the car was waiting for us. We stayed that night with a friend in Plymouth, and next morning were married.

I telephoned back to let the family know where we were, and heard (as I had expected I would) that my father was absolutely furious. He was very, very acid, they said, and not speaking to anyone, just raging silently. That left me in an awful dilemma: I was petrified by the idea of going back, yet the only alternative was to abandon the family and start out on our own – and we had no money for that. In the end my mother agreed to act as peacemaker, and although my father remained quite unapproachable until we walked back into the show, he was fine the moment we appeared, and never said a word about our elopement. No doubt he was remembering his own secret marriage, and knew from his own experience that once the deed had been done there was no point in arguing about it any more. Until then Dicky and I had been sharing a caravan, but when we came back he moved out, and Rosie and I moved in together. Thus a permanent bond was established between the Chipperfield and Purchase families, and in the following year our first son, Jimmy, was born in the wagon at Tetbury.

By then our show was developing well. We were constantly learning by experience and improving our acts at every opportunity. Dicky already had a considerable reputation for his skill with lions and tigers, and the show was renowned for its wild animals – something rare among one-day tenting circuses. I worked the three bears, wrestled with Bruni, walked the wire and did two clown acts. My younger sister Marjorie worked the horses (of which we had about thirty), and my brother John, who was still only fourteen, already showed great promise with dogs, training mongrels to walk on their hind legs, to open gates, and to do other small tricks. With these acts, and a small amount of outside help, we could easily do a two-hour show, and we were becoming known as one of the best of the family circuses. Our tent could seat about six hundred people, and we began to take much better money.

My father was still very much the figurehead and the boss behind the

scenes. He had got the family moulded more or less into the shape he
wanted, and we were gradually taking over more and more of the
administrative work. Dicky was the ringmaster and in charge of the
programme, while I organised the publicity. By then we were fully
mechanised, with Leyland lorries, although the horses still travelled from
one place to the next on foot: with one-day tenting, the distance between
stands was relatively small, and traffic was still so light that we could run
thirty horses loose on the road without danger, one rider at the front and
a couple at the back, just rolling the whole lot forward.

We had established permanent winter quarters outside Stockbridge,
in Hampshire, in some old buildings on Chattis Hill, near the racing
stables, which had been left empty after the First World War, and during
the winter months we seemed to be almost as busy as we were during our
tours in the summer. We would be up at dawn to paint the wagons, repair
our equipment and practise our acts right through the day. We also
secured some excellent contracts for putting on small circuses in department stores: sometimes we worked right through the winter in places
like Manchester, Plymouth and Southampton. Usually a section of the
toy floor would be set aside for us, and we would put on a complete small-
scale circus, with horses, lions and even an elephant. The animals
generally lived outside in their wagons, which were parked in the yard
(although sometimes we had cages on the roof), and they would travel up
and down in the commercial lifts.

It was always very pleasant working in those chain stores. For one
thing it was dry and warm – a marked change from the conditions in
which we often had to struggle – and for another the staff always made
much of us. The girls, in particular, thought we were terrific. Used as
they were to having artistic window-dressers about the place, they
suddenly found themselves surrounded by huge men in breeches and
boots, with all their lions and tigers. We felt almost as pop singers must
feel today: the staff would always invite us to their parties, and we soon
felt we belonged to the organisation.

The store would lend us men to handle the boxes in which we moved
the lions and tigers up and down, and although most of the staff were
nervous with the animals, they were not all nervous enough: in Southampton one man lost a finger to a lion, having succumbed to the tempta-

tion to put his hand through the bars of the cage. Why it is, I do not
know, but if people see a lion or tiger, they must stroke it, no matter how
often they are told not to. The animal's perception – as I have said – is
very keen, and it has nothing to do but wait for those inquisitive fingers
to come within reach. The instant they do, it has them. Even my own
daughter Mary, who should know better, since she spends her whole life
with animals, lost the end of one finger in just this way.

In 1936 we got a big new break when we were invited to make a tour
of Sweden. A family of German clowns who had worked in England
were putting together a show, and they conceived the idea that it would
go over much better with the Swedes if it could be billed as an *English*
circus. They therefore needed some English people to take part, and they
engaged us to provide horses, a lion act, my sister with the rolling globe,
and me wrestling the bear.

Having got their English artistes, the Germans were faced with a new
problem: how to make them *look* English. They found no good answer
to this, the nearest solution they could devise being to make everybody
involved look Scottish. So they called the show the 'Circus Scot' and
issued everyone with kilts. There followed an amazing parade in Stockholm, in which the entire company marched through the city in its
Highland regalia. A real Scot would have gone mad at the sight: there
were tiny Italians with tartan kilts reaching below their knees and
sporrans slung on their behinds, or at their sides: there were Germans,
Swedes and an entire Czech orchestra, all marching through Stockholm
in tartan, and not a Scot among them.

We had excellent audiences at every stop, and the tour was a great
success, especially from our own point of view, as it was our family's
first trip abroad and it greatly widened our perspectives. In a one-day
tenting circus everybody is so busy, and the routine is so unrelenting, that
you scarcely ever have time to look around at what is going on outside
your own immediate little environment. In many ways it is like being on
a ship. From the time you start out at Easter, to the time you come back
in November, you are virtually on board a small cargo boat, cooped up
with the same lot of people for the whole voyage, and with no idea of
what is going on in the rest of the world. You cannot leave the ship –
except perhaps to make a quick dash across country on a Sunday, to watch

some other circus perform – and it is worse if you are one of the family who owns the vessel, for you are on call, if not actually on duty, twenty-four hours a day. I have known some people become so exhausted that they have gone to the wrong town and started building up the show all by themselves, automatically following the route of earlier years rather than the one actually planned.

During the season those Sunday expeditions to watch other shows were our only form of entertainment – and highly enjoyable they were, for we got particularly keen pleasure out of watching other circus families, properly brought up by parents who had shaped their children in traditional ways. We talked exactly the same language as they did, and would always eagerly compare notes about the things that each of us were and were not allowed to do. We never considered these other circuses exactly as opposition: they were more like friendly cousins whom we saw only at intervals. What worried us was not their wealth but their cleverness at their job: if they were better than us, we would go back and practise all the harder; and if they seemed a bit smarter than we were, we would just make that extra effort to smarten ourselves still further. The art of any business, after all, is to make what you have to sell as attractive as possible.

Thus, until the Swedish tour came along, our world had been a very small and confined one, and the trip abroad was an excellent experience for our family, as it took us right out of our normal environment and gave us a new look at ourselves.

I myself had to pull out of the tour before the end and return to England in July 1936, for I had a contract to appear at the London Palladium, wrestling the bear in one of the Crazy Gang shows. By then we had trained Bruni to do a comedy act in which he tore the trousers off the referee who pretended he was trying to control our wrestling bouts; we showed the act to George Black, who was running the Palladium, and although he thought the bear terrific, he wanted me to do something different with him, to fit him in with an act which he was planning. So Bruni and I reorganised ourselves, and became part of an elaborate Hungarian gipsy scenario.

First a band from Budapest played Hungarian music; then gipsy dancers came on, and then I and the bear came on and wrestled in the centre of the stage, with the dancers whirling all round us. As in the circus, I had Frank Turrell as a helper, and we both dressed identically, in boots and breeches, but naked to the waist except for a gipsy scarf round the neck. If ever the bear's attention wandered from me, Frank would engage it, but in fact Bruni was splendid, and he took no notice of the various distractions all round him. Even so, I don't think the act was nearly as exciting for the audience as it had been in the circus ring. In the theatre the people were too far away to get much idea of the bear's power, and many of them thought he was a man dressed up in bear's skin, so upright and dignified was he when he walked about.

Financially, however, the season was very good for me. Our expenses were all paid as a matter of course, and I earned thirty-five pounds a week, which in those days was a handsome amount. Rosie and I lived in our caravan, which I had parked in Kentish Town, and the bear stayed in one of the theatre's dressing rooms, which had been specially adapted for him. Feeding him was no problem, as we could buy fruit and vegetables cheaply at the London markets, and he developed a very sweet tooth, being spoilt by the theatre people with sweets and chocolates.

By then he had become thoroughly reliable, and a great character, and whenever some of the Crazy Gang had friends whom they wanted to frighten or impress, they would get us to take him into their dressing rooms after the show. We would never let anyone tease him, but just to have this huge animal walking about and drinking milk out of a bottle was enough for most people. His room was right at the top of the theatre, and at night he would walk upstairs with me to go to bed: the staircase was a narrow one, and we'd brush past all the other actors going up and down. Frank used to sleep in the same room as Bruni, and during the day we would take him out on the roof. There was someone with him all the time, because he didn't like being alone – and the more we were with him, the better we got to know him.

All went well until one evening in December. Our act that night did not seem unusually rough, and I noticed nothing at the time; but the bear must have caught me a heavy blow in the back, for when I got home that night I had a terrible pain in the kidney area. I went into the Middlesex Hospital for observation, and after I had been there for a day or so the pain just stopped. The doctors had been proposing to take the kidney out, but when I seemed to be better they let me out for Christmas.

I was out of hospital for two or three days, but I felt so rotten that I went back in, and a surgeon immediately operated to remove my left kidney, which he found had been crushed. As I came round from the operation the first thing I heard was the bells ringing the old year out.

I never wrestled with Bruni again. The accident was in no way his fault: my being hurt was just one of the hazards of a very rough act, and the bear was no more dangerous after the incident than he had been before. But it took me a year to recover my strength fully, and, having lost one kidney, I did not want to risk losing the other. We kept the bear for another three years, and Frank wrestled with him; but when the war broke out we had to put him down.

For the whole season of 1937 I was out of action, recuperating, but by the end of the year I was physically restored, and doing even the most energetic things again, including acrobat and trapeze work. Except that I had to drink more, the absence of a kidney seemed to make no difference.

In 1938 and 1939 our circus was the best it had ever been. People had begun to say: 'Now there's a family show that's going places' – and so we were. We were getting bigger all the time, and just finding our strength. It was a measure of our rapid growth that we sent young Jimmy to boarding school as soon as he was old enough. This move was a major departure from tradition: in the past, circus children had always played barefoot among the wagons, and never gone to school, except perhaps in the winter. But now there was so much mechanised transport about, and so many people were involved, that it no longer seemed safe to have the children at large in the show. Besides, we wanted Jimmy to have a proper education, for we hoped that by the time he grew up he would have a major business to run.

During the summer of 1938 my father was suddenly put out of action by a stroke. We were playing in Penzance, and he had already given his normal talk, out on the front; then, while the show was in progress and he was doing nothing in particular, he collapsed. We rushed him to hospital in Hale just outside Penzance, but soon after he arrived there he began to come round, and he started to mutter 'Get me out – get me out,' for he had a horror of hospitals of any kind. If we didn't get him out, he said, he would *walk* out – and I am sure he would have tried to do so. But in fact he could hardly talk, let alone walk, for his right side was entirely paralysed – face, hand and leg. Luckily we knew a particularly good doctor in Plymouth, and he, being familiar with my father's quirks, offered to look after him in his own house in the city. So after a couple of days in the hospital we hired a whole compartment on the train and moved my father to the doctor's home. There he stayed for six months, with this excellent man keeping a professional eye on him, and by the end of his convalescence he had recovered all his faculties. The temporary paralysis had given him a severe shock, and he had to admit that he had been very ill; but after he had obeyed the doctor's instructions and lost a good deal of weight, he was able to get about much as he had before, provided he took things quietly.

During his illness Dicky and I ran the show, but the next summer – 1939 – my father came out and travelled with us again. Once more we had a good season, and we began to feel we were on the edge of a breakthrough into the really big time. Like everyone else, we saw the threat of war growing, but somehow we could not believe that war would really come. In any case, there was no question of stopping the show and sitting waiting for hostilities to break out: the only thing to do was to go on working, building up our strength and hoping for the best.

When the war did come, it caught us in Norfolk. Our immediate instinct was to go home, back to our winter quarters in Stockbridge, even though it was only the beginning of September. To this day I could find the field in which the show was pitched when Chamberlain made his broadcast on that Sunday morning. We chalked on the vehicles: 'We're going to join the Army', and everybody helped us pack up and cheered us off in a gay mood. For those who were mechanised, the trip back to Hampshire was simple enough; but my brother John had the horses to drive home. In three days he rode 165 miles, driving about thirty horses all the way, and when he arrived, after a fifty-mile day, the animals were all as lively as crickets. It seemed odd to be home prematurely, and we had no inkling of how long, or how disastrous to the circus, the interruption of our lives was going to be.

CHAPTER SIX

Fighter Pilot

THE war was obviously a disaster for us in the commercial sense. Our successful progress was abruptly cut off, and the circus had to be disbanded: although we kept the lions as long as we could, the increasing difficulty of getting meat forced us to shoot most of them – a heartbreaking process, for these were animals in which we had invested countless hours of training, and which had become part of our lives. Bit by bit our equipment was requisitioned or sold, and the world we had known was at an end. It took us months to come to terms with the shock and to accept that the situation was inevitable.

And yet, strangely enough, I found that my own reaction was partly one of relief. I think that anybody who goes through a really poor spell is liable to get the feeling that nobody cares about him, and that he means nothing to anyone. For the past fifteen years we had been battling away in an apparently endless struggle, alone against the rest of the world. Everyone else seemed much better off than us, and I had developed a 'They've got it – we haven't attitude. Then suddenly, with the onset of war, everyone was thrown into the same situation. Apart from anything else, the war was a form of rest – but it was also an equaliser. If a bomb fell, it might fall on anyone, rich or poor, circus man or king, without discrimination: the whole country was in the fight together, and I found a sort of satisfaction in the knowledge that at last I was *needed* by some of those people who had seemed so indifferent before – that I, as much as anyone else, was needed to fight the Germans or perhaps just to dig people out of rubble after an air-raid. Looking back, I am not very proud of my attitude at that time, but at least I can see how it had been formed.

Once we had settled in to our winter quarters outside Stockbridge, we felt we should give the Army some practical help, so we drove the circus lorries to the camp at Bulford (where we heard there was a shortage of transport) and offered to hand the trucks over. The Army was certainly short of transport, but it turned out that they were also short of drivers, and they accepted not merely our lorries, but us as well; and so, until the engines were worn out, we became contractors and drove military stores about. We were less pleased when the Army came and demanded our tent in peremptory fashion. When the man asked how big it was, Dicky didn't tell him at first, but asked whether he had the right to take it. '*Take* it?' said the man. 'We can take *you* if we want.' And take it he did. The Army paid us three hundred pounds for it – precisely one tenth of what it cost to buy a new tent after the war.

As for the Army taking *us* – that proved more difficult. Dicky was already thirty-five and therefore too old for immediate call-up. I was only twenty-seven, but was medically Grade Four because of my single kidney, and I could easily have avoided military service altogether, had I chosen to do so. To opt out was certainly a temptation, for entertainers and entertainment ran extremely short during the war, and I am sure we could have made a fortune by keeping some sort of show on the road. But I wanted to make some contribution, and I was reinforced in my determination by Rosie, who knew that I would never be happy unless I was doing something positive. I therefore began trying to wrangle my way into one of the services.

At first I had no luck. I tried to enrol in the Army, and was thrown out. I tried the Navy, fancying a career in submarines, but was thrown out of that too. Then I took a longer look at the R.A.F. The thought of becoming a pilot thrilled me, and I set my heart on getting into the air. Medical considerations apart, there was one major snag: the fact that I knew no mathematics, having never learnt anything except the most basic arithmetic. At that stage, however, the Air Force was running a recruiting campaign with a poster which advertised 'Three Months to Brush Up Your Maths', and I reckoned that if they gave me three months, I should be able to learn enough. I based my hopes on my father's philosophy which had been drummed into me all my life – that you can do anything if you really put your mind to it. The fact that I could not do mathematics – I reasoned – was not because I was stupid: the trouble was merely that I had never had a chance to learn.

The first hurdle, though, was the medical one. I knew that if I just

presented myself in the normal way, I would be sure to fail, so instead I
discovered the name of the man in the Air Ministry who was in charge of
that department, collected some photographs of myself wrestling the bear
– stripped to the waist and bulging with muscles – and sent them off
together with a letter saying it was ridiculous that a man in my condition
should be considered unfit for service, seeing that I could go through any
test that air-crew might have to take. I sent the package to Bush House
by registered post, but for weeks I heard nothing, and when I made
enquiries it transpired that although the Air Ministry had signed for the
package, it had afterwards been lost. The Post Office created uproar, and
the Air Ministry (I heard) was searched from top to bottom before the
parcel could be discovered. I have never forgotten the name of the man
who signed for it in the first place: Flight Lieutenant Poop.

Then I got a letter telling me to report to Bush House at once, and
when I arrived there the doctor said: 'You're the fellow who's caused all
the rumpus.' Apparently the whole place had been ransacked in the
search for the missing photographs. In any case, the manoeuvre was
successful in the end, because I passed fit for service.

My next step was to report to Oxford, where I took the mathematics
exam and had an interview. The exam paper was Chinese to me: I could
not answer a single question, and I scored nil. Then I went before the
board – and they, clearly, thought I was mad. Their attitude made me
angry, and I pointed out that the recruiting posters definitely stated that
one had three months in which to bring one's maths up to scratch. 'How
can you put that on the posters if it isn't true?' I asked, whereupon an
Air Commodore replied that the time was designed to allow recruits to
brush up their maths, not to learn from scratch, adding that it was
impossible for anyone to start from the beginning and learn enough in
time.

That made me even more annoyed. 'How do you know?' I said. I
pointed out that the man was basing his opinion on the average person,
but that I might be different. He didn't know me, any more than I knew
him: he had no idea of my capabilities, any more than I knew his.
'Suppose I asked you if you could learn to do a backward somersault in
three months,' I said to him. 'Do you think you could do it?' By then
they were getting annoyed too, and I think they suspected I was trying to

mess them about. But in fact I was perfectly serious about the backward somersault, for I knew what a difficult thing it was to learn, and how impossible it would appear at first to someone who had never done any of the right kind of training. 'You're basing your estimate on what *you* can do,' I told the man, 'not on what *I* can do,' and I guaranteed that in three months' time I would return and do the paper properly. The Air Commodore still said he thought it was impossible, but the Board must at least have seen that I was sincere, for they agreed to let me have a go.

Thus I committed myself to learning maths, and fortunately I discovered a wonderful ally in the form of John Wilson, the master of the village school in Stockbridge, who agreed to give me lessons both at school during the day and at his home in the evenings. First I had to obtain permission from the education authorities in Winchester, but luckily this came at once, and I was able to start straight away.

To go back to school at the age of twenty-seven was an odd experience, and I think I was regarded as a bit of a freak by the children. Not that they knew exactly what I was doing, for I had a desk in the headmaster's room, and worked on my own in there, so that only Wilson himself knew that I was starting maths from scratch. Even so, the story of how I returned to the classroom seemed to catch the fancy of many people, not least Edward Seago, the artist, whose little book *High Endeavour*, published in 1943, gave a rather fanciful and romanticised account of my struggle to join the R.A.F. For some reason he chose to write the book in an ambiguous form – neither clearly fact nor clearly fiction – and he never gave my full name, referring to me coyly as 'Jimmy' throughout. Even so the book was quite a success, and went through several editions during the war.

After a slow start, I got the touch of the maths very well and became quite good at it. In a few weeks I could do triangle velocities backwards, and I began to enjoy battling with navigational problems. It was hard work, all right, but the concentration was exactly the same as I had needed when training with wild animals or learning a new act in the circus (like walking the wire); and now, as soon as I saw the application of maths, the whole thing became both an exciting challenge and a joy. I am sure that John Wilson and his wife Muriel (who helped with our after-hours sessions) suffered much worse than I did, for they had nothing to gain, and merely had all their evenings wrecked by my endless questioning. But both of them stuck to the work marvellously, and they were so devoted to my cause that by the end Wilson was asking my permission whenever he wanted to go out to the cinema for a break.

And so, three months after my first visit, I returned to Oxford. This ability to travel about the country freely still seemed strange and pleasant to me, for in our pre-war days it would have been out of the question to leave the show in the middle of the season and go swanning off to some place not on our planned itinerary. I arrived in Oxford feeling reasonably confident – and, sure enough, at this second attempt the paper seemed like child's play. I was given the rating 'Exceptional', and this time, when I went before the same board, I sensed that they were both impressed and a little ashamed. The man with whom I had had the exchanges about the backward somersault was there again, but I did not reopen our conversation to ask him whether he had been in training. He certainly did not look as if he had.

I was thrilled to have been accepted for pilot's training; but at once a new snag arose. There was – I discovered – a time-lag of several months before I could expect to be called up. That alarmed me, because I was afraid that I would lose my newly won skill in maths if I did not keep in constant practice. Once again, it seemed, the only thing to do was to pull strings.

I found out that the place where the records were kept was in Reading, so I went there and demanded to know how long it would be before I was called up. I was shown into a room lined with shelves, every one of them stuffed absolutely full of cards. The corporal in charge explained that a person's card came into the room at the left-hand end of the top shelf and had to travel all the way along every row, gradually working its way down the wall until, as it emerged at the bottom right-hand corner, the man received his posting. I asked if he could find my own card, and he pulled it out straightaway, from somewhere near the top. I asked how long it would be before I reached the bottom, and he said: 'Months.' Then I said to him: 'Look – I don't know what it means to you, but would you accept a fiver to take the card out of where it is and put it back in near the bottom?' The poor man was horrified and said that he would lose his stripes if he did any such thing. I pointed out that it probably made no difference to the majority of people concerned if they had to wait: indeed, many of them were probably hoping that their call-up would be deferred as long as possible. For me, though, it was different – and I explained how I was afraid that my maths would go stale if I did not use them. In spite of my entreaties the corporal said he couldn't possibly do what I wanted, and I walked out with my fiver still in my wallet. But in fact the man can never have put my card back into the rack, for I got my call-up papers the very next morning.

So, at last, my service career began. I reported to St John's Wood in London, where I was issued with my uniform, and I lived there for about a fortnight before being posted to Paignton, in Devon, where we did our basic training. From there I went to Hatfield, where the De Havilland company were building Tiger Moths and Mosquitos. (The Mosquito was then the latest type of night-fighter, and I remember how excited I was just to see one, little realising that in a year or so I would be flying one every night.) At Hatfield I learned to fly, going solo in a Tiger Moth after seven and a half hours. I enjoyed flying from the start: the individuality of it appealed to me – the fact that one was on one's own, in charge of a machine, alone in the sky, with nobody immediately at hand to push one about.

From Hatfield I was posted to Eaton Park, in Manchester, and there I ran into another terrible block. There were thousands of air-crew waiting for operational postings, and everyone seemed sunk in gloom. There was no hope of going anywhere quickly, they said, and people were being thrown out by the hundred because there were no jobs for them to do. Again I felt desperate, knowing that if I stagnated I might lose the advantage I had won with so much effort; so, through my sergeant, I approached my Commanding Officer, explained my predicament, and asked if I could possibly get a posting. He, too, was gloomy, and said there were only two places in England to which I might possibly go – but somehow he managed for me to be sent to one of them – Wolverhampton. There I had a further stroke of luck, in that I went on with more advanced flying (again on Tiger Moths), whereas some trainees were posted merely to ground jobs.

While I moved about the country, my family were sitting tight in various bases. My father and mother were living in their wagon at

Wishford, and Rosie was in our wagon at Stockbridge with our three children. Dicky had joined the Home Guard, but somehow he contrived to keep a few elements of the circus in being, and with Rosie's help he preserved a small nucleus of animals right through the war. Everything seemed to be going rather better than we had expected until, at the end of 1941, disaster struck us.

One day in November our eldest son Jimmy – then a fine, dark boy of six – was climbing a ladder to the loft in the stable when he fell off and broke his arm. The skin was punctured by the impact on the floor, and the doctor told the local hospital that they had better be careful, because the accident had happened in a stable, and there was therefore a danger of tetanus. Jimmy's arm was put in plaster, and we assumed he had been given the right inoculation.

About ten days later I was lying in bed in my billet in Wolverhampton, awake in the middle of the night. Light was coming into the room from a lamp outside, and suddenly, as I lay there, I saw the handle of the door turn, down at the end of the hut. A man came in, and with that sixth sense that switches itself on in a crisis I knew at once, before he had spoken, that he was looking for me. I said: 'You want me.' He asked: 'Are you Chipperfield?' and I said: 'Yes, – and my son's ill.' He said: 'Yes – you're to go right away.'

I travelled all that night – a ghastly journey in which I was constantly changing trains and hanging about on station platforms. I reached the hospital at about five in the morning, but I arrived too late: during the night Jimmy had died from tetanus.

Rosie and I were stunned. If we had not had the other two children, I do not know how we would have stuck it out: it was they, Mary and Richard, who made us feel life was still worth living. I am sure that we could have sued the hospital for neglect, because they admitted that they had somehow failed to give Jimmy any injection until it was too late. But I could not bring myself to have a row with anyone about what could not be undone. I did not even go to the inquest, because I could not bear to talk about it.

I stayed on at home for the funeral, and when I eventually returned to my unit I was put on orders for not having filled in the right forms. Even then I did not care. I had the feeling that people could do what they liked to me – it would make no difference. In fact the R.A.F. were very good to me: they marched me in on orders, but when I told them what had happened they said that no charges would be brought. Then the Commanding Officer sent for me, and no one could have been more sympathetic. He asked what I would rather do – stay on with my own course, or wait a while and join in with the next.

He said he had had things like that happen to him, and compared the feeling they induced with having a black spot come over the brain. At first, he said, everything seems impossibly black, but with the passage of time the black starts changing to grey, and life becomes bearable again. Excellent man that he was, he put the alternatives to me very clearly, but personally advised me to go straight on – and on I went. I shall always be grateful to him for his kindness and wisdom, both lavished on me at a time when he was under tremendous stress.

The tragedy had an extraordinary sequel. Only ten days after Jimmy had died I was woken again in the middle of the night in exactly similar circumstances. A message had come to say that Rosie had fallen over on a brick floor, had broken her arm, was likely to lose it, and had been taken to the same hospital. It was almost too much to believe.

The man in the next bed to me said: 'Jimmy – if I were you I'd get in my aircraft and take it up to about ten thousand feet and dive it straight into the bloody ground.' I felt almost like he did: five minutes holding the stick down, and my troubles would all be over. But off I went again, on the same nightmare journey, all the way reliving the memories of the trip before. This time, however, my arrival was not so agonising, for Rosie was getting the best possible attention. The hospital staff, appalled by what had happened to Jimmy, had called in the best bone specialist available in London: he discovered that a chip had been knocked off the main arm bone and had gone into the elbow joint and locked it, so he operated to remove the loose piece, and in due course the arm recovered.

After these shocks my service career proceeded less eventfully. I finished my course at Wolverhampton and then went on to the Royal Air Force College at Cranwell. There I flew Oxfords, got my wings, and passed out as a Pilot Officer. Needless to say, I was delighted to get through successfully, because by then my burning ambition was to become a fully-qualified R.A.F. pilot. I would have done bomb-aimer, rear-gunner or any job offered me, but I wanted a commission too – not for the commission itself, but because I wanted to make a success of my whole attempt to join the R.A.F., and to get my wings, win a commission and become a pilot, all in one go.

At our Wings Party, when we passed out, the Commanding Officer made a very pleasant speech after dinner: first he made the usual complimentary remarks about the course, but then he said: 'There's one man I must mention specially,' and he told a nice little tale about me. Of course I was embarrassed while he was talking but soon afterwards I got a chance to let off steam, for I had arranged to do an old-fashioned clown act as part of the cabaret. Rosie had sent my clothes up from Stockbridge, and I luckily found the only other prop I needed – an excellent White Clown in the form of a very thin Scottish pilot who might have been playing the part all his life. Together we did the egg entrée, and all the air commodores were rolling in their seats. For some reason the act went perfectly, and half the audience were convinced that they had been watching a professional clown at work – which indeed they had.

One other memory remains from my time at Cranwell. I became friends with a Siamese recruit called Varanand, a cousin of Prince Bari, the racing driver. Although he was a very good-looking fellow, he always used to complain that he could never get any girls, and I would tease him by telling him that he ought to pretend that he was a prince, like his cousin. Little did I realise that he *was* a prince – a fact I discovered right at the end of our course, when he asked me to sign his will as a witness.

He had several times said how much he would like to meet my parents, so one weekend, when we had some leave, I took him with me to their caravan at Wishford. Their reactions were marvellously true to form. As soon as I telephoned, and my mother heard that a prince was coming to tea, she flew into a state of great excitement, turned the place inside out and forced my father to put on his best suit. He, by contrast, could not care less who the visitor might be, but of course he dressed up to humour my mother. When we arrived, there he was sitting bolt upright in his Sunday best, and my mother going round the wagon like a bluebottle. She tried to make out that we'd caught her on the hop, and that if she'd had any warning, things would have been different, but my father barged straight in and said: 'That's all rubbish. Ever since you phoned she's been dressing me up and getting out the best china!' My mother could have killed him on the spot – but that was just typical of the old boy. He didn't have to dress up to entertain a prince; he just carried on being himself. Prince Varanand saw exactly what was happening, and thoroughly enjoyed his visit.

As our course passed out of Cranwell, we split up for different forms of pre-operational training. Varanand went on to day-fighters, but I was too old for them, and had determined to go for night-fighters. As always, it seemed almost impossible to get what one wanted, but by then I must have had a bit of a reputation for intransigence, for at a conference some-one asked my instructor what I was going to do, and he replied: 'What-ever you put him on, he'll get on to night-fighters in the end – it'll waste an awful lot of time to send him anywhere else.'

I think it was my hunting instinct that made me want to fly fighters, and the fact that I love the dark that made me want to hunt at night. Besides, in those days the Mosquito was a very glamorous aircraft: there were very few names which one could bandy about, but after Spitfire and Hurricane the Mosquito had no competitors, and everyone I met seemed to be talking about it.

In the end I achieved my ambition – although not until I had gone through some typical ups and downs of postings and counter-postings. From Cranwell I went to Grantham, where I flew twin-engined fighter-bombers, and where we had a phenomenal stroke of luck. Rosie came up in the living wagon to be with me, and we arranged with a farmer to park the trailer in a field adjoining the aerodrome, just beyond the end of the runway. One day, about a week after Rosie had arrived, I was flying round in a circuit when I looked down and saw that another bomber had overshot the runway, gone through the hedge, and finished up (appa-rently) right on top of our caravan. Thinking Rosie must be petrified, I got permission from my instructor to land at once, and when we got down we found the wagon surrounded by people and fire-engines. The extra-ordinary thing was that although the aircraft had skidded to within a few feet of the trailer, Rosie still had no idea that anything was amiss. There she was inside, cooking the lunch, as though nothing had happened.

From Grantham I went on to an operational training unit at Charter Hall, outside Edinburgh, where I flew Beaufighters and was told that I

would be posted to Burma. I didn't fancy that much, but I would have
accepted any operational posting readily enough, and I practised as hard
as I could doing the short landings which would be necessary as we staged
through Gibraltar. Then, at the last moment, as I was on leave and
waiting for orders to proceed to Burma, I got a telegram telling me I had
been posted to the Mosquito squadron at West Malling, in Kent.

By an odd coincidence, on the day the telegram came I was talking to
a man called Parker who ran a bicycle shop and petrol pump in Stockbridge, and it turned out that his son Jack – a navigator in the Fleet Air
Arm – had just been posted on temporary attachment to the very squadron
I was about to join. As soon as Jack's father heard that I too was bound
for West Malling, he telephoned him to say that I was coming, and of
course we met as soon as I arrived, delighted to see each other again. But
on only the third night after our reunion Jack went missing, never to
reappear.

I have always remembered how he sat on standby in the operations
room that evening, scribbling away at a letter and looking slightly out
of place in his Fleet Air Arm uniform, with his hat on the table in front
of him. He was a great big, good-looking man, pleasant and generous and
keen, and at one point he said wistfully: 'I'd give my eyes to get a Hun
tonight.' To me that seemed an awful thing to say – exactly the kind of
remark which tempted fate and which my father had taught me to dread.
Then the alert came, and off Jack went with his own naval pilot. We
listened to them take off, and later we got a slightly garbled radio message
in which they said that one of their engines was running hot. But after
that there was nothing: they never came back, and it was assumed that
one of their engines had caught fire, and they had come down in the sea.

Our Commanding Officer, Wing-Commander 'Cats' Eyes' Cunningham, asked me, as a friend of the family, to go and break the news to
Jack's father – and this, with a heavy heart, I did. But when I arrived
back at the house in Stockbridge the father's reaction was so tremendously
brave that I felt ashamed of my own timidity. 'Don't let it affect you or
get you down,' he said. 'Go back and carry on flying. Jack's only missing
– perhaps he's gone to Norway.'

Back I went to start my own operational tour. But my first week or so
with 85 Squadron was anything but comfortable. The Squadron was very

posh and experienced: its pilots had all seen action, and they were not very keen to have complete novices dumped on them. Cunningham looked at us as though we had some foul disease, and in fact he was so disgusted with having inexperienced crews landed on him that he got two of them posted straight on somewhere else. I, however, was stuck there, and although I was desperately keen to learn to fly a Mosquito, at first I couldn't even get anyone to show me over the aircraft.

At last I arranged for George Houghton, another of the pilots, who later became a great friend, to take me up in a dual-control version, but so precious was the aircraft that he would not let me fly it. Then, eventually, a really clapped-out Mosquito was found, and I was told to go out and fly it on my own, without a navigator.

The runway at West Malling was extremely short for an aircraft that size, but I got back as far as I could and took off successfully. Almost at once I went into cloud, and then I found myself in the middle of a swarm of American bombers returning from a raid, some with their engines on fire and most of them shooting off Very lights. The only thing to do was to climb straight through them, and this I did, heading south, because to the north there was the balloon barrage guarding the approaches to London. I came down through the cloud again somewhere over Brighton, but because of the strict rules about observing radio silence, I couldn't call up my base to find out exactly where I was.

In a few minutes it was clear that I had once again performed my well-known trick of getting lost. I seemed to have done this in almost every type of aircraft that I had flown. I had taken off in a Tiger Moth and come down in a farmer's field; I had landed an Oxford by mistake on the wrong airfield, and had been forced to put a Blenheim down on a strange aerodrome by the onset of darkness. Now I was lost in a priceless Mosquito.

Not for long, though; soon I spotted an airfield, and after a very careful approach made a perfect landing. Yet hardly was I down when I saw a sheep walking along beside the runway. A sheep! That seemed to me very odd – to have animals loose on the airfield – and while I was still taxi-ing an Army jeep came racing out to meet me, with a man waving out of the window. 'That's marvellous!' he exclaimed when I got out. 'This is the first twin-engined aircraft we've had land here' – and I found

I had come down at Ashford on an experimental runway made of felt, not designed for an aircraft the size of the Mosquito at all.

The Army officer was thrilled, but I was much less happy, as I reckoned that the runway was barely long enough for me to take off again. Rather than risk it, I rang up 85 Squadron to discuss the problem, and when Cunningham heard what had happened he was absolutely furious. 'HAVE YOU BENT THE BLOODY AIRCRAFT?' he kept shouting, and at least I was able to assure him that I hadn't. After some discussion, he told me I had better not try to take off, but to wait while he sent a fully-experienced pilot down in another aircraft. So I stayed there the night, and in the morning the pilot stripped every possible bit of weight off the Mosquito, took it to the very end of the runway, and just managed to get it off.

The names Cunningham called me after that! He was such a perfectionist himself, such an expert, that he had trouble appreciating the problems of people less skilled than himself. No more, he said, will you fly without a navigator. Never again! But once the heat had gone out of the situation, everyone made a good joke of it, and often when I came in from operational trips people would ask me whether I had seen any sheep lately.

I soon found that the Mosquito was a lovely aircraft to fly. Some people were nervous of the fact that its skin was made of plywood, but from the point of view of the crew it made no difference: the plane handled beautifully, and you couldn't tell that it was not made of aluminium, like most others. The cockpit was so small that the seats were staggered: the pilot sat on the left, slightly forward, with his navigator a few inches further back on his right and their shoulders overlapping. The only way in and out was a small door down by the navigator's right hip, and often when we were flying at night I used to think what a performance it would be if we had to bale out suddenly through that tiny opening: first I would have to feather the propeller on that side, then I would have to trim the aircraft on the remaining engine, then send the navigator out, then at last go out myself. Luckily no such necessity ever arose, and I and my navigator Jimmy Stockley (who later married my sister Marjorie) flew a whole tour together.

By the time I joined the Squadron – in the summer of 1944 – the bombing raids on London had dwindled to a shadow of what they had been, and the main menace was the Doodlebug. To intercept the flying bombs we would patrol over the Channel and wait for the radar stations to vector us on to an incoming V1. The Mosquito was hardly fast enough for the job, and on nights when there was any sort of moon the much speedier Spitfires and Typhoons would come rushing in and tip the Doodlebugs over or shoot them down before we had a chance. Our one real superiority lay in our radar, which was absolutely first-class: once we had locked our beam on to another aircraft, it could never get out of it except by superior speed, and it was by means of the radar that I scored my only kill of the war – a Doodlebug which we shot down into the Channel. Its end was not as spectacular as one would have hoped: although we saw our bullets striking it, we never saw it crash, but Ground Control rang the Squadron later and credited us with its demise.

Intense though it was, the Doodlebug campaign was relatively short, and the Mosquito squadrons were soon switched on to other tasks, among them that of escorting the bomber forces when they raided targets in Europe. Our object in this was to confuse the radar defences by acting as decoys, going in either before or after the main raid, or even making phantom attacks on places which were not in fact to be bombed at all that night. I shall never forget a classic remark made one evening by 'Babs' Babington-Smith, the intelligence officer who briefed us for our mission. 'You may find the defences rather *restless*,' she said – and 'restless' proved the understatement of the year. We flew to some place in the Ruhr which was very heavily defended and arrived just after the first main phase of the attack had gone in. The gunners were letting fly with everything they had, and evidence of extreme restlessness was bursting at every conceivable level in the sky.

But the job I most enjoyed was intruder work. The intruder system – which proved highly effective – was another measure designed to take the heat off the bomber squadrons during their night attacks on targets in Germany. If Hamburg, for example, was the objective, a squadron of Mosquitos would go out just before the raid and a single aircraft would take up station above each airfield on which German fighters were based within reach of the target city. The presence of one intruder overhead was enough to keep the entire fighter squadron grounded, for no pilot dared expose himself, during his laborious take-off, to a hostile aircraft already airborne – and the result was that large sections of the German fighter force could be put out of action for the night without a shot being fired. The Germans were reduced to bringing in fighters from bases so far away that the aircraft scarcely had any fuel with which to do battle: often they had hardly reached the scene of the raid before they had to turn round and go home again.

I found those nocturnal expeditions fascinating. The Squadron would take off together, but once we were airborne we would separate and head for our allotted fields. Each pilot was allowed to choose his own route over the Channel, and I generally went across at some height between nine and fifteen thousand feet. The cockpit was cramped, but the temperature was comfortable, and for a few minutes everything would seem very cosy as I sat there watching the purplish glow from the instruments and the faint glitter of the sea far below. As we approached the coast I would try to pick the blackest-looking spot, away from any lights that were showing; but no matter where we crossed the shore, guns would open up from all sides. Because of the engine-noise in the cockpit, I generally wore head-phones throughout the flight, and in them we would pick up the howl of the direction-finding radar. As the beams swept back and forth, hunting us, the sound would come and go, come and go, with a wow-wow-wow kind of undulation; but as soon as the operator got a fix on us the noise changed to a steady, penetrating yowl that went right through our heads. That was one sound I could do without, so as soon as it started I would take the headphones off. At the same moment, the searchlights would blaze on and the guns would start. I had a simple system for dealing with the lights: whenever one caught us I used to dive straight down the beam. Whether it made the aircraft any less conspicuous, I am not sure, but at least it enabled us to work up a tremendous speed – and that alone made us feel better. In any case, it was better than stooging along horizontally, caught in the beam and a prey for the gunners.

Our reception when we arrived over the fighter airfields was entirely different. Almost always, as soon as they became aware of us, the defenders would lie doggo, putting out every light in the place and evidently hoping that they could bluff us into thinking the airfield was a dummy, or that we had come to the wrong place. They hardly ever fired at us, and we were not allowed to fire at them, especially in Holland, because we knew that there were Dutch workers on the airfields. Our job was merely to sit there above them and do circuits at exactly the same height and speed for the allotted time, at the end of which – to the minute – another aircraft would arrive to replace us. But although the role was mainly passive, several members of our squadron caught German fighters coming in: obviously the aircraft were running out of fuel, and the pilots must have told the control tower that they had to land regardless of the fact that an enemy was overhead – and our lads blew them to pieces during their landing approach.

Once, on one of my first intruder missions, our target airfield was Leeuwarden, on the Dutch coast. Jimmy Stockley found it easily enough, but the place was absolutely dark and quiet, and after we had been going round for half an hour he said he reckoned the field was a dummy. I said to him: 'Well – when we arrived here you seemed very sure it was the right place – and in any case, we can't leave now. But I tell you what I'll do. When one hour's up I'll get back a little and make a pass along the runway, and we can have a proper look.'

This we did. The runway lay at right angles to the sea, and I drew away inland a little to dive at it from the landward end, so that if anything happened we could shoot straight out over the water.

The second we reached the end of the runway, every light on the airfield blazed on, and every gun opened up. Tracer came streaking over us from all sides like barrages of confetti. Jimmy, who had been so sure that there was nobody about, cried 'Open the taps!' and I said 'Don't worry – they're open!' The runway seemed a terrible length, even though we must have been doing the best part of four hundred m.p.h., but luckily we were so low that the gunners could not hit us without also hitting each other, and we escaped unscathed into the friendly night – by which time Jimmy had no doubt that we had been doing our job properly.

Altogether I did intruder patrol over a dozen different airfields, and often, as we cruised through the night, I used to think about my mother and father, and Rosie, all wondering where I might be. My parents, I knew, were in their wagon at Wishford; Rosie and the children were at

Stockbridge, and here was I, ten thousand feet up over Germany. If anything goes wrong, I used to think, the odds are that they'll never know what happened to me.

One thing which always amazed me was the speed with which, every evening, we learned the German colours of the day. This was the code of coloured Very lights which a pilot could fire to identify himself if he was caught up in a mêlée at night: there were always two colours – for instance red followed by green, or green followed by blue. The code-word for them was 'Sisters', and we would take it for granted that news of the Sisters arrived every evening. We assumed that Dutch workers on the German airfields were passing the word out, but, however it worked, the intelligence link was highly efficient, and we seemed to know the colours almost as soon as they had been issued. The system certainly paid off, for once a member of our squadron found himself in the middle of a German squadron on an exercise. As each Luftwaffe pilot fired off his colours to protect himself, the Mosquito methodically shot six of the aircraft down, one by one.

As it turned out, I flew only one operational tour because my eyes began to give trouble. After one five-hour trip in cloud, during which I had sat staring fixedly at the small dials of my instruments, the muscles of my eyes somehow locked so that I could not turn them from side to side. I myself had not noticed anything wrong, but the interrogation officer who debriefed me saw that, instead of turning my eyes, I was turning my whole head from side to side. As a result I was taken off flying and became the passenger and freight officer – a dull job which I did not enjoy, but which was cut short by the end of the war in Europe in May 1945.

No one could pretend that my war career had been very dramatic or distinguished. I never killed a German, because the chance of doing so never came my way – although had the need arisen, I have no doubt that I should have met it without any qualms. And yet, even though I achieved nothing spectacular, I was pleased to have played a modest part in the national struggle for survival; if I had taken advantage of my physical disability, I should never have felt easy afterwards, for people would surely have assumed that I had fiddled things. As it was, whenever someone asked 'What were you in the war?' I could cheerfully answer

'Petrified', because it was true. I had been as frightened as anyone else, and I didn't mind admitting it. But at least I had been *there*.

Besides, apart from questions of conscience, I had very much enjoyed my life in the R.A.F. I loved the flying, and people had been very good to me all along the line. I had met a wide variety of characters, especially during training, and the whole experience had broadened my outlook enormously. The men I was with were mostly interested in the circus, but many of them were completely ignorant about it, and often people would be astonished to find that I was a circus man, especially if they discovered the fact after they had known me for some time. They expected me to be some sort of freak – or at any rate a gipsy. On the Continent things are quite different: there the circus has always been treated as just another profession. But the war taught me that in this country the circus man is regarded as an odd creature – romantic, perhaps, but above all very strange. Somehow I had never noticed this attitude before, perhaps because I had always lived within such a close-knit group. Now, as one small bonus of the war, I had gained an outside view of my own profession.

CHAPTER SEVEN

The Big Show

THE remains of our pre-war show made a sorry sight. During the war Dicky had moved from Chattis Hill to some farm buildings at Sandy Down, which John Lewis had let us have at a very low rent, and there nettles had grown up head-high, over and through the rusting remains of the lorries which we had worn out in the service of the Army. Apart from those wrecks, all we had left were a few beast-wagons, one or two lions and tigers, and a few horses. Our worst loss was of all the show's main equipment: not merely had the tent itself gone, but also the seats, the ring-fence and the ring-entrance. Dicky had done wonderfully well to hold on to anything at all. He had shown wild animal acts in the few circuses that had survived, and he had played in one or two of the shows which went round the theatres, using a ring on the stage instead of a tent. For some of the war Rosie had worked bears, and with help from my younger brother, John, they had just managed to keep things ticking over. Even so, our pre-war existence was in ruins, and would have to be built up again from scratch.

The will to succeed was there, all right: I was determined not just that we should revive the show, but that we should make it one of the biggest and best circuses in the country. By then, with my extra age and experience, I found the idea of the hand-to-mouth life we had once led even more distasteful, and I vowed to myself that we would never again become swept up in an existence so hard-driven and at the same time so precarious. I applied for a quick release from the Air Force, and in due course got one, but before I was actually demobilised I returned to Stockbridge several times and began to collect bits and pieces together. It was quite a shock to come home and start doing some real work again. After my pampered life in the officers' mess, looked after by a batwoman, my hands were like silk: it took a real mental and physical effort to harden myself off and pull back to the condition I had been in before.

We began building the ring-entrance and seats ourselves from any old wood we could get hold of, and we scoured the local scrap-yards looking for second-hand vehicles. We tried several, among them an ancient steam model, very much like some of the ones we had had in the 1920s; but we eventually bought a big old Scammel petrol lorry with chain drive to the rear axle, strong enough to tow three trailers. Our biggest problem was to get a new tent; canvas was still subject to a form of rationing, and we first had to obtain a licence from the Board of Trade. As soon as this came we commissioned a large new tent from a firm in Truro called Penrose who in the past had made tents for my father and grandfather. The cost was staggering – three thousand pounds, which of course we did not have, so we only paid a deposit and owed the company the rest, which was to come out of our first season's takings.

For the rest of 1945 and the early months of 1946 we laboured away, building, painting and practising our acts. As before, Dicky trained the wild animals, but I was to work some of them, and also to do the clown acts. It was not as easy as I had expected to pick up the threads of our old life after such a long gap; but at least we had plenty of time to get ready, and gradually we began to shake down again into an efficient family unit.

We opened again on the common at Southampton at Easter 1946. The omens looked good: the Easter Fair was on, the weather was fine, people were in a festive mood, and our show was coming together well. We should, we felt, be able to do all right – but we could hardly have foreseen that things would go the way they did.

We started with a terrific bang. At nine o'clock on Monday morning people were queuing up for the show that began at midday, and we were packed out for every performance we gave in Southampton on that day and the next. Our plan was to do a mixture of one- and two-day tenting: Monday and Tuesday in Southampton, Wednesday in Totton, Thursday in Lyndhurst, and Friday and Saturday in Christchurch. On paper the programme did not seem too ambitious, as all the grounds were within a few miles of each other – and had the weather held, I daresay we should have gone through our first week easily. As it was, the weather broke and we nearly killed ourselves.

On Tuesday night, after our two shows, we pulled down and began to travel – and down came the rain. From then on, for at least a week, it

rained relentlessly, day after day, night after night, and for half the time
we were wet to our skin. What kept us going was the fact that, wherever
we went, we sold every seat: never in our lives had we taken money like
this, and we could hardly believe it. But how we had to work for it! The
tent – the biggest we had ever used, and seating about nine hundred
people – was in six pieces known as quarters – two for each end and two for
the middle; we had worked out a drill for handling each piece, whereby six
men heaved it up, crossed their hands beneath it, grabbed each other's
arms in a kind of lock, and carried the bundle away to the lorry. But on
some of those first nights, when the signal *Up!* was given for levitating
each quarter, the canvas just did not move, so sodden was it with rain.

So foul was the weather that it took us twice as long as it should have to
pull down and build up, and at Lyndhurst, as we were struggling to build
up in a downpour, someone appeared with the news that the ground at
Christchurch (where we were supposed to be the next day) was under
water. 'Good,' said Dicky. 'That means we can miss tomorrow and get
ourselves sorted out.' But I couldn't agree. 'How can we turn away the
kind of business we're doing?' I asked – and I sent Rosie on ahead to
Christchurch, to find another ground, which she did. There the story
was exactly the same: still raining, and the show still packed to the roof.
On Sunday morning, when we tried to pull out, the vehicles sank to their
axles in the mud and became hopelessly stuck. By a miracle I remembered
that there was an Army depot near by, and I decided the only thing to do
was to find the senior officer and persuade him to give one of his tank-
crews a mud-recovery exercise, and pull us out. Again Rosie was our
envoy, and again she was successful: back came an enormous tank, which
pulled our trucks out as easily as if they had been match boxes.

Away we went, through the rain – and from that moment we never
looked back. Whenever we played we were full: people seemed to be
starved of entertainment, and many came twice in a day to see a good
old-fashioned family show. More than anything else, it was the sheer
excitement of success that gave us the stamina we needed to survive the
strain of that first season. But also we were tasting again the intoxicating
freedom of life on the road: once more we were free to go where we liked,
to play when we liked, to stop when we liked – servants of nobody except
God and the King. Furthermore, we were exhilarated by the joy of

operating as a family again: although we had brought in one or two outside acts to strengthen the show, the family all pulled together as though
they had never been separated.

All these influences served to supercharge us and send us through that
first post-war summer on the crest of a wave. By the end of the season we
had saved enough to pay the balance on the tent. Our worries on that
score, however, were by no means over, for the Inland Revenue, refusing
to recognise the cost of the tent as a business expense, tried to make us
pay income tax on the money we gave for it, and it was only after a long
wrangle that we won our case.

Our success had raised our ambitions to an altogether new level, and
that winter we despatched Dicky to Ceylon to buy elephants. For years
before the war we had wanted elephants in the show, but – apart from
Rosie – we had never had any, and now, for the first time, we had both
the money and the ambition to acquire some. Dicky went off in December,
and a few weeks later he cabled us from his ship on the way home saying
that he had bought nine. Nine! That was incredible. Bertram Mills, the
biggest circus in England at the time, had six elephants, and they were a
sensation. But nine – that was phenomenal. Dicky was worried that he
had overdone it, and in his telegram asked whether he should sell some of
them off. I answered 'Certainly not.' If we were going to be big, I thought,
we might as well be the biggest. So back he came with nine baby elephants, and as I write this, nearly thirty years later, three of those original
batch are still working for him today.

In our second post-war season we again went from strength to strength.
By then there were really four different families taking part – Dicky's,
mine, my sister Marjorie's and my younger brother John. This meant that
the money we took had to be divided into four, but even so, we all did
much better than if we had had to hire a large number of outside acts. As it
was, we did at least three acts each. Dicky trained and worked the wild
animals; John worked the horses and was also the stud groom; Marjorie
also worked the horses; and I, besides doing the clowning, was the tent-
master, in charge of building-up and pulling-down. To the public the
picture was very much one of a family in action, and we managed to run
quite an expensive-looking show economically.

During the summer of 1947 we made another big break-through by getting several of our acts booked up for a winter season with Tom Arnold, the leading impresario. We got the contract through a combination of luck and nerve on my part, for one day I just drove the whole way to London from Cornwall, where we were tenting, and walked into Arnold's office without an appointment. He was one of those tycoons whom you cannot reach without going through about five other people's hands on the way, and in fact I never did succeed in getting through to him that day. But I left messages and some photographs, and just as I was about to leave a man called Ronnie Blackie, who arranged all Arnold's bookings, walked out of his office and asked me to come in for a chat. He and I liked each other immediately, and he said he thought something could be arranged.

Next week we got a telegram asking where Arnold himself could see our show, and eventually he caught up with us in Bath. Since the clown entrée was one of the acts which he had his eye on, I wanted to be sure of doing it when he arrived; at the same time, I did not think it would be a very good idea to try to conduct business discussions with one of the most important London impresarios while wearing clown's make-up. So, the moment the show was finished, I washed off and changed, and appeared in the wagon, where Arnold was by then having a cup of tea, in ordinary clothes. The session was very cordial, and (from our point of view) extremely successful, and Arnold signed up the majority of our acts for his winter season. Only at the end, when everything was settled, did he ask who played our clown – and when I said that *I* did, he was amazed. Why hadn't I told him before? he demanded – and I said: 'Well, I didn't want to prejudice our discussions.'

This was a big step forward in our career, for it meant that we continued earning a very high salary right through the next two winters instead of just sitting about in winter quarters. Then Arnold announced that he was going to establish a huge permanent winter circus at Harringay: again he wanted all the acts we could give him, but this time he also wanted one really major attraction – something that had never been seen before. I immediately thought of a really big troupe of elephants, and suggested that he should have twenty elephants all in the ring at once. He liked the idea, but asked if we could get them in time. Yes, we said, of course – and we agreed that, although the nine animals which we had already trained would do most of the work, we would get another eleven to make up the number. Thus a second visit to Ceylon was set up, and this time it was Rosie who went, to return in due course with the eleven elephants we needed.

Our winter engagements with Tom Arnold did an immense amount of good to our own show, for the money we earned out of season enabled us constantly to improve our own equipment, to buy more animals and larger tents, and so on. We became bigger every year. In all this expansion – I think it is true to say – none of us had the slightest *financial* ambition. We wanted to earn more and more, of course – but only so that we could go on improving the show. None of us wanted money for money's sake – none of us does today – and we ploughed everything we got back into the business.

As soon as I saw the way our show was growing, I stopped clowning and gave up ring work altogether, reckoning that it was more important to spend my time on publicity and management, and gradually I became fascinated by running a big business. I found I loved organising things and people – and I think it was sheer organisation which enabled our show to reach the size and complexity it did. I know that I often annoyed people by my insistence on getting every detail right; but if our show had not been run with absolute precision, everybody would have been miserable. My enthusiasm for punctuality is one obvious manifestation of my outlook: if I say I want lunch at one o'clock, I do not mean that I want it at five past. I want it at one. I believe that details of this kind are important simply because, if one keeps fixed standards in small matters of this sort, life is made that much easier.

By the middle 1950s we had become the biggest show in England, having overtaken even Bertram Mills. Until then the Mills brothers had not reckoned us much, but in the spring of 1954 I met one of them and said: 'If I were you I'd miss Plymouth and Exeter this year, because we'll be there a month before you, and I think you'll be wasting your time.'

'Nothing ever alters our route,' he answered. 'We go the same way whatever happens.'

'Well,' I told him. 'This year I think you may change your mind.'

Off we went, and in Plymouth we did the most enormous business – the sort of business that no one on earth can follow. A month later along came the Millses, and they absolutely starved – the expression we use when you do not take enough money even to pay for the diesel that generates the lights. In Exeter the same thing happened – they starved again, and after that they reckoned us properly. I wasn't exactly sorry, because I remembered, years ago, going to watch the Mills show and wondering when, if ever, we should reach that size and sophistication.

Our own show had grown at an astonishing speed, until we had two hundred and fifty people working for us, and newcomers could live in the circus for a couple of months without meeting everyone else in it. Our tent was the biggest in the world: it seated between eight and nine thousand people, and had been specially built for us by a German firm called Stromeier, near Lake Constance. The main danger with a really large tent is that it may be blown down in a gale, so I had made a study of wind pressures and designed the tent myself. This one had twenty masts; the pulley blocks alone weighed two and a half tons, and there were three thousand lights on the outside. By then we had cranes to handle the canvas, as there was no question of lifting the pieces by hand; but even so building-up and pulling-down were such large operations that we had to have two complete sets of poles, iron stakes and exterior lights. Sometimes we tried split weeks – that is, playing three days in each place – but that killed the men, and generally we stuck to weekly stands.

Although we employed a full-time tent-master, and an assistant, I used to stay up all Saturday nights to watch the tent come down: those thousands of square feet of canvas were the mainstay of our life, and it would have been a disaster if anything had gone wrong. Everything depended on a number of different people dovetailing their individual operations smoothly. Each section of the seating was in somebody's charge, and while that went out, the ring-fence was being dismantled, together with the ring-entrance. Next, the high-wire equipment was taken down, usually by the artistes themselves. Occasionally we had a difficult person who was slow over dismantling, and whenever there was a hold-up the tent-master would come to me, rather than risk offending the man by making a direct approach. Even so, the tent-master was really in charge: he was the key man, and no one could hold him up.

As soon as the canvas was down, away it went to the next ground, where the spare poles and lights would already be in position. The whole operation had to be conducted with military precision, and even in heavy rain pulling-down took only about five minutes longer than in fine weather.

The moving of the vehicles was no less rigidly controlled. The lorry towing the canvas trailers had absolute priority. If it broke down, the driver had the right to commandeer any other towing vehicle that came past. The next most important vehicle was the one that towed the seats, and even the animal wagons had to give way to these two. (The point about the animal wagons, though, was that they were driven by the keepers, so that even if they had to surrender their tractors, the animals would still be fed and watered while they waited.) Many of the animals went by train, including the elephants, llamas, camels and eighty-odd horses, but even without these on the road we needed about forty-five drivers, some of whom towed three trailers, and we had about a hundred wagons in all. Because of the sheer numbers, we never travelled in convoy: rather than cause enormous jams, parties of two to three would be going off all night.

Simply to keep all the vehicles' tyres at the right pressure was a job in itself, and at first we employed a man for this task alone. But then, of course, he left, and rather than train someone else who might also disappear, we gave the job to one of the clowns, telling him that we didn't care how he spent his days so long as every tyre on every vehicle was at the right pressure when the time came to pull out on Saturday night. This worked very well, for the job needed a conscientious man, as many of our trailers had twin wheels, and if an idle person failed to see that the inner tyre was at the right pressure, the fact would not become apparent until the truck was loaded and on the move.

On the ground itself we had a strict pecking-order for the layout of the living wagons, which had to be parked in exactly the right pattern. The reason was partly a practical one – so that anyone arriving on a new ground in the middle of the night could easily find his place. But social considerations were even more important, and the rule was that the artistes who had been on the show longest lived nearest to the ring door. Feelings about the positioning of wagons were extremely strong, and I have known people leave the show because of them: disputes generally arose between newly-arrived, expensive acts, who thought they were the tops, and the people who had been with us longer. Tradition ruled that it was length of service which counted most, and the newcomers just had to accept it. Apart from these delicate social features, there were perfectly sound practical reasons why people wanted to avoid certain areas: no one wanted to be near the generators, for instance, because of the noise, or close to the dog and sea-lion wagons, because of the sudden outbreaks of barking. We – the directors – lined all our wagons up together, along with a wardrobe van and a bathroom. Designing the lay-out of the ground (one of my jobs) was thus quite a complicated task.

For entertaining visitors we had what we called the Big Wagon – a modern caravan luxuriously fitted out with oak panelling, concealed lights, close carpeting, a fireplace and a bar. In this we would hold press conferences every Monday, do business with our contacts, and entertain any V.I.P.s such as the mayor who might come to the show. Sometimes, when the evening performance had finished, I used to take a guest into the wagon and give him a drink. We would talk pleasantly for an hour, and then I would say to him, 'If you look out of the window, you'll find that the enormous tent has gone.' Almost always he would say, 'Impossible!' but when he looked out, an hour to the minute after the show had ended, the tent would be down.

Although the tent was so large (a man standing at the other end of it was so far away that you could not recognise him) we never varied the size of the ring, which remained at forty-two feet diameter – the standard ring in which everyone was used to working. Each time we arrived on a ground we would have between ten and fifteen tons of soil dumped and spread out into an even layer six or eight inches deep. This was then topped with sawdust, and the ring-grooms would fashion a star or some other pattern, with a big C in the middle. A really good ring-groom could make the surface a work of art. One big problem was finding everyone enough time to practise. Nobody was ordered to practise – what they did was a completely professional matter, up to them. All the same, the pressure on the ring was intense, and much practising had to be done late at night, after the show had finished.

In building the show up, the vital requirement was that everybody should stick to his own job, and I went to great lengths to ensure that nobody poached on someone else's territory. My war-cry, endlessly repeated, was, 'You do *your* job, because if *your* horse or *your* elephant isn't ready on time, it's you I'm to blame. Don't tell me that you made yourself late by helping someone else, because I just don't want to know. I want *you* there with *your* equipment, ready for the first show of the day when it opens at four forty-five.'

Another key part of our policy was to keep everyone as quiet as possible. This we had learnt from our father, who had always insisted that during building-up and pulling-down no one should shout or call unnecessarily. If someone wanted a person, he always said, the thing to do was to go and find him, not to yell for him. In some shows, you can hear a wife calling her husband to lunch; but no one ever called my father, or me, because we both knew that lunch would be ready at one, and that if we were late, the food would be getting cold. Dicky was just the same: he hated any shouting or commotion. The result was that both in our pre-war family show, and in the Big Show later, there was hardly any noise; and if anyone *did* scream or yell suddenly, you knew at once there had been an accident. We used to say that the only thing we should be able to hear was the clatter of the seat-boys at work: that, we reckoned, was the lazy man's dream – to be able to lie in bed and listen to the lovely clatter of the seat-boys working.

Accidents, of course, were bound to happen. People were kicked and bitten, and occasionally tentmen were hurt, but everyone was properly insured. We also had some lucky escapes. Once a man was pinned between two vehicles when a driver backed his truck on to a trailer: as soon as he found himself being squashed the man gave a yell and the driver went forward again; but another person who saw the incident said that the trapped man's eyeballs bulged right out of his head with the pressure, and then popped back in again. I saw him next day, and the whites of his eyes had turned blood-red; but apart from that he was none the worse.

To accommodate the whole of our enormous menagerie, both animal and human, in the winter, we had bought a two-hundred-and-fifty-acre farm about ten miles from Stockbridge, on a south-facing slope of the Hampshire downs. We let the land to a neighbouring farmer, but on a site beside the road I built three enormous sheds, about a hundred and forty feet long and seventy wide, in which we stored and maintained the vehicles, quartered the animals, and still had space for a full-size practice ring. The people lived in their wagons along the front, and altogether the place made a pleasant and efficient base from which to operate.

Our family, meanwhile, had been increased by two. When young Jimmy died, during the war, Rosie and I were so grief-stricken that we did not think we would ever bring ourselves to have any more children. But with the healing passage of time we had changed our minds, and when Rosie again became pregnant I sensed (although she never said so) that she wanted an exact replica of the boy we had lost. The moment I heard that the baby had been born I rang the hospital and said: 'Don't tell me – I know. It's a boy, with brown eyes, and he weighs nine pounds exactly.' The hospital staff were astonished, because I was right in every detail, and the resemblance between John (as he was christened) and Jimmy was indeed extraordinary. At the age of a year their photographs were indistinguishable, and I have often wondered whether Rosie, by longing passionately for another Jimmy, had somehow influenced the new child to develop in the same way. Our last child was another girl, Margaret.

Our older children, Richard and Mary, were both at boarding schools. Richard went first to Marsh Court, a preparatory school near Stockbridge, and then to Marlborough College: he always hated going back, and quite often could not be found as the dreaded moment of departure drew near – whereupon we would have to search the entire show, generally finding him hidden under the seats. Dicky's eldest son (another Richard) was even worse. He used to hold his breath for so long that he turned purple, and made himself so stiff that they could not get him out of the wagon. One day they had to send for the tentmaster – a huge man – to heave him out: Richard bit him clean through the thumb, but the man hung on and forced him sideways into a car. Those journeys back to school were diabolical: nobody would volunteer to be the driver, so that the task was usually left to me, and all the way back the children would be in floods of tears. The ridiculous thing was that once they arrived at the school, they forgot all about us: sometimes I used to peep round the corner after they thought I had gone, and there they would be, playing and fighting as if I had never existed. I always felt a brute to force them to go back, but with our nomadic existence, boarding-school was the only means of giving them a proper education.

Mary also gave us trouble to start with, for the first school to which we sent her did not suit her, and she made very little progress. Then, however, I heard about an excellent school in Heidelberg, and we sent her there – although not before I had been over and gone through a gruelling inquisition in front of the all-female board. By a strange fluke, at the first English lesson she ever had in Germany the class was given a story to read about a lion-trainer being killed by a lion in Manchester. When Mary quietly remarked that it was her grandfather about whom they were reading, the teacher thought she was decidedly odd; and later, when I myself visited the school, one of the mistresses said to me confidentially: 'Oh, Mr Chipperfield, there's only one thing that worries us about Mary: she will keep saying that this story we read was about her grandfather.' 'That's right,' I answered. 'It was.' After which they stopped complaining, and Mary went on to learn perfect German.

By then she was already an outstanding horsewoman. She had been riding ever since she was old enough to walk, and during the holidays was constantly doing something or other with ponies. Richard was less enthusiastic, but like any other boy brought up in a circus, he picked up a good many tricks of the trade.

For me – in effect the managing director – the planning and organisation demanded an enormous amount of travelling, and to cover the ground I had a Rolls-Royce and two light aircraft. In my search for new acts I used to travel thousands of miles on the Continent, and I would see between thirty and forty different circuses every summer. Often I travelled with an agent, and most of my bookings were made through some agent or other, for it was not done to negotiate directly with the proprietor of a show. Whenever I found an act I liked I would first ask the proprietor what the people were like – whether they were reliable or difficult, and so on. Then, if I wanted them, I would get his permission to make a booking with the agent. I would never think of trying to buy the act off him by offering the artistes more money: that is not the way to operate, for the circus world is too small, and everyone is too well known to each other, for that kind of competition.

There were always other scouts on the look-out as well, and as I drove through Belgium, Holland, France, Germany, Switzerland and Spain word would keep reaching me about marvellous acts in other shows that

I had not yet visited. 'Have you seen so-and-so?' someone would ask, and off I would go to investigate each new report. But the most exciting thing was to stumble on an exceptional act that no other talent-spotter had yet discovered – and sometimes it would happen, in a remote, tiny circus that no one had heard of, perhaps in Spain, where, during the fiestas, there might be three or four circuses playing in the same town. In general, that was an exceptional period for the circus: on the Continent, as in England, the demand for live entertainment was insatiable, and shows of every description flourished as never before. There were many with whom I would have liked to go myself – to have done a tour or two with them; and our name, I was glad to find, commanded as much respect as anyone's.

The period for which we took acts on was generally three years, for that was the time it took us to cover the whole of England, and Wales and Scotland, doing one year in the south, one in the midlands and one in the north. Our aim was never to show the same act more than once in any one place, so that unless a family had an entire alternative repertoire, to which they could resort during a second cycle, three years was the most we would want them for.

A vital requirement of any act was that its members should be reasonable and easy-going: if they had a reputation for being difficult or cantankerous, we would hardly ever touch them, however great their professional skill might be, for the amount of trouble they could cause by feuding with other people in the show might be out of all proportion to their worth as an attraction. There were so many essential people with whom they might fall out – the tentmaster, the transport men, the electricians, the ring-grooms, to say nothing of the other artistes – and it simply was not worth having our normally harmonious atmosphere disrupted.

On the whole I found circus people wonderfully professional and dedicated, and in our Big Show we built up a marvellous *esprit de corps*. The feeling emerged most strongly in moments of crisis – as happened once after a violent storm in Birmingham. I had gone down to the farm to shoot hares for some lion cubs that we were rearing; there was a tremendous gale, and as I always had a great fear that the tent would be blown down, I telephoned back to the show as soon as I had arrived in Wiltshire to find out what was happening. The news was that the tent was

1 The original James William Chipperfield.

2 My great-great-grandfather James William Chipperfield.

3 My great-grandfather James Chipperfield. The picture was taken on 22 April 1908, when he was 84.

4 My grandfather James Francis Chipperfield.

5 An early poster for the show.

6 Rosie's parents, Captain and Mrs Purchase.

7 My father Richard.

8 The show after the comeback, between the wars: my father tells the tale, while Marjorie walks the rolling globe.

9 Myself working tigers in the early days.

10 More tiger training.

11 I wrestle Bruni the bear at the London Palladium, 1936.

12 Fighter pilot: Edward Seago's portrait.

13 The Big Show: myself, with my brother Dick, and comedian Arthur English in the outsize tie.

14 The Big Show: the Raluys' human cannonball act.

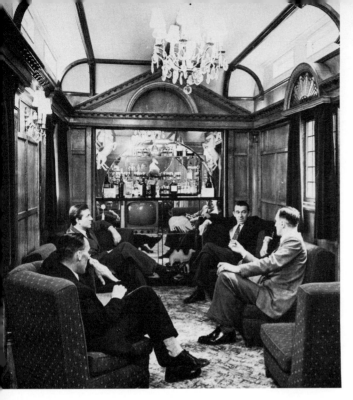

15 The big wagon where we entertained visitors to the Big Show.

16 A worm's-eye view of the Big Show.

17 The Big Show from the air. Its tent, the world's largest, seated between eight and nine thousand people.

18 In Africa with my son
Richard, then thirteen.

19 Among the Tuareg.

20 This was my life – with Eamonn Andrews, Monday 13 March 1961.

21 The monkey jungle at Longleat shows the shape of things to come: the road, deliberately convoluted to open as much ground as possible to view, is solid with cars.

22 With James the chimpanzee and
my daughter **Mary.**

23 With Suki the tiger.

24 Catching an elephant.

25 One lion's reaction to a car driven into the Longleat reserve with a tailor's dummy and some luggage lashed to it. The BBC were filming a warning to the public about the dangers of leaving their cars. Other lions tore the dummy apart.

(*Photo: Syndication International*)

26 Princess Anne visits Blair Drummond.

27 Partners: Lord Bath on my right, the Duke of Bedford on my left.

28 With giraffes at Woburn.

29 A baboon hitches a lift at Blair Drummond.

30 At Woburn, I teach young African elephants 'trunks up'.

31 Richard on safari.

32 This baby hippo, Esme, was born at Longleat and hand-reared by Mary.

33 With Mary's daughter Suzanne, at the age of three, and Dandy Lion, at the Pheasantry, Longleat.

still standing, but that it had split – so I drove straight back, and for the rest of the night we stood about, anxiously watching the wind battering our most precious possession. In the morning, as soon as the storm abated enough to make it safe, we got the members of the high-wire act to take down their apparatus, and then lowered the canvas on to the seats – whereupon the high-wire team, without being asked, set to and spent the rest of the day sewing up the split so that the show could go on that night. Naturally I gave them something afterwards for having worked so hard, but they did not know that I would, and they had done the job spontaneously.

High-level people in general, I found, were extraordinarily careless about their equipment. With their lives literally depending on it, you would expect them to check every wire and fastening; but one team arrived with their entire apparatus worn out. There was not one piece of wire that I myself would have passed. People's attitudes to heights vary enormously. I hate them, and could never work at any altitude. Even to walk up the outside of our big tent (which I had to do to check the bale rings, which carried the highest peaks of the canvas), and to peer down through a hole and see tiny people working in a little saucer of a ring eighty feet below – that was enough for me. But some people are absolutely impervious to vertigo: although a few will go to thirty feet but not more, there are others who think that once they have gone beyond thirty or forty feet, there is no difference in going all the way to eighty – even though at that height any movement you make seems enormously exaggerated.

In the high-wire acts there is very little danger so long as the walker keeps hold of the balancing pole, for with a pole in your hands, it is almost impossible to fall off. The trouble starts when the team do things like pyramids – and for the proprietor of the show it is the worst thing in the world to see a man come down. One night I was standing outside during the high-wire act: the audience was dead quiet as the people watched the figures high above them. Then suddenly there was this sickening thud: I half heard it, half felt the impact come through the earth. I looked in, and there was a man lying on the ground. He had been doing his act on a swinging rope, and as a finale he used to dive off into space, with little straps round his ankles that were supposed to pull

him up well clear of the ground. But that night the straps broke and he
plummeted into the sawdust, just managing to turn his head to one side
at the last instant. His partners rushed in, picked him up and carried him
off, and outside they began bending him all shapes. As he seemed to be
all right, they told him to go back in and take his bow, but I knew that
he must be badly hurt and insisted that he went straight to hospital. Sure
enough, he came out purple with bruises from head to foot, and although
he was not permanently damaged, the accident finished his circus career.
His nerve had gone, and he never went up again.

One of our most careless performers was Raluy, a Spaniard who played
the Human Cannonball. His act was highly spectacular, and one of our
best draws, as both he and his wife had themselves shot through the air,
high across the centre of the ring. Everyone enjoyed the build-up we gave
their performance. We would bring in the cannon, mounted on its lorry,
and the barrel would gradually go up. Then Raluy would get behind it
and start to align and sight it, while somebody told the tale about it over
the loudspeakers. Then Raluy would get up and let a blast or two of
compressed air into the barrel, so that everyone could hear the *ssshhh,
ssshhh*. Next he would climb up and lower himself into the mouth of the
barrel, but wait there a moment, with just his head showing, before
sliding down out of sight. As soon as he had disappeared the ringmaster
would call for silence, so that he could hear any instructions that might
be given from the bowels of the great gun, and then, when everyone was
well keyed-up, he would blow a whistle – whereupon there would be a
deafening bang, and the human missile would go sailing fifty feet or more
across the ring, to land in a net.

Most of the audience believed that a real cartridge had been fired; but
in fact the bang was made by a thunderflash, and the gun was fired by
compressed air. In theory the act should never have given any trouble,
because the cannon was pumped up during the day to a pressure slightly
higher than was needed, and at the last minute the pressure was bled off
until the needle was on exactly the right line. Difficulties occurred only if
the operator failed to take enough trouble, or, as a further stunt, demanded
a very short net. This, in my opinion, was an extremely foolish thing to
insist on, as the size of the net made very little impression on the public.
They wouldn't have been any more impressed if the man had said he was

going to be shot on to a *handkerchief*. What they wanted was to hear the bang and see the body go hurtling through the air. The other important thing was the thrill of the explosion: we always found that if something went wrong, and the thunderflash failed to detonate, the act fell flat – no matter how finely the human bullet might fly.

Raluy did not demand short nets, but his approach to the act was extremely casual. On the first day of a winter show which we put on in Belfast he failed to align the barrel properly, shot out of it in much too high an arc, hit the lights, dropped to the floor of the ring, and was taken off to hospital, where he had to stay for six months. When he returned, ready to start again at Easter, I told him that before he had himself shot off again, he must test the cannon with a sack the same weight as himself. He refused, saying that it was quite unnecessary, so I told him that if he did not test the thing, the act would not take place. Then he said: 'Just to please you, I'll shoot my wife out and try it with her.' I told him he was crazy, but said that provided he tried it with a sack first, I did not mind if he shot his wife off afterwards. So we found a sack, made it the right weight – and needless to say had an exact repeat of the accident: the barrel was angled too high, and the sack flew straight into the lamps. After that Raluy did deign to adjust the barrel's angle, but, believe it or not, he then proceeded to shoot his wife across the ring before he ventured to go himself. He really did not deserve to survive.

Altogether the act was a fairly dangerous one, and we once had a man killed by it when the circus was on tour in South Africa. What happened to him exactly, we never knew: he flew out of the barrel and dropped short, but it seems that he may have had a heart attack before he was fired, rather than have been killed by the impact. Certainly it was an alarming and claustrophobic experience to descend into the polished barrel, and on another occasion a man lost his nerve at the last moment. Just as we were about to press the trigger, we heard him shouting: 'Help! Get me out!' so we had to lower the cannon and let him crawl out ignominiously. In Africa, where cannon-fodder was more easily procurable than in Europe, we heard all sorts of stories about how the act was performed: in some circuses, it seemed, the practice was to get two Africans identically dressed, on the assumption that the one who was fired off was not likely to be in very good shape when he landed. Most of the tents, we heard, were far too low, and the wretched human bullet would go scorching along under the canvas, with smoke pouring from him and the skin going off his backside, to drop right out beyond the ring doors, missing the net altogether. If – as usually happened – he was knocked out by his landing, his double would go in and take the bow.

In spite of its hazards, the cannon was one of our best acts as far as crowd-pulling went, for it had the great merit of being easily depicted on a poster. Another in the same category was Dicky's prize invention of a tiger riding on an elephant. This act was extremely difficult to bring off, for most elephants do not like other animals riding on their backs, and most tigers do not like jumping on to anything that is moving. Only by extraordinary patience did Dicky achieve it. He started training the elephant with a big dog, which he taught to jump up, and he started the tiger by getting it to jump on to a pedestal on wheels, which was about as high as an elephant and could be towed round the ring. Even with these preparations, nothing would have been achieved unless both animals had been completely confident in their trainer.

The acts that I myself most enjoyed were the flying trapeze and the high-school horses. I still loved the wild animals, but to me there was something particularly graceful about the flying trapeze: the people who did it were very fit, very physical, and if the act was well lit, its magic was inexhaustible. *Haute école* – really an advanced form of dressage – is the same: with good lighting, good music and a pretty girl, I think it is unbeatable.

Perhaps the most thrilling part of the show was the chariot race, which took place on a large oval track that ran round outside the ring fence. It was not really a race at all – in the sense that no one was trying to beat anyone else – but the horses became so excited that the event did invariably turn into a competition of sorts. To warm the audience up, we first had the 'Roman riding' – two men riding four horses between them, each standing up with one foot on the middle of a back. This was an excellent spectacle, but was not particularly dangerous for the men, because if one fell off he merely landed on the soft track. The danger came in the chariot race itself, for the wheels and axles of the chariots were so low that if they hit a man on the ground they rolled him over and over – and indeed one of the directors of Tom Arnold's circus was killed by being hit on the head by a chariot wheel. Not surprisingly, half the men we trained for it lost their nerve before the season was through, and we always had to have replacements ready.

The horses, who knew the form precisely, would be so keyed up waiting for the starting whistle that they were off the instant it sounded and frequently knocked down the men holding them. But the charioteer's real difficulties set in when his horses tried to overtake. There was only one place in which this was possible, but I have seen horses become so excited that they jumped with their front legs into the chariot ahead of them and carried on galloping with only their back feet on the ground. On the corners the wheels would slew round and fling earth and sawdust all over the audience, who had to be protected by strong barriers of metal-bound wood.

To dovetail all the different acts together, and to work out the timing of the programme, was an exceedingly complex job. Once we had got it all settled, we tried not to vary it even by a few seconds, but it was a constant struggle to keep all the acts short enough. We had never liked long acts: ten minutes, we thought, was definitely too long, and the audience tended to become bored, no matter how good the artistes might be. Six minutes seemed to us the practical working maximum, and as most foreign acts were used to working for longer, we would write exactly what we wanted into the contracts. Even with every detail specified, it was still sometimes quite a job to get the people out, and Dicky, who was in charge of the programme, would go mad as he stood at the ring door and start muttering: 'They'll be *living* in there next – they'll soon be having their meals in there too.' We had to resort to threatening that if they went over their allotted time, we would start the next act regardless. 'If you're still up there,' Dicky once told the high-wire act, 'we shall just ignore you and bring the elephants into the ring.' That fetched them down all right.

Another recurrent difficulty was that the humour in Continental circuses was traditionally much coarser than in ours, and unless we maintained the strictest control, the clowns would do things that seriously upset British audiences. Usually it was little, apparently offhand touches that made the difference: for instance a horn might sound whenever a clown kicked up his leg, or a little puff of smoke might come out of the seat of his trousers as he left the ring. In Germany or Spain people would hardly notice those things, except to laugh briefly at them; but here they caused a surprising amount of offence, mainly among family or school parties, and we had to be tremendously careful to keep any form of blue gesture out. We used to tell our clowns that they ought to be able to be really funny without any of that kind of thing – and the best of them certainly were.

One of the funniest was Fiery Jack – so called because he was so absolutely silent and miserable – probably the most miserable fellow we ever had in the show. He was tall and thin and wore white make-up, with tight black trousers and a bulge in the seat. He did a lot of little gags, like smoking a bundle of firewood as a pipe, but his main act was a comedy turn with a car that exploded, squirted out water, blew its horn, drove itself and so on. In this he was helped by his wife, whose job was to come on with a bucket and paste and, during one of his spells of intro-spection, while he was standing with his back to the car, pondering what to do next, to slap a poster on to the vehicle, so that it was there when he turned round.

Both Fiery Jack and his wife were tremendous animal cranks: they hated other people, and children particularly, but they absolutely loved dogs, and we would tease them mercilessly by telling them they would be far less upset if they saw a child die than if a dog was killed. There was too much truth in the joke for it to be comfortable, but one day I could not resist exploiting the situation, and just as the wife was waiting outside the ring with her bucket and brush, ready for her cue to go on, I slipped up to her and said: 'Have you heard about those pups that have been born?'

'What pups? she asked immediately.

'Oh,' I said, 'it's wicked. They've tried to drown them in a bucket, but they're not properly dead. . . .' Of course the pups did not exist, but she, hardly pausing to find out where they were, set off in a state of high indignation, entirely forgetting her cue. The result was that a nasty gap developed in Fiery Jack's act, and he missed one of his best laughs. Afterwards he seized hold of his wife and shook her, and gave her the most terrible verbal roasting, all the angrier because he knew he had been made a fool of.

He himself was besotted about animals. Nor was his passion for them in any way abated when the midget who worked in his act had his arm bitten off by a tiger. Of course, said Fiery Jack (and for once he was right), it was not the tiger's fault, for the midget had put his arm through the bars of the animal's cage.

Cranks like him are one of the worst banes of the whole circus business. I have known them spy on the lion-trainers and complain to the boss that the animals are being maltreated – and almost always, it seems, these people are the ones without children. The love that they would have lavished on children is channelled, in a twisted way, on to animals, and only a sort of bitter contempt is left for the rest of the human race. This was so in the case of Fiery Jack – and it was to try to make him value humans more highly that we played tricks on him; but at least he did not spy on anyone, and he was a marvellous clown.

These, then, were some of the characters who lived and worked in the Big Show. A circus that size is an entire community, and it moves from place to place like a nomadic village, a living entity, complete in itself. Inevitably, with so many diverse people thrown together, there are certain frictions, and tensions are inclined to build up, however carefully things are managed; and we made it our policy to throw at least two lavish parties every season at which everyone was encouraged to talk uninhibitedly. One was on or near my birthday in July – a huge supper party held in the ring after the last show had finished – and the other was in a hotel after the season had ended. Besides the artistes, we invited all our accountants, booking staff, insurance agents and so on, and every occasion was well worth its expense simply as a kind of lightning conductor – a means of bringing grievances into the open and releasing them harmlessly. Much useful business was done, mainly in the field of human relations.

My father never really came to terms with this huge private world which we had created so suddenly. He and my mother saw the show, and in a way he was proud of it, for he realised that everything we had achieved sprang from his own rock-like determination, which we had inherited. Once he said quietly to my mother: 'We started quite something, didn't we?' Yet he never really liked the idea of us running such an enormous enterprise. He was alarmed by the amount of money and people involved, and he dreaded the responsibility that such big business imposed on the people who ran it.

As for us, our lives were completely given to the show, and we became intensely familiar with every sound and smell of that existence. In the evening during the performances, we could sit in our caravan talking, with the windows open, and even though a conversation was in progress, I would be listening subconsciously to the rhythm of the show. Every sound would register, and if the note changed or things suddenly went quiet, I would know at once that something had gone wrong. Often we would walk round the ground late at night, just listening to the noises. Sometimes the lions would roar – perhaps because rain was coming, or because one of them was in season, or simply because they wanted to let people know where they were. But most of the sounds were much gentler, and one of the loveliest to me was that of the elephants snoring. In their long tent one of them would always be on its feet, guarding the rest, but the others would be lying like mountains and breathing like the sea. It was a measure of their confidence in humans that they did not bother to get up as we went along the line; but of course as we moved we would be talking gently to each of them – 'All right, Jane? Sally? Any good dreams lately?' and so on – for no good animal man goes into a stable without some soothing words to let his charges know who it is and that all is well.

The nocturnal smells were no less distinctive than the sounds. I could have picked out the elephant, lion and tiger areas by the smell alone. Smells, to me, are intensely evocative, and I would always remember how, when I was a child, I used to think the smell of tigers the most expensive and exciting in the world. To many people it would be just a sharp, bitter stink, even stronger and more musky than that of a lion; but to anyone brought up poor in a circus it is a wonderfully exotic perfume – a scent which one is lucky to have a chance of smelling. When I was a boy we sometimes played with another show which owned a tiger, and to catch a whiff of its scent was a rare event; now, in the Big Show, we could smell it every night, but its expensive connotations were exactly the same.

The Big Show changed my own life completely. From being an acrobat and clown, used to working in the ring, I had become a full-time business man, working in an office wagon from early morning right through the day. I did not miss the physical side of my earlier life very much, for I still did a good deal of manual work around the ground; but what I did miss was the one-day tenting, and the mobility and constant change that went with it. With the Big Show, although we were moving from place to place, we were so much a self-contained unit that you sometimes got the impression that you were not moving at all – or, at least, that the world was moving with you, and the problems of running the show hardly altered from one place to the next.

It was not this, however, that made me decide to leave and branch out on my own. Rather, it was the realisation that there was just not going to be room in the business for all the members of our families. I and Rosie, by then, had four children; Dicky and his wife Myrtle had three, my sister Marjorie had three, and my younger brother John four. In another generation, I could see, the show would have fifty directors, and the situation would become impossible. I do not believe that any family business can carry on in the same form past the second generation. Not that there had been any serious friction between myself and Dicky: we had had one or two minor disagreements, but on the whole we had always got on perfectly together. Yet for some time I had been feeling that bad rows might break out. The root of the trouble was the fundamental difference between Dicky's character and mine. I was always for pushing ahead, for expanding, for getting bigger, longer, faster, heavier – for becoming the biggest in the world. I could never just stroll along. Dicky, on the other hand, could not see the point of continually increasing our effort. 'Why not relax and stay as we are?' he would say. 'We're quite big enough already.' In this he was very like my father who (as I have said earlier) hated having responsibilities and preferred everything on a small scale. I, by contrast, had much more of my mother's ambition.

Another factor was that as I grew older I became more aware of my own qualities. I am not the easiest person in the world to work with. I like punctuality and discipline. I am inclined to be dogmatic and ruthless, and if I get an idea or a project under way, nothing must obstruct it. I suppose I am too single-minded; but that is the way I am, and I cannot change.

In any case, I could see that my particular qualities were difficult in a big family. On the other hand, I believed that my principles *would* work with just my own four children: they, I hoped, would accept them, and see that my ideas were good ones. I did not want the children, in the end, to become managers in a family show: I hoped to find them something more individual and independent to do – although what it might be, I had no idea at the time.

My decision to break away was not sudden or impetuous. I pondered it for months. I discussed it with my wife and children, and with Dicky, and although neither of us liked the idea of my going, we both in the end decided that it was the right thing for me to do. And so, in the autumn of 1955, when the Big Show was drawing towards the end of its second season, I finally took the plunge. We were playing to full houses in Grimsby; the rest of the programme was all arranged, and everything was going well. There seemed to be no particular need for me to stay. Thus on a sunny morning, with every kind of emotion churning inside me, I hitched up our wagon and drove away from the show which I had done so much to create.

The statistics of the Big Show tell their own story. It contained seventy-five tons of seating, twenty tons of canvas, fifteen miles of rope and rigging, fifteen thousand electric lights, four thousand yards of cable and more than two hundred animals. It was certainly the biggest show in Europe, and probably the largest there has ever been.

CHAPTER EIGHT

Casting About

THE change was a drastic one. From running a business which employed two hundred and fifty people, from owning two light aircraft, I was suddenly reduced to sitting on a tractor, ploughing some fields in Hampshire. As my share of the circus business the family gave me the two-hundred-and-fifty-acre farm and the buildings which we had put up as winter quarters. It was a good piece of land – a series of fields along a face of the Hampshire Downs, which sloped up to a couple of copses near the top of the hill. Right on the top was Danebury Ring, an Iron Age fort. Until I went to live there, the place had been only lightly farmed by a neighbour; but my son Richard and I went to work to bring every possible inch under cultivation. We pulled out the scrub that had grown over some of the hill and ploughed up headlands that had never been touched before, and eventually grew some marvellous crops of corn. At first we got a lot of help from Lyn Pond, our friendly neighbour, who was constantly advising us about what fertiliser we should use, or how much seed we needed. Under his expert eye we gradually taught ourselves to do every job that presented itself. I found I loved ploughing – one of the most relaxing occupations I know, and one highly conducive to thinking. Sitting there on the tractor, hour after hour, with the gulls and plovers wheeling into the fresh furrows behind me, I had time to think about my life so far and to ponder over what to do next. My immediate aim was to make a living from the farm, but deep down I knew that I must somehow get back into business.

For the first two or three years I was at a loose end – and also worried about money, for, with the children at boarding-school, our outgoings were greater than our income, and we began to eat into the small amount of capital that I had saved. Casting about for a new line, I tried all kinds of things, among them running horse-shows which featured big prizes.

At Leicester, for instance, we had a hundred-pound prize, which in those days was enormous. But although the show was a success, it only just broke even – and although I ran other shows that turned out well, I made no money from them.

My next venture was equally unsuccessful. I had the idea that at airports, where passengers had to hang about before catching their planes, there might be scope for small zoos, or pets' corners, so that people (and particularly children) would have something to amuse them during their enforced wait. I tried the idea at Lydd, in Kent, but in spite of getting a great deal of help from the local airline manager, the scheme never looked like making money.

Then, for one summer, we went out with a small show which we called the Carl Purchase Circus, and which consisted largely of members of Rosie's family. Our star attraction was to be a hypnotist who had been a great hit in all the town halls. Thinking he would be a big draw, we booked him for the season, only to find that we had made a frightful mistake; far from attracting people to the circus, he scared them all stiff, and word travelled ahead of us, so that no one came to the show at all.

The year after that I tried managing a circus for Bob Fossett, but this, too, was a failure. Although the circus itself did well, the show had a distinct style of its own, and did not want to be changed by an outsider. It soon became clear both that the members of the show were not amenable to being managed by a stranger, and that I was not suitable to be their manager, so at the end of the season I gave it up.

None of these fumblings-about was very productive. But I think the mistakes we made at the time were typical of the sort of thing people do during a period of fundamental readjustment: you must try anything that comes to hand. Throughout that time of trial and error my conviction persisted that we must get back into business; but at the same time we hankered after some occupation that would once again involve us with animals.

Richard, although strong and practical and already a terrific worker on the farm, never showed any great enthusiasm for working animals; but my daughter Mary – by then sixteen – was passionately keen on them, and had already shown that she was going to be a genius at training. She and

I – both having plenty of time in the evenings – together trained Taurus, the most intelligent dog I have ever owned.

He was an almost pure-bred Alsatian, but with just a touch of Labrador somewhere in his ancestry, for his tail went up slightly more than it should have. He was advertised as a puppy in Wishford, where my parents were living in their wagon, and my father, hearing that I was looking for a dog, insisted on buying him for me. Knowing everyone in the village, my father could easily have found another puppy for nothing; but with typical generosity he bought Taurus for me, since he knew that I had set my heart on him. It was the last present he ever gave me, but I often told him afterwards that he had given me the best dog I would ever have.

There was nothing, it seemed, that Taurus could not do. We spent hours in the evenings training him, and in the end he would work entirely on words of command, without any movement from either of us. He would walk on his hind legs, jump, sit down, roll over, drop dead, or say his prayers – all without me moving a muscle. As I worked on him, hour after hour, I kept thinking that this was how my grandfather must have trained the fortune-telling pig, with endlessly-repeated commands. Perhaps Taurus's best trick was clearing the table: I would just say to him: 'Clear the table,' and he would take off it every cup and plate and carry them carefully, one by one, into the kitchen. He had a wonderful mouth, and would carry day-old chicks about without damaging them in the slightest. We taught him to grab people by the wrist and hold them without biting. If I said: 'Bring him over here,' he would drag the person across, gently but firmly. He would also go into the stable and lead out the horse, pulling on the rope attached to its head-collar. Oddly enough, the one thing we had trouble teaching him was to bark on command: try as we might, we could not make him understand what we wanted, until one day we discovered accidentally that he barked at once if we said 'Land-Rover' – because he was excited, thinking it meant we were about to go out. Thereafter we used 'Land-Rover' as the signal for barking, but gradually modified it to 'Land-Rover – bark – good', and finally just to 'bark'. Once he had mastered that, he was invaluable for film-work (as we were soon to discover), for a dog that barked reliably on command was what every producer seemed to want. Tricks apart, Taurus was a marvellous guard-dog. When strangers appeared on the farm he would go for them if I gave him the slightest word; and in the little bungalow in which we lived he adopted an intensely protective attitude towards Mary, lying across the door of her room and growling like thunder if anyone approached it. He was extraordinarily sensitive to human moods, and hated it if people started to argue, or, still worse, to push each other about. Altogether he was an ideal combination of toughness and sensitivity.

In 1959 we suffered a heavy loss when my father died at the age of eighty-five, having enjoyed wonderful health right to the end. He and my mother had been living happily in their wagon, which was parked in a pleasant field behind the pub in Wishford, and there he had continued to delight in the village life which he had loved ever since he was a boy. He had a little shed which had begun life as a pigsty but which he had converted into a workshop and paintroom, and there he was constantly pottering about making toys or painting pictures. For the last twenty years of his life he was blissfully happy: he had no worries at all – and that, we reckoned, was only fair, for in his youth and middle age he had had worries by the score, having so little money and so many mouths to feed. At Wishford he always used to say that he thought he must have done something quite good in his life, for God to reward him with such an enviable autumn span. One of the rituals he relished most was his evening game of draughts with the village policeman, a man named Ransome. Every night he would get out the board and set it up with due ceremony, and the combatants always had a drink or perhaps a cup of tea together. Sometimes my father would argue like the devil, but he always loved the game.

He remained fully alert and active until the day before he died. Then, one morning, he remarked to my mother that he felt very lazy, staying in bed so late. She said: 'Why not enjoy it? There's no hurry to get up.' But get up he did, and at once he fell over, knocked down by a stroke. When I reached Wishford he was breathing easily, but unconscious, and he died the next day, never having come round again. It was the best possible way for him to go, as he did not suffer at all. After his death my mother left the wagon and went to live with relations, and now, as I write this, she is a lively ninety-three.

The year after my father's death, by a great stroke of luck, we made a breakthrough into a new line of country – films. We were not entirely new to the film business, for back in the 1930s we had supplied horses for a picture called *Alf's Button Afloat* in which the Crazy Gang attempted to go hunting but were frustrated when their horses, hearing circus music, would do nothing but canter round and round in circles. Since then we had had nothing to do with the cinema industry, but it was a contact we had made in those early days who brought us back to it. Before the war Hugh Attwooll had been an electrician at the Gainsborough film studio in Shepherd's Bush, and we had met him during the filming of *Alf's Button Afloat*; by the 1950s he had become an Associate Producer with Walt Disney at Pinewood Studios. We met him briefly again in 1953 when he borrowed an elephant from our Big Show for a film called *Beachcomber*, but it was in 1960, when he was making *The Horsemasters*, that he first called on us in earnest. For this film they needed a wild, free-running stallion, and the people who had contracted to produce the animal proved useless. Hugh came to Dicky's circus while it was playing at Kingston to see if there were any suitable horses about; by a fluke I happened to be there for the evening, and at once was able to offer him the very creature he was looking for, since Mary then had a splendid chestnut stallion called High Endeavour, named after Ted Seago's book about my war career.

In a very short time High Endeavour earned us two thousand pounds. Although most of the film was being made at Shepperton, the horse shots were taken at Burnham Beeches: what the film people wanted were sequences of the stallion knocking down the girl (played by Millicent Martin), and of him rearing up to fell the villain. There was no problem in getting him to charge the girl down, for he was one of the most spirited stallions we have ever owned; the only trouble was that in the violent scenes Mary had to stand in for the star, and got quite badly knocked about. The action, however, was so convincing that we instantly made our name with Walt Disney, and from then on, for the next ten years, we were in demand for film work with animals of every kind.

After *The Horsemasters*, our next epic was *In Search of the Castaways*, made in 1961. The stars were Maurice Chevalier, Wilfrid Hyde-White and Hayley Mills. The story involved two children (one of them Hayley) searching for their lost father, who they believed was still alive, and the quest took them to (among other places) the Andes and New Zealand. The animals used included crocodiles, horses, mules and a leopard – the last of course being the most difficult and spectacular. Not having a leopard of my own at the time, I borrowed a beautiful female called Chico from Dicky, and for the seven weeks during which I had her available we were paid £120 a day.

The whole set had to be wired in with netting – overhead as well as at the sides, to stop the leopard going up into the flies – and the cameramen worked inside wire-mesh cages. I spent most of the day on the set, with the animal running loose so that she would get to know everything on it and not be frightened by unexpected discoveries. People often say that film work is dreadfully boring, because of all the delays and repetitions – and I daresay that for the actors this is so. But for anyone working with animals it is fascinating, as you have hours of time in which to study the creatures closely and really get to know them. So it was with the leopard: I never tired of being with her on the set – and I must say the film crew was marvellous, always sending out for cold drinks or asking if I would like them to switch off the lights for a while so that we could all have a break.

For the sequence in the Andes Disney decided he must have a condor, which was supposed to swoop down and carry off the boy. Could I get a condor and train it, he asked? 'Certainly,' I said, but I warned him that it would cost a lot of money. His reply was typical: he wasn't asking what it would cost, but whether I could do it. So off I went to Belgium (where I had heard a tame condor was available) and I came back with this huge bird, which soon would follow me about like a dog. That condor was a tremendous character, and – except when he was in a temper – an extremely good worker, easy to train. As long as he was happy, he would do anything for you, but if you took something away from him, or tried to push him into a place where he didn't want to go, he was liable to go into a sulk and peck you (once, in another film, he did just this, removing quite a large piece of skin from my hand and eating it while the cameras were turning, so that the whole process was recorded).

In *The Castaways* his role was to fly down from a high peak in the mountains – supposedly to swoop on the boy and carry him off. By the time we had got the bird, trained him, rented an immense studio and built part of the Andes in it, the three-second shot had cost seven thousand pounds. But money – as usual – was no problem, and all that mattered was that the sequence should turn out as Disney wanted it. Getting the condor to swoop down was no trouble. I knew that he would come to me as soon as he saw me, so I got a man to take him to the top of the artificial mountain in a box and stationed myself on a bale of straw at the bottom with some pieces of meat. To stop him landing too soon, I got a whole lot of men to lie down on the floor between the bale of straw and the foot of the mountain. When everything was set, the man at the summit loosed him from his box: I called him, and down he came, first time – the biggest wingspan of any bird in the world. It was a thrilling sight, and it made a splendid sequence.

Disney himself was in Hollywood at the time, and at the end of every day's shooting the latest rushes were flown across to him for his approval. The rushes of the condor scene were checked in the normal way, and, being technically excellent, were sent off to him. As soon as they had gone, the artificial Andes were demolished, for the studio was needed immediately for something else. Hardly had the mountains disappeared before Disney was on the telephone from California: the condor rushes were terrific, he said, but he wanted them shot again with the cameras running even faster so that when the film was shown it could be slowed down to give the impression of the huge wings flapping even more impressively. So we had no option but to build the Andes again and reshoot the entire sequence. Yet once more no one worried about the expense: what Disney wanted, he got.

Thereafter, Mary and I became steadily more professional. The film company found it easiest to hand us a copy of the script before shooting began and let us get on with providing all the animals required. We formed a first-class working relationship with Disney, yet in all the years we furnished him with animals we never had a contract or signed a piece of paper. He soon found that when we said we would do something, we did it, and there was no need for any formality: we simply told him what each project would cost, and he paid. We made a lot of money in those years, because although our expenses were high, and there were always a lot of people to tip, as well as animals to feed, we earned enormous fees. Much of our success was due to Mary, whose skill with horses and small animals such as dogs and cats soon earned us a wide reputation in the industry as a whole and brought us many jobs in films other than Disney's. There was no animal which we would not take on: we worked lions, tigers, elephants, snakes, alligators, badgers, foxes – anything that was needed.

Few animals, however, gave us so much trouble as cats, of which we used about forty for the Disney film *The Three Lives of Thomasina*. The story – told from the heroine Thomasina's point of view – included a cat's dream of going to heaven, so we had to create a feline Valhalla, with a mass of Siamese cats sitting around, and an Egyptian-type priestess-cat in charge. Thomasina herself was played by three different Siamese, so that when one got tired we could carry on with the next. We chose cats that were as nearly identical as possible, and made them all still more alike with judiciously-placed dye.

We went to endless trouble to make the scenes realistic. In one Thomasina was put out of the house, and decided to go for a walk to visit the girl whose bedroom was on the first floor: she had to go along the ground and climb a tree, from which she could cross into the upstairs window; but on this particular occasion she was supposed to change her mind half-way up the tree, and suddenly turn round and come down again. That may not sound too difficult – to make a cat walk along, climb half-way up a tree and come down again; but in fact it takes a bit of doing. We took enormous pains to make it all look natural. First we dug a trench along which the camera could travel, tracking the perambulating cat. Then, for a whole week, we trained the cat to climb the tree – mainly by having one of the girls (who devoted all her time to the animal) call her constantly from the upstairs window. Then, on the day when we wanted to take the actual shot, the weather was foul – very wet and windy – and none of us thought the cat would work properly. But – all credit to her – she did her stuff perfectly. Instead of having the girl in the upstairs room, we had her hidden on the ground, and just as the cat was half-way up the tree, she called out. Thomasina turned straight round and came down again.

Much more frustrating were our attempts to make the cat wink. We could make her *blink* easily enough – both eyes together – but Disney had insisted on having her wink with one eye only, and we spent two whole days, with colour film running continuously, before we got what we wanted. The animal spent most of the time under the arm of a stand-in, and we blew at her eyes through straws, one after the other, hoping that the fine jet of air would make her wink. But it was not until, in desperation, we thought of putting a drop of contact-lens fluid into one of her eyes, and thereby partially anaesthetising it, that we succeeded in producing what we were after.

Another stunt was needed to produce shots of Thomasina rising through the sky towards the cat-heaven above. To achieve this, we ran the cameras at tremendous speed while we dropped the three leading ladies upside-down from a distance of a yard or so on to spring-loaded foam mattresses. Even in that short drop they righted themselves, and the film, slowed down and run backwards, showed them apparently rising, as they turned lazily over and over, against a background of bright blue sky.

While we were working on these films, I generally lived in a room in the studio, and in the evenings we would go out to eat at one of the local restaurants or hotels. Sometimes Mary would bring a trailer up, and live in that. But at weekends we would always dash home and work flat out on the farm, where Richard was holding the fort. He, by then, was there all the time, for he had lost patience with school at Marlborough, and I had taken him away.

That in itself was quite a drama. One day his housemaster rang me up to say that he had gone out on a cross-country run and, instead of coming back with the others, he had lit off across the Downs and just kept going. Since then he had not been seen, and the police were out looking for him. As Marlborough was only about twenty miles from the farm, I felt fairly sure that Richard would have made for home. I consulted the farm manager whom I was employing at the time and asked him if Richard had ever talked about running away. He said he had, and that he had once remarked what a great idea it would be to go to France without any money and hitch-hike about the Continent. But, said the manager, if he had to bet on it, he would put money on the fact Richard was hidden somewhere about the farm. So we searched the place, and there Richard was, sure enough, curled up asleep in an old caravan parked in one of the buildings, still wearing his singlet and shorts, his feet covered with blisters.

I rang the school and told them what had happened, and the house-master was extremely generous all the way through. First he told me not to send Richard back in a hurry; then he said that if the trouble was financial, there was no problem, as the school had a fund which could find the remainder of Richard's fees. Altogether, the school's attitude was exceptionally pleasant and fair, and it was flattering to find how keen they were for Richard to stay on – he had done very well at Marlborough, and apart from anything else had been in his house cricket team. He himself, however, had had enough of the place. For one thing he was nomesick, and for another he felt that – at nearly seventeen – he ought to be getting out into the world and doing something useful. I told him he would have to go back and face the consequences of running away, but he didn't mind that so long as I did not force him to stay at school much longer. In the end we agreed that he should finish the current term, but after that he could leave; so I drove him back, and the school – seeing that he was having real emotional difficulties – did not punish him at all. Thereafter he helped us run the farm – and extremely useful he was.

Meanwhile, between farming and filming, I had developed another bent which in the end was to prove a decisive influence in my life – a liking for Africa. I made my first visit soon after the war, while we were building up the Big Show. The journey was really a reconnaissance trip, the aim being to explore the animal-catching possibilities. I flew out and went first to Kenya, spending a few days in Nairobi, but I found I did not like the atmosphere there, for the whole place was still very much old-school-tie and colonial. Nor did I think a great deal of the men in charge of the game department. So I soon pushed on to Dar es Salaam and Mozambique, whence I took a small plane out into the wilds and stayed for a week with a Portuguese farmer.

The sights I saw in Portuguese East Africa filled me with excitement. I saw herds of buffalo and zebra two or three miles wide, moving in their tens of thousands across the plains. I saw hippos by the thousand, some of them – an extraordinary sight – disporting themselves all round the wreck of the German cruiser *Königsberg* whose captain had taken a rush up a river when he was being chased in 1915 – an episode that later gave rise to the film *The African Queen*. Obviously there was an abundance of animals in that huge country – in fact, I judged that there were far *too* many – but as yet very little had been organised in the way of a system of catching and dealing: the dealers were there all right, but they were still hampered by shortages of vehicles and fuel caused by the war, and they had not got back into their stride. In Uganda, too, I heard, the situation was much the same: it was the lack of organised facilities that made me baulk at the idea of catching there. With the advantage of hindsight, I know that we would have done best if I had gone straight to Uganda that first year, but at the time the idea of transporting animals eight hundred miles to the nearest port seemed out of the question.

My first African visit thus produced no concrete results, but I thoroughly enjoyed the trip, in spite of having a rough passage on the way home. Commercial flying, in those days, was still a bit of an adventure. As I came back through Johannesburg there was some sort of strike on, and I just managed to get the last seat on the one plane that was leaving – an old Constellation. When I bought my ticket I said to the girl in the booking office: 'Do they get there?' and she, with a charming smile, answered: 'Sometimes!'

That flight was an amazing experience. The aircraft belonged to El Al, the Israeli airline, and it was full of Jews going home to their newly-founded country. I swear five thousand people had gathered to see them off, and every one of the passengers was loaded down with food to offset the strict rationing which—they knew—prevailed in the new country. Seeing the extra weight which they were taking on, I went up to the pilot—an American—and asked him if it mattered. He knew exactly what was going on and said: "No—it doesn't matter, because we've hardly got any freight." So off we went, with the whole plane stuffed full of food.

The first set-back occurred when the air-conditioning broke down and the temperature inside the aircraft rose to a frightful height, and the boxes of chocolate the passengers were carrying began to melt. But the final blow came when one of the engines packed up and the pilot announced that, instead of refuelling at

Cairo, we would have to land at Khartoum. Now the heat at Khartoum (I knew from landing there on the way down) is like that of a furnace: when it first hits you, you can hardly believe it. But none of the people coming from Johannesburg in the winter had any inkling of what it would be like. The second we landed I shot out of the aircraft and made for the lavatory, where I changed into a pair of shorts. The rest of the people thought the plane was on fire, such was the blast of heat that hit them when the doors opened. Out they came, pouring with sweat in all their heavy clothes—but pouring with chocolate too, for it was melting and running out of their coats like water. I have never seen people so bewildered or in such foul tempers. To cut short a long and painful story, we were grounded in that baking oven for four days, while another engine was flown from Tel Aviv. Not only did the chocolate and sweets melt: all the food went bad and had to be thrown away—and that did not please the passengers at all. Suddenly, as one, they all turned against the airline and began threatening to report it for inefficiency when they eventually reached Israel. In Johannesburg they had been all for El Al, telling me again and again that it was the best in the world, but now they tried to take it out on the crew, pretending the delay was their fault. They, of course, were in no way to blame. On the contrary, the pilot was an excellent fellow, and I felt so annoyed on his behalf that I got a kind of petition typed out which I forced all the passengers to sign. The document proclaimed that the pilot had done everything in his power to make the passengers comfortable and to minimise delay, and I blackmailed the people into signing it by the simple expedient of telling them that, if they refused, I would get the national papers in England to publish a full account of the incompetence of El Al as soon as I reached London.

Being intensely nationalistic, and very touchy about the prestige of their new country, the emigrants could not stomach such a possibility, and soon all except one of them signed. This one man held out long after the others, but I wore him down in the end by putting on pressure through his friends. Even if just this *one* man did not sign, I said, I would still publish my account and not only would I tell the world what a rotten airline El Al was: I would also reveal how the Jews going to strengthen the new state all came home to it with their coats stuffed with non-kosher food, not least the rabbi, who was taking with him a side of bacon. That finished them: the defaulter signed, and I handed the completed manifesto to the pilot, who of course, was delighted. He thought the whole episode a huge joke, and when we eventually took off again he let me fly the Constellation part of the way home.

Not that I blamed the other passengers for complaining, as the delay was certainly very irritating: what annoyed me was the self-righteous way they went about it, and the fickleness with which they switched their enthusiasm for El Al into instant contempt the moment something went wrong.

For me, the enforced wait was enlivened by another little incident. Since we overflowed the main hotel, some of us, including myself, had to stay in a boat-hotel on the Nile. One evening in the restaurant I vaguely noticed the Arab waiter looking at the fancy cigarette-case with built-in lighter that I was using.

At the time I thought no more of it, but later that night I suddenly woke up, aware of the presence of someone else in my room. I was in the top bunk of two, and for a moment I lay absolutely still. Then I saw a dark figure clad in a white shirt immediately beneath me. Without thinking, I rolled out of the bunk and dropped on the man, clutching him to me and gripping him by the throat. He screamed with shock and began to struggle, but I held him tight against me in case he had a knife. Then I got the light on and found that my visitor was the waiter from the restaurant, who had obviously come for my lighter. He pretended he was trying to find out the time, so I dragged him out on to the balcony where there was a great big ship's clock, and said to him: 'There's the bloody time.' And I promised him if he ever came near me again I would drop him straight into the river. Then I went back to bed, having balanced a thermos-full of cold water on the handle of the lock-less door.

Another winter, while we were still running the Big Show, Dicky drove down into the Sahara, partly for a holiday and partly to see if he

could catch any animals, and he came back with such stories of the
strangeness and vastness of the desert that I became determined to go and
see it for myself. Accordingly, the following winter, I assembled a small
expedition: three well-equipped Land-Rovers, four men from the show,
Rosie's brother Tommy, and my own Richard. We drove down through
France to Marseilles, took the ferry across to Oran, and struck south-
eastwards through the Atlas Mountains and into the desert.

For me the whole trip was an astonishing experience – a glimpse of
a world of which I had scarcely even dreamed. The journey down through
the Sahara was an experience in itself. In those days there was no road:
sometimes tracks were visible in the dust, but often there were none,
and we just followed the oil-drums set out as markers. At night we
camped in the open, surrounded by an infinity of flat volcanic ash.
Until then I had never realised how much the human eye depends on
seeing a variety of objects at the same time to preserve a sense of scale;
then, one day, we all sighted what we took to be a grove of trees in the
distance. Good, we thought: when we reach them, we'll pull into their
shade and make tea. But we never reached trees at all: there were none
to be found – only a few scrubby bushes as high as your knee.

It was the sheer space and emptiness of the desert that struck me most.
At one stage we overtook a woman carrying a child, and we picked her
up to give her a lift. There was absolutely nothing in sight – not a track,
not a rock, not a tree. We drove for three or four hours, and suddenly,
by signs, she indicated that it was time for her to disembark. Again, there
was no mark to be seen in the wilderness, but off she went, at an angle
to the course we were following, entirely confident and unworried.
Clearly some instinct which we could not fathom told her exactly where
she was.

Later, far in the south at Abalac where we camped among the Tuareg
tribesmen, we found the same instinct no less highly developed. We would
drive out of camp in the evenings, hunting gazelles, and often dark would
have fallen before we turned to head for home. In each vehicle we had
a Tuareg guide, and sometimes on the way back mine would fall asleep:
if he did, I would deliberately let the other Land-Rovers draw away out
of sight and start heading in a different direction. Then I would wake
the man and say 'Which way – Abalac?' – and immediately, without

hesitation, he would point out the right bearing. Like homing pigeons, those people apparently have compasses built into their heads, and it seems extraordinary to me that, with all our scientific knowledge, we have no idea how such navigation-systems work. Certainly they are highly efficient and precise: if they were not, the people who use them would not last long in their trackless, signless environment.

I myself loved the desert, and would happily have stayed in it for a year or more. We established an easy relationship with the Tuareg, and after we had lived among them for a few weeks they began to treat us like kings, bringing presents to our camp, and even lending me one of their slaves, which at that stage they still owned. Most of the gifts were of dates or pieces of camel's cheese, but I, as the leader of our party, was also favoured with more and more goats, and in the end I owned so many that I had to employ a man as a goat-herd. As the Tuareg's confidence in us increased, they began to show us their guns, all of which they held illegally: they brought out the most amazing weapons which they had wired up and screwed up and nailed up, and through which, in any case, they fired bullets of the wrong calibre, many from cartridge cases that had been loaded three or four times already. The guns looked as though they would be at least as dangerous to the people firing them as to the opposition, but they were their owners' most treasured possessions, for each one had been acquired only by the desperate expedient of killing its owner, and it was with these antique weapons that the tribesmen took on the hated French Foreign Legion.

We, in turn, gave them presents of tea and sugar, and at night they would sit round our fire, telling stories, which were interpreted by an American missionary whom we had picked up in Tahoua, a small town about a hundred miles away. During the day we let them fire the Holland & Holland .500 big game rifle which we had brought with us. It was a marvellous sight to see these tiny, light-weight Africans being blown backwards, heels over head, by the recoil, but coming up smiling and demanding another shot.

A more practical service that we performed for them was to take them hunting in the Land-Rovers. Their customs forbade them to eat any animal whose throat had not been cut, so several of them would accompany us to make sure that every victim died correctly: even after we had shot a gazelle with the rifle, they would leap on it and cut its throat. Once I shot a gazelle which wasn't quite dead, and as I was about to put another bullet through its head, one of the men lay on top of it to stop me firing, so that he could finish it off in the traditional way. I shouted to him that if he didn't get off, I would shoot him too – and, of course, he was up in a flash. Not that it stopped them eating the meat afterwards.

Nor, if they were hungry, did their scruples prevent them eating a female, even though their normal practice was to eat males only. They had extraordinary eyesight, and could pick out a buck antelope from a doe at hundreds of yards' range, even though both animals carried identical sets of antlers. Yet sometimes we did shoot a doe by mistake, and they ate the meat readily enough, burying chunks of it in the hot coals of a fire, leaving it covered over for some time, and then taking it out coated in ash. It made a delicious smell roasting, and, once one had knocked the ash off it, its taste was no less good.

Our European idea of cruelty had no meaning for these people. Once when we were short of food we came across a flock of guinea fowl, so I leaped off the truck and blasted two barrels into them with a shot-gun. Several were killed outright, but several were wounded, so I sent the slave I had with me off to catch the runners. He had a simple method of making sure they did not escape: instead of knocking them on the head, as any of us would have done, he pulled one leg off each and left the wretched thing still alive, flapping on the ground. Tommy, who is very touchy about people being cruel to animals, was absolutely furious and wanted to kill the fellow there and then, but I pointed out to him that what the man had done was obviously quite natural to him, and I realised that it would be useless to remonstrate.

There were several very strange features of that environment. One was the fact that animals and birds seemed to be able to exist without any water. As far as we could see, in most areas there was no water at all, and we ourselves had to drive a hundred miles to find a decent well. Another odd feature was the way the Tuareg seemed to know instinctively how to regulate their own diet. Having lived mainly on dates and cheese for weeks, they would suddenly gorge themselves on meat when we shot them an antelope; but then, having eaten so much lean flesh, they said they must have fat – otherwise they would be ill – and they made me shoot them a bustard, for the neck of the great, tall bird was completely lined with fat, and they cooked that up and ate it, almost as a kind of medicine or an antidote to the meat.

Altogether, it was a fascinating experience to live with such primitive people. I really made my mark with them one day when they persuaded me to join in a spear-throwing practice. They had a gourd which they would roll along the ground, and they threw spears at it as it went. Rather reluctantly I agreed to have a go, and by a miracle I put the spear right through the middle of the gourd at the first shot. They were all immensely impressed – they rushed at me, shaking me not just by the hand, but all up the arm, as they do in moments of excitement, and they clamoured for me to do it again. I was too crafty for that, and rested on my laurels, but ever afterwards they looked on me as a kind of visiting king.

And yet, although we enjoyed ourselves, we did not accomplish very much, for we had really just come on a swan, without any clear idea of what we wanted to do. The only thing we did try, in a rather half-hearted way, was to catch some ostriches; we had a vague idea that we might use them in the circus, but as we had no means of getting them home the whole plan was rather futile. That did not stop us having a go, and in the process we learned a good deal about ostriches, not least that they have phenomenally good eyes. We found that if we drove towards them they would start to move off at ranges up to a mile: at first we could hardly believe that they were taking evasive action at that distance but it soon became clear that they were, and we realised that the only way to catch any would be to push them down a narrowing funnel of thorn bushes into a corral. We did succeed in cornering a few, and although most of them broke out again, we actually captured one – which, of course, the Tuareg were all too keen to slaughter.

Throughout our stay in the desert, the Tuareg never ceased to surprise us, whether by the exercise of some inbuilt skill which we allegedly more civilised people did not possess (like that of direction-finding), or simply by revealing some unexpected possession. When I announced that I was going to drive to Tahoua, for instance, it suddenly became apparent that, in spite of their poverty-striken appearance, they had a considerable amount of money about them, in gold and notes, for one chief offered me twenty pounds in cash to take him and his slave with me. Of course I gave them a lift for nothing – and a nightmare journey it was, for the old man was desperately sick in the back of the jeep throughout the five-hour trip. When we reached Tahoua he staggered out, and the last we saw of him, he went crawling off along the gutter at the edge of the street, with his slave trotting beside him, in such an extremity of retching and groaning that we were seriously afraid he might die. But later, to my astonishment, I heard that he had enjoyed every moment of the ride (his first in a motor vehicle) and that he was clamouring for a return trip.

In January I flew home from Kano to rejoin the circus, leaving the others to bring the vehicles back. The main snag about all these early trips to Africa was that, even if we had caught animals and shipped them out successfully, we would have had nowhere to put them. Apart from the circus and our own films, which needed only a few, we had no market, and it was not until 1960, when I built and opened a small zoo in Southampton, that we had a base of our own into which we could put the animals we caught.

It was purely by chance that we became established in Southampton. I was driving through the town one day and happened to see some workmen taking down a hoarding. I asked one of them if there had been a horse-show, and he said No – it had just been the general Southampton show. I told the man my name, and that I would be interested to hear about any other shows which were staged there. After that I thought no more about it, until suddenly a message came from the Council saying that they had heard I was interested specifically in horse-shows. I went along and explained that there had been a slight misunderstanding, and that I had made only a general inquiry. But then it turned out that there had been horse-shows in Southampton in the past, and that the Council were again looking for a person to run one. So I agreed to do it, organised the show, got it on television, and managed to make the event a success. I ran the show for several years, and one summer it struck me that the piece of ground next to the show – a sort of open field on which the Council grew plants for the gardens in the town – would make an ideal site for a zoo. So I casually said to a member of the Council: 'When are you going to have a zoo on the Common?' – and suddenly a new project was born. The Council liked the idea; I applied for permission, got it, leased the site, and designed the buildings myself. At first the zoo was a very modest affair, with just a few animals, and it did not cost us a great deal, for Richard and I put up most of the buildings with our own hands, going over from the farm in the evenings, when we had finished there, and carrying on until ten or eleven at night, helped by an enormously strong young man called Rodney Dring who was with us on the farm.

Probably the most expensive single building was the bungalow which we built inside the zoo compound, for, as soon as we made the decision to go back into the animal business, we decided also to live on the new site. Many were the animals that shared that little house with us, but none gave us more fun – or trouble – than James the chimpanzee. A dealer brought him to the zoo one day when he was about a year old, and Rosie, who is far too soft-hearted in these matters, felt sorry for him because he had a cold and a runny nose. So sorry did she feel that she allowed the dealer to relieve her of a hundred and fifty pounds. I bet the wretched creature would not last a week, but she nursed him so well that he recovered full health and in due course grew into a magnificent animal over four feet tall.

We brought him into the house nearly every night, even when he grew up, and the result was that he got to know us both extremely well. But whereas I was always very much his trainer, and a person to be obeyed, Rosie was definitely his mother and his refuge. Whenever trouble threatened, he would run to her and cling on tight. So long as he was small, this was no problem, but when he became adult his sheer strength made him potentially very dangerous – for a chimp is several times stronger than the most powerful man, and, no matter how good his temper, is liable to hurt people without meaning to if they get in his way. An adult chimp with a bad temper is an exceedingly unpleasant proposition – so much so that I would rather handle an adult lion, any day.

James was a splendid animal to train because, like all chimps, he was so intelligent that he more or less copied what I did, without my having to din things into him by repetition. I taught him to do backwards somersaults, for instance, by merely lifting one of his feet and giving him a push. Very soon he got to like the feeling, and would start doing it himself. I had only to say to him: 'Come on, James – somersault,' and over he would go. He also learnt to walk on his hands – but this he taught himself. How he managed it, I never knew: one day I just saw him going along upside down, and thereafter he would do it to order. I think he did it originally to show off, and of course as soon as I praised him and played him up a bit, he was keen to do it some more.

Having travelled about in cars since childhood, he was a thoroughly experienced motorist, and often drove up from Southampton to Pinewood with me when I was working on films. He sat up in the other front seat beside me, just like another human, and sometimes in traffic jams I would see other drivers do the most tremendous double-take as they suddenly realised what it was sitting a foot or two away from them. James never interfered with the gears or steering wheel, but all his motoring life he remained a dreadfully nervous passenger, putting out his right hand and laying it gently on my arm whenever he thought I was going too fast. Speed was one thing he hated, and hump-back bridges another: at any moment of crisis he would reach out for me, as though physical contact increased his confidence. Occasionally, when he got bored, he would climb over into the back and survey the scene through the rear window – to the amazement of anybody following.

In general he was very little bother, although, in his special room at the studio, he had to have somebody with him all the time to stop him getting worried and breaking out. It was his habit of escaping that really caused trouble. Once he broke out of the studio while we were filming and ran off down the street, but luckily I had Taurus the Alsatian with me: he and the chimp knew each other well, and when I sent the dog after him, James was happy enough to turn back. The odd thing was that the people he passed took hardly any notice of him, as though they did not realise what they were seeing.

Another time I arrived home in Southampton from America to be greeted with the news that James had escaped from the zoo and gone to ground in a public lavatory just down the road, at the corner of the park. I rushed straight there and found the place surrounded by police and firemen, with the doorway barricaded up with boxes and cages of every size. Inside, James was having a high old time ripping out the plumbing: for once he ignored my voice, but luckily Mary arrived at almost the same time, having also been summoned by the family, and when he heard her call, out he came – with two hundred pounds' worth of damage to his credit.

His longest and most alarming escapade, however, came when he got out of his cage in the zoo and went to ground in our bungalow, where, for four tense hours, he was incarcerated with Rosie and her mother. I was away, making a film, and knew nothing of the episode until it was nearly over, but I do not think many other women would have played it as coolly as Rosie did – if indeed any other woman would have survived at all.

The trouble began when James's keeper went in to feed him. Instead of first shutting the chimp into his sleeping quarters, the man went straight into the main cage, and in a second James had rushed past him into the open. The other keepers tried to block his way, but James took a kind of Kung Fu jump at one of them, hit him in the chest with his feet, and sent him flying. Then he ran straight to our house, but, finding he could not get in, set off down the road, only to turn back and try the house – his normal refuge – again. This time he got in, and he rushed straight into the smaller of the two bedrooms, where my mother-in-law was in bed. Having briefly terrified her by bouncing on the bed, he went out again into the sitting-room, where Rosie was – and instantly my mother-in-law barricaded herself into her room with the furniture piled against the door.

This left the chimp with Rosie in the main room, in the middle of the house, but she could not reach the telephone, which was in the hall, for fear that James might bolt again if she opened the door. Outside, zoo staff brought up various cages and manoeuvred them against the door; also they brought up a long rope with a clip on the end that could be attached to James's collar. But the chimp had no intention either of leaving or of allowing himself to be caught: although he wanted to be with Rosie, whenever she tried to go right close to him to slip the clip on, he pushed her gently away. She then sent our younger son John (whom James for some reason hated) away to the vet to fetch tranquillisers, and when these appeared she administered them to James ground up in glasses of whisky, which he loved. He would take big gulps, and then gasp and groan and make terrible faces, but always come back for more. On this occasion he put away an entire half bottle of whisky, together with several tranquillising tablets; but far from knocking him out, they seemed only to make him livelier, and he began bouncing up and down on the double bed in our room, doing backward somersaults and thoroughly enjoying himself.

And so, for four hours, Rosie was cornered with this potentially lethal animal. That she was never in the least frightened shows what marvellous confidence she has in animals, and they in her: it never occurred to her to be scared. But everyone else was terrified, including myself, for in the middle of the drama I happened to ring up just to see if everything was all right. No, they said; everything is definitely *not* all right. The only advice I could give John was that if the chimp should really turn nasty, the best thing to do would be to throw a bucket of warm water into his face, as that would scare him. Having said that, I set out for home like the wind.

The saga ended abruptly when James, seeing his arch-enemy John walk past outside, smashed the window in an attempt to get at him. John immediately threw a bucket of water into the animal's face, and James rushed straight into Rosie's arms for protection – whereupon she at last managed to slip the catch on to his collar, so that he could be reeled in, like a fish on a line, through the doorway and into a travelling box. I arrived just after he had been captured, and by then he looked thoroughly ashamed of himself: he knew he had been taking liberties, and when I got him out of the box, to walk him back to his cage, calling him all the names I could think of, he was really creeping along.

No harm came of the incident – but the fact that everyone survived intact was in no way due to the trainer who was supposed to be in charge of James while I was away. There he was, a qualified animal trainer, too scared to go into a house where a woman was stuck with a full-grown chimpanzee. As it turned out, there was no need for him to go in. But what made me sweat was the thought that if Rosie *had* got into trouble, he still might not have dared to go and help her.

James's subsequent career has not been entirely happy, and he personifies the dilemma which is liable to overtake anyone who brings up a wild animal in domestic surroundings. Had Rosie not nursed him when he arrived as an ailing infant, he would almost certainly have died, so that it can fairly be said that we saved his life. The trouble was that she became strongly attached to him, and he to her, with the result that he grew up almost more human than chimpanzee. The consequence was that he would never again happily associate with other chimps, and all our efforts to find him partners have failed. When we tried to furnish him with a wife, for instance, the experiment was disastrous. We introduced him carefully and gradually to what we thought was a thoroughly desirable female, placing her in an adjacent cage, so that the two animals could touch each other through the bars, until she came in season. As soon as that happened, we put her in the same cage as James, but he, far from making her welcome, bit out the whole top of her arm, causing such a bad wound that she had to be put down.

A later attempt to settle him on the chimpanzee island in Woburn safari park was no more successful: all he did during his two weeks of island life was to ignore the other chimps he was with and to smash the attractive old gazebo to matchwood. Whenever Rosie or I hove up in a boat, he would scream to come off, and we had no alternative but to take him back to Southampton.

Now, at the age of twelve, he is still a terrific animal, but a confirmed bachelor, with set habits. People often ask why he is on his own, and the answer is that he prefers to be. Rosie and I are constantly visiting him, and whenever I appear he puts on a tremendous performance. First another chimp, who lives in a separate enclosure near the entrance, sees me and shouts out some message. That starts James screaming and banging: he storms up and down his cage making an appalling noise, as though he would like to kill me. For as long as I shout at him to shut up, he goes on doing it; but the moment I say quietly: 'All right, then; if that's how you're going to behave, I'm off,' he stops and goes all soppy, waiting for me to play with him or give him some little titbit.

In a way it *is* sad that he will not live with other chimps, for that would be more natural. But at the same time Rosie and I cannot believe that we should have let him die when he was a baby: I think he has an interesting and enjoyable life and as far as I can tell he is happy enough.

Since his arrival we have often found ourselves in a similar situation, and every time we have taken an orphan into the house we have done so knowing full well that one day we will have to attempt the difficult, if not impossible, task of reuniting it with others of its kind. It is just not in our nature to let any creature die if we can possibly save it. My daughter

Mary faced exactly the same problem with her lion Marquis, whom she reared as an orphaned cub. As he grew up he became her inseparable companion, but when he reached maturity she had to wean him from his semi-human existence – and now, he, too, is in Southampton Zoo, where he has sired several litters of cubs. Just as Rosie and I can still go in with James, so Mary can walk into Marquis's enclosure and have a conversation with him – to the amazement and horror of any strangers who happen to be around.

When we opened Southampton Zoo, one of the people I asked to the ceremony was George Houghton, an old friend from the R.A.F. who had flown with me in 85 Squadron and had since become a civilian pilot, working for B.E.A. and flying all the commercial airliners up to and including Comets. As a side-line he ran a small market garden, with greenhouses, and I asked him to lay on the flowers for our opening. When he saw the zoo he was so pleased with it that he said he would like to come into some other similar project with me. Thus it was that, the following year, we designed and built another zoo, together with an animal quarantine station, at Plymouth.

These new projects stretched our financial resources to their limits. We were short of money anyway when John suddenly went down with appendicitis, and to pay for the emergency operation I sold the Rolls-Royce, which I had kept from my days with the Big Show. We put what money we had left, from that and from our film work, into the animals and buildings for Southampton; and then, when Plymouth came on the horizon, we decided to commit ourselves full-time to animals, and we sold the farm to our neighbour Lyn Pond for thirty thousand pounds.

It was this lump of capital that enabled us to meet the considerable cost of building the twin installations at Plymouth. We chose the city partly because of its docks, at which we would be able to unload animals coming from Africa, and partly because the place as yet had no zoo. One requirement of a quarantine station is that it should be at least a mile from any farm, and in Plymouth we found an ideal site – an area of the park in the city centre which was not really used as a park at all, but was more or less just a field. I approached the council, and they sent a representative to look at Southampton Zoo, which they liked, so that they were happy to give us permission to go ahead. Nor did we have any trouble obtaining a quarantine licence from the Ministry of Agriculture. I had often worked with them before and found them very helpful; they liked the way we handled animals and knew that we did things properly. So I got them to give me an exact specification for the construction of the quarantine buildings, and we went ahead in Plymouth and built a much bigger zoo than the one in Southampton, with the quarantine station attached to it. The combined project was very expensive, for the quarantine buildings all have to be fly-screened or in some cases air-conditioned. Animals coming in spend their first two months inside the fly-screens, and anyone going in or out has to pass through a lock of double doors, so that there can be no chance of any insect escaping. After these first two months the animals move out into the open, but they remain in the station for another ten months in case they are carrying any diseases internally, such as liver complaints. We built the station at Plymouth to hold about seventy animals at a time, the air-conditioned giraffe-house alone having a capacity for twenty-five.

By then, with the two zoos and the quarantine station, we were at last properly equipped for bringing animals into the country. At that stage, not having any other outlets of our own, we were really acting as dealers, selling to other zoos, from which the demand was quite strong. But there was one serious snag about handling animals which other people had caught: we did not know how they had been trapped, or how they had been handled since capture, or even where they had come from, and a considerable number died for no particular reason that we could discover. Clearly, there was only one way of ensuring a supply of animals in good condition, and that was to catch them ourselves.

CHAPTER NINE

Animal Catching

OUR first opportunity of catching animals in Africa came quite by chance. In 1961, while working on *In Search of the Castaways*, I heard that a man called Bombo Trimmer – the Director of the National Game Parks in Uganda – was trying to send two hand-reared lions to England. He had offered them to Chessington Zoo, but Chessington did not want them, and in the end I took them into Southampton. Later, when Trimmer came over on leave, he paid his former cubs a visit, and he liked our little zoo so much that he asked if I would go out to Entebbe and design one there. Naturally I agreed; and a few weeks later, while we were still filming, a cable came to say that although the Ugandan Government would not be able to give me a cash fee for laying out the zoo, they would, as a form of payment, grant me licences to catch animals in the country. This sounded an excellent arrangement, so as soon as the film was finished I flew out to Entebbe.

There I met Lawrence Tennant, who was then Chief Game Warden of Uganda, and together we sketched out plans for a zoo in the capital. Because of the chronic shortage of money the project never got off the ground, but the Game Department's offer of hunting licences held good, and after I had had a look at some of the country, I decided that we would be able to operate there. By a great stroke of luck a trapper from Kenya called Tom Mann appeared and offered us the use of his transport, so we joined forces with him and, quite suddenly, were in business. Before I left I promised to send Richard out; and he, when he arrived in Africa, took to the life and work as though he had been born for it.

Our first camp in Uganda was up country at Fort Portugal, in an area where the Game Department told us there was a surplus population of elephants and buffalo. Our main purpose was to catch elephants, and now, when I think back on the amateurishness of our first efforts, and the danger we put ourselves into through inexperience, I am amazed that none of us was killed. Our main weakness was that our vehicles were far too small: we used ordinary, ex-army jeeps, and to drive among a herd of elephants in one of them is the most terrifying experience imaginable. The animals tower over you, more than twice your height, and you know perfectly well that if a big one really went for the vehicle, it could trample it flat as a sardine-tin, so that you would have no protection left, and nothing to shelter behind.

Although we have constantly refined our methods, and now use a three-ton truck with four-wheel drive and specially protected engine, our basic catching tactics have always remained the same. First we get the herd moving, by chivvying it with several trucks. Then the catching vehicle drives in among the cantering animals until we have selected the beast we want – generally a youngster of two or three. Once the target is pin-pointed, we edge up alongside and slip a noose on a long pole over its head. At the touch of the rope the animal stops, whereupon everyone on the vehicle leaps off and swarms him – two or three men clinging to every leg – while the other trucks keep the herd going. With any luck the shock keeps the animal still for a minute or two, during which other men place a crate in front of him and manoeuvre it backwards past him until he is inside. Sometimes, however, the animal takes off before he can be crated, knocking down all the men and setting off after the rest of the herd. The strength of even a small elephant is astonishing: a three-year-old, weighing perhaps twelve hundredweight, is extremely agile, as well as strong, and he can really throw people about. Even though he is still a baby, no one can hold on to his trunk – I once saw a Swedish girl who had come out with us knocked horizontally the width of a big room by a single blow.

To drive in among a herd of wild elephants is the most exciting and dangerous activity I know. It is like being in the middle of a tank-charge, except that these tanks are trumpeting and squealing, and half of them have enormous tusks which can pierce the side of your vehicle as though it were made of paper. The Africans in the back are yelling with fright and urging the driver to go faster, and the driver is frantically trying to keep with the chosen elephant and to avoid the ant-hills. Once we took a scientist out with us – a professor who was studying animal brains – and he was so terrified by one not particularly dangerous pursuit that he had to spend the next four days in bed. Even in a big vehicle the chase is thrilling enough, for sometimes the elephants try to climb up into the back, and once we had a pair of tusks come through the windscreen. Funnily enough we had a new driver, out for the first time that day, and Richard had just told him that he would be perfectly safe whatever happened, since a charging elephant always lowered its head at the last minute and that therefore, if one came, it would hit the heavy mahogany shield that covered the engine and radiator. Hardly had he uttered these comforting words when an animal came straight for the cab, shattered the windscreen, and filled the driver's beard with chips of broken glass.

We can, in the last resort, always shoot an animal, for the African game guards who accompany every expedition carry rifles. But to me it is a horrible thing to see an animal shot when we are out catching, for the whole point of the operation is that everything is *alive*, and we are trying to catch animals *alive*. To see one dead in an awful anti-climax. Yet sometimes one is forced to shoot by the demands of self-preservation. On one occasion a big cow elephant came for the jeep I was in: she was right beside us, touching the vehicle, travelling at twenty-five miles an hour, and the African guard, who was absolutely terrified, fired into her at point-blank range. I didn't blame him at all, as I thought that in another few yards the elephant would have turned us over and done her best to trample us to death. Richard, on the other hand, was very upset. 'There goes the price of a licence!' he said furiously. I pointed out that, for the price of a licence, he still had me, which was rather important, but he was not at all impressed, especially as he had to go back and finish off the wounded elephant, which had stopped and was standing forlornly on its own, sick with a bullet through the stomach.

Once we have got a young elephant in the crate, we hoist him on to another lorry by a system which Richard devised of raising each end of the box gradually higher on piles of old tyres. If the day is particularly hot we occasionally pour a bucket of water over the animal to help cool him off during any wait there may be, and then we drive him back to the camp, where, inside the *boma*, or stockade of big wooden stakes, we have a supply of fresh fodder already cut. Most elephants settle down very quickly; many start eating the same day as they are caught, and from the moment they enter the camp their taming and training begin. The

Africans who look after them are wonderfully patient, and spend days on end persuading them to eat more, trying them with one different kind of green fodder after another until they find something that they like. We find in general that although Africans have no natural aptitude for looking after animals, they do, with training, become immensely conscientious: if you tell them that a certain animal needs ten buckets of water a day, the animal will get ten buckets a day, come what may.

Chasing elephants is undoubtedly the most dangerous form of animal catching; but – no less certainly – catching giraffes is the most exhilarating, mainly because of the speed at which it happens. Whereas an elephant normally trundles along at twenty or twenty-five miles per hour, a giraffe can do about thirty-five for short stretches; and in any case, quite apart from the speed of the pursuit itself, we have made it a rule that every chase must be short and sharp. If we do not get an animal within two minutes of starting to run it, we let it go, for our experience has taught us time and again that to run any animal (but particularly a giraffe) too far is the surest way of ending its life prematurely.

When you start to chase a giraffe, he thinks at first that he will just trot away from you. Then he finds that the vehicle is still with him, so he goes a bit faster. At that pace – about three-quarters speed – he is still going easily. But then, as he suddenly realises that he cannot shake off his pursuer, he panics and puts in a terrible spurt. If that spurt lasts more than a few seconds, he will surely die. He may not die there and then; he may even live for six months, but he will almost certainly die within a year, for his heart has been strained. Similarly, if, after being caught, he is left in a crate for any length of time, he will either kick himself to death on the spot, or, even if he survives the immediate crisis, he will expire within a few months as a result of the nervous stress. As we gradually gained experience, we realised that many of the animals which we had bought from other trappers in our early days, and later lost in the zoo, must have died from this kind of delayed reaction.

We ourselves killed at least one giraffe by chasing it for too long, but we have now refined our technique to such a degree that we have entirely eliminated this kind of mistake. The first requirement is to select the right animal – something which is by no means easy for a person with little experience. When we started, we caught several animals which proved, on closer examination, quite different from what we had expected. From a distance, we had misjudged them completely, not yet having got our eye in. Later, however, Richard became such an expert that he could instantly spot the kind of animal he wanted – a young adult, which is fit and lively and used to running about anyway.

Most giraffes will let a vehicle come to within a hundred yards, or even seventy-five, before they start to move off. So we make a slow first approach and choose an animal from the herd. The next task it to push him away from the rest: as soon as he is separated from the others, they ignore him and carry on grazing as though nothing was happening.

Away goes the quarry – and from the moment he starts to run, a stop-watch is ticking to make sure that the chase does not exceed the two-minute limit. Not only does the giraffe go fast: he is also adept at sudden changes of direction, and we need a first-class driver, both to keep up with his twists and to avoid the ant-hills. All being well, we are alongside in less than a minute, and at the first touch of the noose on the end of the long pole, the animal skids to an abrupt halt in a cloud of dust. Off jump the men – one on each leg and one on the tail. This last sounds a desperate position to be in, but in fact the man is perfectly safe provided that every-one hangs on, for a giraffe can only cow-kick, out sideways, and anyone straight behind him, hanging between his legs, is out of the animal's reach.

In a few more seconds a second truck has deposited a crate beside the captive animal, and he is bundled into it, in a state of shock. Then we put him straight on to the lorry and keep him going, right back to the camp. Usually he does not come to his senses and realise what is happening until he is released again inside the *boma*. There he finds other giraffes again, and although he may canter round once or twice, he settles down in an hour or two. Other catchers use several crates at the same time, and once they have got the first animal, leave him incarcerated while they go for a second; but this, in our experience, is always fatal sooner or later, for once the animal comes out of his state of shock, the stress is too much for him.

Exactly the same, we found, applies to eland. It is quite possible to chase an eland (or, for that matter, any other antelope) until he is so exhausted that he can only walk, and you can go up beside him and slip a noose over his head with no trouble or danger. But to do so is utterly futile, for that animal's heart has been strained and he will not last more than a few months at the most.

People often ask me why we do not use tranquillising darts to slow the animals down before we catch them. The answer is simple: for one thing it is extremely hard to judge the right dose even in the calm, controlled conditions of a zoo or European safari park. With giraffes it is particularly difficult, and one leading zoo I know of has lost four out of five giraffes which it has attempted to sedate. In the bush one would be even more likely to kill the animal by mistake.

With elephants there is a different reason: if you dart one animal and it begins to slow down, the rest of the herd all slow down as well. Sensing that it is sick, they stay behind to help it; and if it stops altogether they cluster round it in a tight circle, urging it to come on with them and thus making it impossible for the catchers to approach. Altogether, in spite of the hazards, we find it is far better to stick to the methods we know.

In the course of numerous catching expeditions I have come to love Africa. I love the enormous open spaces, the silence, the heat, the clarity of the air. To me, life in camp is always a delight: to wake up as dawn is breaking, when the air is cold enough for you to want a jersey, to strike out into the crystal freshness of the morning, to drive for maybe an hour before you see anything, but then at last to come on a herd of elephants, giraffes or antelopes – this has been one of the great experiences of my life. For me, a circus man by birth and upbringing, the most astonishing thing at first was to see all these animals that nobody *owned*. Until I went to Africa, every animal I had seen had always belonged to somebody, but here were these huge herds, free, wild, and able to go wherever they liked. Just to see them all at large gave me an enormous thrill.

And yet – as I already knew subconsciously and soon discovered in all too precise detail – that freedom was largely an illusion. For one thing the animals *did* belong to somebody – to the Ugandan Government; but a far more sinister factor was that every kind of animal was under pressure, either from other species which preyed on it, or from poachers, or simply from the gradual erosion of living-space brought about by increasingly efficient agriculture and the spread of civilisation. Very soon I could see that there was simply not room in Africa for all the animals, and that what space did remain was shrinking fast. It was this single fact that enabled me to catch a few of the animals with no compunction. Often, in fact, we actually save an animal's life by catching it: on one of our first trips to Uganda, for instance, the forty giraffes for which we were given a licence would have been culled by the game department if we had not caught them alive, for they were raiding new farms in the area and had been declared surplus to the number that the district could carry.

Anyone who imagines that a giraffe or an elephant in Africa lives a life of ease, free from anxiety, has no conception of the real state of affairs. In fact every animal has constant worries, whether they are caused by other animals or by humans. Far from living in a beautiful meadow, where everything is laid on for them, they are heavily preyed on and poached. In a single herd of giraffe I have seen one animal with an arrow sticking out of its stomach, and another with an arrow through its ankle. Sometimes, out of twenty elephants captured, we have found only five without defects of some kind: the others have all had tails missing, ears torn off, deep wire-cuts round their legs, or, worst of all, the ends of their trunks severed by poachers' snares. There is no more pathetic sight than an elephant that has lost the end of his trunk. He cannot pick things up properly any more, and to eat he has to go down on his knees, to grovel on the ground, so that he can shove things into his mouth.

I cannot say I blame the poachers. To them, a giraffe or an elephant is just an immense quantity of meat walking around, and of course they will get it if they can. I am sure that if I were a penniless African, with six children to feed, I would be as big a poacher as anyone. It seems to me that poaching is inevitable. But the result of it is that many of the animals which look so good from a distance are in fact quite heavily disfigured.

On the other hand, I cannot believe that an animal which is caught and brought back to Europe to live in a park or even in a zoo is any worse off than its fellows left in the wild. It suffers a relatively brief period of agitation, inevitably, in the first few weeks after its capture. But every facet of its behaviour thereafter suggests that its loss of freedom is more than compensated by the banishment of the insecurity which was a constant factor in the animal's life in the wild.

Once an animal is caught, it is obviously in our interest, as well as in that of the creature itself, to look after it as well as we possibly can, and we have learnt by experience that it is best to keep the two activities of catching and looking after the animals quite separate. My son Richard was one of the best catchers in the world, if not *the* best, but he was *not* the world's best person at looking after what he had caught. The point was, however, that he recognised this, and did not attempt to do both jobs. For handling the animals, we have full-time experts who do not go out on the catching expeditions, but remain in camp and then travel home with their charges. It is not fair to expect a man who comes in exhausted after a long day in the bush to go and spend hours coaxing some animal to eat: someone else must do that, and that man must be a specialist at the task.

Over the years our catching expeditions have taken us to many parts of the world. Probably the longest trips – in terms of distance alone – were two visits that we made to the Falkland Islands in the early 1960s. Our object was to catch sea-elephants and king penguins, and, in spite of the time and the expense involved, both journeys were very successful. To reach the Falklands at all in those days was quite a business, for there were no regular flights between the islands and the mainland of South America. On the first trip, in the autumn of 1964, Richard and I flew to Montevideo and then took a ship for the three-day voyage out to the islands. The catching itself was simple enough, once we had reached the right place: a small boat took us out to the island from which we had permission to take the sea-elephants, and we had a rough time coming in to land. Because of the rocks, we had to use a dinghy to cover the last quarter of a mile, and we got soaked to the skin by the surf. Once we were ashore, however, there was no problem, because the sea-elephants lay basking on the tussocky grass and took no evasive action beyond making rather slow attempts to bite. Some were far too heavy to lift, so we chose six young ones, about three-quarters grown, and hustled them into the nets which we had spread out. When we had them properly enmeshed – but with their flippers sticking out – we walked them down to the water, attached a line and towed them out to the ship, where they were winched on board. Altogether we took back six sea-elephants (worth a thousand pounds apiece by the time they reached England), and fifty penguins (worth fifty pounds each) which were caught for us in South Georgia and brought up to the Falklands on the *A.E.S.* (its owner's initials), the ship which had taken our gear out from England.

In those days the Falklands were quite a place. As yet there was no international telephone, and it was a well-known fact that the girl in the post office read – and circulated to her friends – the contents of all the telegrams that passed through her hands, so that the person to whom the message was addressed was usually the last to hear about it. One day I went into the post office and found her nearly dying with frustration, for a cable had come from Mary asking WHAT PAINT SAFE TO PAINT ELEPHANT? For one thing, she could not imagine why anybody should want to paint an elephant – and I could see that she was so desperate to find out that I felt I must explain. What had happened was that Mary was just starting work on a film called *Maya the Magnificent*, and the story demanded that one of the elephants should be white.

Another fact about the islands which surprised us was that no one bothered to catch or eat the abundant fish. We caught masses, both for ourselves and for our sea-elephants and penguins on the way home. Yet the islanders turned their back on the wealth of food in the water, relying instead on the ubiquitous mutton, which was eaten so unfailingly every day of the year that it was known as '365' and appeared in everything, even the sausages. Another odd fact was that none of the people we met could swim, even though they lived by the sea: the reason, I suppose, was that the sea-water was always too cold, and there was no swimming pool on land. Something that surprised us less was to find that people drank prodigiously – so much so that some wives had their husbands blacklisted at the shops and the pubs, to prevent them getting any more alcohol. We could understand how the drinkers felt, for in that bleak landscape, which was usually under cloud and always swept by a damp wind, there was practically no other form of entertainment.

CHAPTER TEN

The Idea of the Parks

IT was two separate strands of my background, woven together, that gave me the most important idea of my life – the idea that it should be possible to release lions from their traditional cages and arrange for the public to drive about among them. One strand was my experience in Africa, where I had seen so many animals at large, walking about in the open: as I watched them on successive catching trips I began to think how marvellous it would be if we could somehow give them part, at least, of the same freedom in England. The other strand was my upbringing in the circus: having worked lions in the ring since I was twenty, I was not frightened of them, and I knew that I would be able to deal with them physically if they became obstreperous. My lifelong knowledge of lions suggested that the animals themselves would tolerate cars easily, provided they had plenty of space in which to move about, and my ring experience made me confident that I could control them.

This, I think, was the big difference between myself and other zoo proprietors. Most zoo men are very nervous of lions, for the good reason that they have never made any physical contact with them, but have always been at a safe distance from them, with bars in between. Had I never worked with lions myself, I am sure I should have felt the same; as it was, I reckoned I knew lions well enough to be able to dominate them: if they did start to fight or to attack the cars of people driving through their enclosures, I personally would go in and sort them out. An ordinary zoo man, by contrast, would have no idea what to do once he had released a lion into an open space: he would be terrified to go in and try to get the animal out again.

The idea was not born suddenly. It grew gradually in my mind, but my basic conviction was that to be able to drive about among lions would be a tremendous attraction for the public, because lions are killers, and danger is a very strong attraction. Everyone likes to court death a little, without getting too near it – even if they only do it vicariously, by watching films or television, or by talking to racing drivers or pilots. From the start I felt certain that thousands of people would be glad to pay for the thrill of going within a few feet of a lion, and that although the expense of setting up the kind of place I had in mind was obviously going to be enormous, we would soon recover the cost.

The other aspect of the idea that fascinated me was that of the spectacle. I am not an artistic person, but I do love to see animals properly displayed, and I kept thinking that lions had never been properly displayed before. In a zoo, whether you look at a lion through bars or across a ditch, you can see him from only one direction: you see him one-dimensionally, and never in the round. My aim was to give people the chance of seeing him from *all* directions – of being able to drive right round him, and of watching him run or climb or mate or fight in something approaching the freedom of his natural element. The more I thought about it, the more I was convinced that this would be a far better way to show animals than any other yet devised.

It is perhaps worth recalling that, at the time, the scheme was revolutionary. Today the idea of driving around among lions has become so familiar in England – and in many countries on the Continent – that people are entirely blasé about it: they think nothing of having a lion lean against their car, or a baboon pull off their windscreen-wiper. But in 1964, when I first thought of it, the concept was unheard of – a fact that soon became all too apparent when the public and Press reacted against it in a typically British way, denouncing it as highly dangerous and anti-social.

Expecting a reaction of this kind, I took care not to mention the project outside our family circle, but quietly set about finding a site. The first candidate presented itself quite by accident. Mary was hunting with Harry Llewellyn in Monmouthshire, and as the horses stood waiting while hounds drew a covert, the man next to her asked her if I would come and look at his home – Hale House, in the New Forest – to see if I thought I could instal some attraction there to bring in tourists. His name was David Booth-Jones, and the moment I heard about his suggestion I made an appointment to go and see him, for this sounded precisely what

I was after. Thus it was that I found myself invited to tea with him and his mother, a dear old lady in her eighties. The house was in good order, but the grounds had been let go – a perfect site for my purposes. I had already given the man an outline of my idea, and in the middle of tea I thought we had better break it gently to his mother; so we started to explain – whereupon she broke in and said to him: 'I know what you're like: you'd go off, and I'd be left to feed the lions myself. Besides, we're quite busy on Sundays: last weekend we sold twelve teas.' I saw at once that the situation was hopeless: the old lady was not going to think on the right scale, so I began back-pedalling immediately. But the meeting was far from useless. As I left, Booth-Jones came out on to the drive with me and apologised for having given me a wasted journey. I said: 'Not at all – I enjoyed coming,' which was perfectly true. Then he asked what my next choice would be, and I said 'Longleat', for I already had my eye on the Marquis of Bath's stately home in Wiltshire. 'Well,' he said, 'Lord Bath's son is a friend of mine – I'll give him a ring.' I bet him he would forget about it as soon as I had driven out of the gate – but he didn't: he gave Viscount Weymouth a call, and arranged for me to go and meet Lord Bath himself.

Now I had watched Lord Bath on television: I saw that he had a broken nose, and I reckoned that he must be a sportsman. He might be an aristocrat, but I thought he looked the sort of man I could talk to. Even so, it was with mixed feelings that I drove slowly down the long drive into his lovely park at Longleat, set among steeply-rolling hills and studded with ancient trees: if *I* owned this lot, I was thinking, I wouldn't have a *dog* walk in it, let alone a pack of lions and millions of people looking at them.

Our first meeting, in early November 1964, went very well – but it nearly didn't take place at all. We had agreed to meet at eleven a.m. I was there at five to eleven, but Lord Bath did not arrive until half-past. In that sort of situation I normally wait ten minutes and then, if the other person still has not come, I go away. But this occasion seemed so important to me that – luckily for both of us – I mastered my normal instincts and hung around, looking at all the pictures in the hall.

When we eventually met and started our talk, Lord Bath was cautiously enthusiastic, but it took him some time to grasp the point of what I was saying – probably because I did not put it clearly enough. 'But the cages will have to be awfully big if the cars are going to be able to get into them at the same time as the lions,' he kept saying, and I kept telling him: 'No, no: the lions won't be in any cage at all, except the fence round the outside. It's the people who'll be in the cages – in their cars.' I could see his enthusiasm growing by the minute, so I thought I had better warn him of the possible snags, the main one (as I saw it) being the sheer numbers of people that the scheme might attract. So I laid it right on the line with him and said: 'Look – you must think very hard about this, because if it works there'll be millions of people here, and I wouldn't want you to blame me for bringing them all in.' But he wasn't in the least worried, and kept repeating that there could never be too many.

Altogether, that first talk was a great success. But as I was about to leave, I said: 'There's just one thing. Our date was for eleven o'clock, and you came at half-past. Normally I leave after ten minutes.' I put it quite quietly, quite smoothly, but I could see that he was rather shocked, and he began to apologise. 'It doesn't matter,' I said. 'It's just that I do come on time. I don't care *what* time you suggest for another meeting. I'll come at midnight if you like. But I don't wait. It's one of those things.' His two retainers were trying to disappear behind the curtains or vanish out of the window, for they had never heard Lord Bath being spoken to like that before. But he was never late again.

At our second meeting three weeks later we had another slight tiff. Again our talks went well, and we progressed as far as discussing the finances in some detail: we agreed that we would form a special company to run the project, with both costs and profits to be shared fifty-fifty between us. But because of the physical situation – with Lord Bath owning the land and me having access to the animals – it was agreed that he should pay initially for the fences and roads, while I would buy the lions and pay for their transport, houses and keep until the park opened. We had already worked out that the roads and fences would cost about £75,000; the cost of the animals was impossible to predict exactly as, apart from anything else, no one had ever tried to assemble the kind of numbers I was after (at least forty), and I had no idea where I would be able to get so many lions from. So it was agreed that if my costs came to less than Lord Bath's, we would balance accounts up afterwards.

Then Lord Bath suddenly said: 'Just one point: with the roads and fences, I can get receipts to show exactly what we've spent. But how do I know what the lions have cost? You could tell me anything you like.'

I suppose I am a bit too touchy about our word and our name, but that is the kind of remark that I cannot stand. So I said straight out: 'If you don't trust me, you shouldn't go into a business partnership with me. I'm going to India tomorrow, and while I'm away perhaps you'll make up your mind whether you want to do a deal or not.'

Everyone went dead silent. The publicity man and estate agent were wishing they could disappear. Then Lord Bath said: 'Oh – now I've upset you.' I said: 'Not at all. But you must make up your mind whether I'm the right person to do this with you. If *I* didn't like *you*, I wouldn't be here – and I hope it's vice-versa.'

After that Lord Bath wanted to continue the discussion, but I refused, urging him to make up his mind about me before we went any further, and off I went to India, where Mary was already working on the film *Maya the Magnificent* and where I was due to join her. A couple of days later Lord Bath telephoned Richard and said he was afraid I had gone cold on the project; but Richard had already been in touch with me, and was able to reassure him that I was as keen as ever.

Looking back, I realise that I must have sounded awfully blunt, and perhaps even arrogant. In fact I am not arrogant at all; but what I *am*, I know, is very direct, and I often say things straight out that other people might have wrapped up in a little flannel. Part of the reason for this is that I have never been much of a conversationalist: if I could have asked for one gift in the world, it would have been for complete command of the English language, and the ability to shade my language perfectly to every situation. Not having any such gift, I am inclined to put things more abruptly than I mean to, and I know that this sometimes disconcerts other people.

Lord Bath, however, was not put out for long, and we went on to form not only a successful business partnership but also a close friendship that has meant a great deal to me. On the purely commercial front I believe that my directness paid off, for I do not suppose there are two other people in the world who have done the volume of business that we have together, with less fuss. If we had not soon established complete confidence in each other, we would have needed huge teams of lawyers to keep everything straight. On the personal front I came to like Lord Bath enormously, and also greatly to admire the devotion with which he worked to preserve Longleat. We soon made a huge joke out of our first uncomfortable bout of fencing.

The trip to India gave me a valuable break, and time to think again about the project I was trying to initiate. For two months Mary and I worked on *Maya the Magnificent*, an American film for which we took two tigers and a cheetah all the way out from England. We charged an enormous fee, but we needed to, because the King brothers, who were making the film, were a difficult company to work for, since, in an attempt to economise, they refused to wire in the set properly, and for much of the time we had to work the animals free. Fortunately we had an exceptional tigress called Suki, whom we had brought up on a bottle in the zoo at Southampton; instead of having to be boxed up between takes, she would lie on the rocks in the sun with Mary, like any other actor, waiting for the next scene to start.

Another help was that the star, Clint Walker, was man enough to work with the tiger himself, instead of having to use an understudy all the time. Since our sequences included a good deal of swimming in a fast-flowing river, some shots of the animals chasing humans, and an attack by the tiger on an elephant, we had quite a lively time, especially as both the tiger and the cheetah several times nearly escaped. The film was shot near Mysore, and for me the first sight of India was a sobering experience. Never had I seen such poverty – not even among the Tuareg tribesmen – and never had I seen so many people sleeping in the streets: half the population of Mysore, it seemed, had nowhere to lay their heads except on the town's filthy pavements.

But throughout my stay in India my mind was playing constantly on Longleat and its possibilities. As soon as the film work was finished I resumed negotiations with Lord Bath, and he applied to his local council for permission to build a fence 'to contain animals'. The necessary permission was soon forthcoming, and later, when a furious argument broke out about the alleged dangers of what we were doing, much play was made of the fact that the original application had been so vague, and that we had never got permission for a change of use on the land that we were going to enclose. At the time, however, there seemed to be no legal objection – and this in fact proved to be the case: the kind of reserve that we were proposing to build did not fall within the scope of any planning law.

Still I took care not to mention the project to anyone except the people immediately involved: it was my idea, and I did not want my plans for an entirely new form of zoo adulterated by anyone else. The only other professional animal man I consulted was Hermann Ruhe, an old friend and the leading animal dealer in Germany. I was doing business with him anyway, and mentioned my plan to him casually: he thought it was a marvellous idea, and that it would really go. The main point I discussed with him was the height of the fences: I was planning to build a twelve-foot-six fence, with a two-foot-six overhang tilted inwards. Ruhe told me that some tests done at Hagenbeck's zoo in Hamburg had shown that, if really stressed, lions could jump twenty-five feet. But when I checked this with Hagenbeck himself, he admitted that this was exceptional, that the lions in the experiment had been starved for days, and that meat had then been hung up high above them.

In spite of this news, I felt certain the fence I projected would be safe enough. In all my experience of circuses I had never known a lion go over the top of the twelve-foot ring cage, even though, in some shows, the animals were trained to go right round the top of the cage, like wall-of-death motorcyclists. In my view, everything depended on the degree to which the animals were going to be stressed. At close quarters – as I have explained in an earlier chapter – a lion does feel highly pressured by the proximity of humans; but the whole point about the park was that the lions would never experience this degree of pressure: they would be in a large enclosure, with plenty of withdrawing room. Given enough distance (I was convinced), and properly fed, a lion would have no incentive to tackle the wire. Even so, I decided that it would be prudent to build a relatively low buffer-fence a short distance inside the big one, to stop any animal taking a run at the main barrier. I thought (wrongly) that for the inner fence five or six strands of barbed wire could be enough.

We had a stroke of luck in buying the main wire, as I discovered a stock of Government-surplus chain-link fencing which had been ordered during the Mau Mau emergency in Kenya. Having been designed for defending camps and other installations against terrorist attacks, it was exceptionally strong, and this, I foresaw, would be good for publicity later.

Piece by piece, we worked out a system for manning the park and controlling the animals. I realised that wardens mounted in Land-Rovers would have to be on duty in the reserve all the time it was open to the public, so that they could both break up any fights that might occur and drive immediately to the rescue of anyone who broke down or got into trouble. For extra safety, I decided that the wardens, or rangers, must be armed with shotguns and both blank and loaded cartridges, so that they could, if necessary, scare a lion off or in the last resort shoot it. For the entrance and exit we devised a system of locks like those used on canals: double gates at about fifty yards apart, so that cars could collect between them and be let through in batches of thirty or forty. Outside the park we planned a large cold-store, or meat-room, in which to keep the bullocks' heads that were to form the lions' staple diet.

Another of my ideas was to have a twisting, serpentine road winding through the reserve. At the back of my mind all the time was the thought that what people would want to do, more than anything else, was to photograph the animals; so I designed the road in such a way that, no matter where a lion might happen to be, a car would be able to approach within a few hundred feet of him. I was also anxious that no one should feel hurried or pushed along by other cars behind: I wanted everyone to be able to stop easily, and to watch or take pictures at their leisure – and this meant that we had to make the road wide enough for at least two lines of cars, one moving and one stationary. But in planning the road, we made one serious mistake, in that we failed to put the entrance and exit in the same place. By siting them separately, we forced ourselves to build two complete sets of double gates, and also to deploy twice the number of staff that a single installation would have needed.

While these preliminary preparations went ahead, I myself was dashing all over the world trying to round up the lions. At that time there were not fifty lions for sale in the whole of Europe, let alone in England, and in the end we had to go as far afield as Israel and Nairobi to make up our numbers. But I began by writing to a number of zoos in England – and of course word soon went round that I was trying to buy up every lion in the country. Since no one could imagine what I wanted fifty lions for, a lot of people thought I had gone daft. Others thought it was some monstrous publicity stunt, but for the moment I did not bother to enlighten them.

Then, by accident, news of what we were doing escaped. One evening Lord Bath went to the annual Bristol Press Club Dinner, without any intention of spilling our particular beans. But, feeling a bit merry, he suddenly stood up and said: 'Well, I'm going to have *fifty* lions at Longleat.' That did it. The Pressmen really woke up, and from that moment we were bombarded with inquiries and criticism.

Every conceivable theory was advanced to show that the project was a menace, the main claim being that the lions would present an intolerable threat to the safety of people living near the park. The next most common complaint was that it would be suicidal for anyone to drive through an enclosure with fifty lions in it, and that the idea was therefore a dangerously irresponsible way of trying to make money. Soon people began to invent even more far-fetched objections: one person said that the scheme would be cruel to the lions, who would fight to the death if all put together in such a large collection; another, that the lions would escape and disappear into the Welsh hills, where they would breed and start attacking the sheep; another still that, since there were no vultures in Wiltshire, the only other natural scavengers available – rats – would move in and over-run the park and surrounding countryside. Sometimes, I must admit, I got rather short with the objectors, and said to them: 'Well, you'd better make your mind up. Are the lions going to kill people? Are they going to eat each other? Are they going to die of cold? Are they going to get out? They can't do all those things – so you'd better decide what they *are* going to do.'

In an attempt to damp things down locally, we held a Press conference to witness the laying-out of the road. Lord Bath, Richard and I forced our way through a bramble-infested wood, carrying an eighteen-foot pole and putting in markers to show where the road would go. We managed to work out the route so that very few trees had to be felled, but at the end of the exercise all our trousers were in ribbons. Lord Bath complained that he had ruined a good suit that day – to which I replied that *I* certainly had, but that I did not see how *he* could have, since he had never had a decent suit anyway!

We also laid out the main fence together, choosing the line so as to make it as inconspicuous as possible, and also to keep it out of sight of the house. Lord Bath was extremely generous in providing land: I had been afraid to say how much I really wanted, and had begun by saying that forty or fifty acres would probably be enough, but he, straightaway, suggested that a particular area of about a hundred acres would be the best. That seemed ideal to me – although I would have asked for more if I had known how our idea was going to develop.

As the news of what we were doing spread, comments began coming in from all over the world and suddenly we got a letter from the company which had just made the film *Born Free*, imploring us to buy the lions which they had used. In Nairobi, it seemed, nobody wanted these animals; members of the film company had got it into their heads that they could not be released into the wild, and if no one bought them, there was a good chance that they would be killed just for their skins. By then I had already got enough lions, and did not really want any more; but it seemed to me a scandal that the lions should just be abandoned to their fate, so I cabled WILL TAKE TEN LIONS AT TEN POUNDS APIECE – and to my amazement the offer was accepted.

Now Lord Bath really began to appreciate why I had been unable to tell him exactly what the animals for the park would cost. Those ten lions from the film were bought for ten pounds apiece; but in order to get them back to England, Richard had to fly to Nairobi to complete the deal. Then he had to have travelling boxes made, at thirty pounds each; then he had to hire a man to look after the lions, and pay their freight back to England. When they arrived here I had to quarantine them for six months, and by the time they reached the park they had cost us three hundred pounds apiece.

Another important factor was that some lions were used to living together, whereas others had always been on their own. A group of five living happily together were worth ten times as much as five individuals who might fight the moment they came into contact. Altogether, it was impossible to say what the total animal bill would be: all we could do was to press ahead and collect what we could – a task in which Mary gave invaluable help.

Throughout all this, the controversy about the park rumbled away, mainly at local level. 'We are making utter asses of ourselves,' one of the Frome councillors announced one day – but the obvious truth of his remark unfortunately did not put paid to the council's campaign against the reserve. The main worry seemed to be that the fence was not high enough, and that the lions would escape to terrorise the local inhabitants. Our cause was not helped when Virginia McKenna, the film-star who had played Joy Adamson in *Born Free*, began writing impassioned letters to the *Daily Express* deploring the whole idea of the park and saying that such lions as did not escape from it would be utterly miserable.

The debate really came into the open in September 1965, when, to our astonishment, *The Times* carried an extraordinary Fourth Leader about our enterprise. Normally the paper's Fourth Leaders were urbane and humorous essays, not supposed to be of any importance or to carry any heavy message. But this one was quite serious, and in spite of its scattering of literary allusions betrayed an attitude of almost hysterical alarm:

> Sporting competition between owners to make their stately homes and broad-acred parks the mostest for visitors is all very well. But there are limits, and in proposing to enlarge a pride of lions in a compound on his Wiltshire estate, the MARQUESS OF BATH has overstepped them. No amount of soothing assurance that the fences would be too high to be jumped, the visitors warned to stay put in their cars, and that the game wardens roaming day and night would be crack shots, can persuade sensible people that a quite gratuitous and unnecessary risk to life is not contemplated. Up till now the man-eating propensities of lions in England have happily been left in the realm of light verse, of MR STANLEY HOLLOWAY's little lad Albert who was swallowed whole and the Bellocian little gentleman whom Ponto got. But there was the grim case in 1956 of the ten year old Boy Scout who died after being mauled by a lion at Whipsnade. How long will it be, if LORD BATH has his way, before that tragedy is re-enacted?
>
> The fecklessness of a minority of the great British public knows no bounds, and who will deny that sooner or later a fatal accident is likely to occur? A start is planned with fifty of the great beasts. But allowances have been made for this number to be doubled by breeding. This is one of the most fantastically unsuitable uses for a stretch of England's green and pleasant land that

can ever have entered the head of a noble proprietor. The wildest follies of
the past pale before it; the old landlords, though they had some odd ideas,
seldom lost their feel for their native soil. They seldom went in for stunts.

Lions in an African game reserve are at home. A few at Whipsnade and
at Regent's Park, under the auspices of the Zoological Society, are justified.
But a lion in Wiltshire is as out of place as a Wodehousian Empress of
Blandings pig would be in Kruger Park. Cattle, sheep and deer ought to
be good enough for a Wiltshire man. The proper place for lions in an island
that is spared them in the wild state is in heraldry. Although some planning
permission has inexplicably been given, there is still time for wiser counsels
to prevail. LORD BATH's dangerous folly is not due to be open to the public
until next Easter. Ordinary citizens who seek to make modest changes on
their property are often checked by a miscellany of planners with power. Here
if ever is a just cause for official intervention — if necessary from Whitehall.*

The call for Government intervention really put the opposition on its
mettle, and a number of local petitions were raised. Frome Council,
belatedly realising what it had let itself in for, made representations to the
Minister of Housing and Local Government, Richard Crossman, but,
fortunately for us, got no rise out of him. Several Members of Parliament
took it upon themselves to protect the helpless British public; one, a local
man, acted with the best intentions of allaying the fears of people in the
area, but the other – who had nothing whatever to do with Wiltshire –
clearly took the matter up only to gain personal publicity, and his
behaviour was so fatuous that I had better not name him. In an attempt to
calm everybody down, we called another Press conference at Longleat
during November, and invited not only all interested journalists but also
M.P.s and members of local councils. This did something to clear the air,
yet no one seemed entirely satisfied with the assurances we gave them. Nor
was the continued anxiety really surprising for – it is worth repeating –
nothing of this kind had been done before, and nobody could tell exactly
how the lions would behave. Even I myself, though I pretended to be full
of confidence, was by no means certain what the animals would do when
we let them out: I could only proceed on the basis of my own experience
and hope that my intuition was right. My biggest worry was that the lions,
seeing faces through the windscreens of cars, might jump straight through.

* Reproduced from *The Times* by permission.

Agitation against the idea of the park continued right through into the New Year, and several national papers predicted that the enterprise would be stamped out at any moment by the revocation of our planning permission. If that happened (I told one journalist) we would demand one million pounds compensation from the council which gave us permission in the first place. I knew that we hadn't spent anything like a million pounds, but the figure sounded a good one, and I said that it was based on the amount of business we would lose if the venture was called off.

People were at us day and night with some niggling point or other, and through all the bombardment Lord Bath kept his head magnificently. Many people would have chucked the whole thing, but he never faltered. Since he did not have the expert knowledge to refute most of the arguments brought up, he was constantly referring inquiries to me, and it was pleasant to find that he trusted my judgement entirely, believing anything I told him about the animals.

By the end of the year every cage and loose-box that we owned in Southampton and Plymouth was stuffed with lions. They had come from all over the world – from Hanover, Barcelona, Holland, Denmark and Jerusalem, to say nothing of those which had taken part in *Born Free*. Not one came from the wild: all had been living in zoos or circuses, and they varied a great deal in quality, one lioness dying almost as soon as she arrived, presumably from old age.

That autumn was further complicated for us by the fact that Mary decided to marry Roger Cawley, a thoroughly able young man who had once been manager of Bertram Mills's circus. But the extra distraction of having to organise a wedding was handsomely compensated, for Roger became the first manager of the park at Longleat and moved in with Mary to the Pheasantry, a pleasant old estate house standing right beside the entrance to the park. To have the family thus reinforced at such a critical moment was a great comfort and encouragement.

For the rest of 1965 the weather was mild and open, so that we made good progress with the roads and fences before frost and snow came in the New Year. No one worked harder than Richard, who toiled from dawn to dusk. Our opening day was already set for Tuesday, 5 April 1966, a few days before Easter, and as the deadline approached I started to get nightmares in which I saw thousands of cars driving straight past our gates, and the people in them looking out contemptuously and saying to each other: 'That's where that idiot had those lions' – and not one of them going in.

Looking back, I do not think I was ever seriously worried by the opposition we encountered, although the sheer volume of it became a nuisance, as it took up a great deal of time. Nor (in spite of the nightmares) did I really believe that the lions would fail to draw the crowds, for the intense interest shown by the Press was a good indication of how strongly the idea had hit the public imagination. What worried me much more was the studied hostility of the zoo establishment. Almost to a man the directors of conventional zoos cold-shouldered the whole project, refusing either to come and look at what we were doing or to give sensible criticism that might have helped us. Even when the park opened and we issued a general invitation to them all, the only man sufficiently large-minded to accept was George Mottishead, Director of Chester Zoo: he was delighted by what he saw, and said that the only reason he did not copy what we had done was that the lack of space in Chester prevented him.

Him apart, we met only indifference and resentment. We invited representatives from London Zoo to come and inspect the park, but they refused on the grounds that they could not be associated with so controversial a project – and all the time we were aware of a constant undercurrent of animosity and criticism. One zoo hinted that the lions would certainly die of cold and wet; another that no animal park with only a single species could hope to attract any large number of people. To me, a dedicated animal man, it seemed extraordinary that none of these people should bother to come and see what was essentially a revolutionary innovation in their own field. I should have thought that sheer professional curiosity would force them to come and have a look. I cannot see that there is any excuse for a man who works with animals to ignore a new project in this field, however much he may dislike it: even if it is only a factory farm, I think he should go and see it for himself before he starts to criticise it. If I heard that someone was planning to keep animals under water, I should not dream of criticising him until I had gone and seen for myself exactly what it was that he was doing.

The only conclusion we could reach was that none of these people who criticised from a distance had any real interest in the welfare of the animals, but were motivated by jealousy. It was particularly galling for them that this new concept of a zoo had been invented by a commercial man – and of course it was the commercial nature of the project that most came under attack. Had I been an ordinary zoo proprietor, rather than a showman with a circus background, I am certain that the idea would have been far better received; as it was, the establishment was particularly irritated by the fact that this was the second occasion on which, during this century, a commercial man, rather than a zoologist, had made a major step forward in animal keeping. The other was when Hagenbeck had pioneered the removal of cages and their replacement by open ditches in his zoo in Hamburg fifty years before. Like myself, Hagenbeck was formerly a circus man and had travelled widely, in Africa and elsewhere; he too had seen animals at large in the bush, and I think he must have been fired by the same ambition as I was – to make the animals as free as possible and to banish the feeling of captivity.

CHAPTER ELEVEN

The Parks in Action

As Easter approached, the welter of last-minute problems kept us busy every waking minute, and there was no time to worry about what other jealous zoo-keepers might be thinking. One major snag was that the radio sets which we had ordered for installing in the Land-Rovers and the control centre had not arrived, so that we knew in advance that our communications would be less than perfect when the park opened. For me, however, the most pressing anxiety was not what would happen on opening day, but what would happen on *release* day, when we first let the lions go. For months I had been assuring everyone that the animals would have no problems in adapting themselves to their new environment, but as the moment of truth approached I became more and more apprehensive about exactly what they would do when they first tasted freedom.

On the appointed morning we towed all the lions down into the park in big circus wagons. We originally intended to release the first of them at about half-past ten, and by that time everyone had assembled, amid growing tension. Richard and I were ensconced in separate Land-Rovers, armed with broom-handles with which to separate any lions that might start fighting. Lord Bath was in another vehicle, and members of the staff, armed with loaded shotguns, set up patrol outside the perimeter fence. Our plan was to release the lions in three separate lots, each round one of the huts, in the hope that they would form themselves into three different prides, each with a base.

At the last moment some snag developed, and we had to postpone the opening of the wagons for a couple of hours. As we went back to the Pheasantry for a cup of tea, I felt like a condemned man who has been granted a reprieve. It was I who, after all these months of preparation was going to say: 'Let them go.' And it was I who would be responsible for what happened when I said it.

At last I could wait no longer, and I said to everyone: 'Well – we've got to face it.' So back we went, and all resumed our positions. The first lions to go, we decided, would be a group of four who had known each other and lived together all their lives: they, at least, were compatible – or so we thought. We had a man on the door, to pull the rope, and finally I gave him the signal.

For a moment none of the lions moved: they just lay there looking out. Then one came to the door and jumped down. A few seconds later a second followed him, and the instant he hit the ground he started the biggest fight you ever saw – *with his lifelong friend*! Richard and I were alongside in a flash and prised them apart with our sticks. The lions looked round, saw us, and immediately took off, one racing down to one end of the park, and the other bolting in the opposite direction. Their two mates from the same wagon also lit off, but without fighting.

Next we let the *Born Free* lot out, all ten at once. Away they streaked in all directions, as though a bomb had burst where we were standing: they went all over the place swiping at tussocks of grass with their paws and bolting into the trees. For a moment I was appalled, thinking they would charge headlong into the fence. Then I saw them all stop among the trees, and I realised what a wonderful sight they made. What a sight! I kept thinking. People are going to go mad about this. I'd never seen a lion out, free, in the open before in England. No one else in the world has seen this, I kept telling myself: fifteen lions loose in an English park. I wondered wildly whether I'd made a terrible mistake – whether what I'd done was right or wrong. Then I thought: well, whatever it is that I've done, I've given myself a fantastic thrill.

Everybody else was just as excited as I was, and kept saying how marvellous the lions looked. People were shouting and pointing out different animals to each other, so I urged everyone to keep calm and stay still, to give the lions a chance to settle down. Gradually they began to come out from the places where they had hidden, but very gingerly, and when they moved at all, they tried to keep some cover over their heads. I then realised that they were so used to having roofs above them that the sky was a terrifying phenomenon: that great light canopy, so high, so far away, was something with which they had never had to contend before, and some of them took months to lose their fear of it. To all those cage-reared lions the most familiar object in the whole park was the fence, and several of them began to pace up and down it – not because they were trying to escape, but because a barrier was something which they knew and which made them feel at home (later experiments proved that if we erected a short strip of fence, only ten yards long, right in the middle of one of the enclosures, some of the lions would spend hours padding up and down it, just because it gave them reassurance).

Of all the lions we released, the adolescent animals were naturally the least inhibited, and it was not long before four of them had squeezed their way under the bottom strand of the low buffer-fence, so that they were right up against the main perimeter wire. To get them back into the main section we had to cut the inner wire, and Mary went in on foot to drive the strays back through the gap. There was never the slightest chance of their going through or over the main fence – but that did not stop some journalistic spy, who had got in without our realising it, spreading alarm in that evening's papers with a large picture and a sensational story about how some of the lions had escaped – a story taken up by next morning's *Daily Express* which printed the headline LORD BATH'S LION CUBS ESCAPE and gave a graphic account of how they had been pursued for hours by armed hunters of all descriptions, some on horseback and some on foot. In fact the main event of the day was that we managed to feed a good many of the lions back towards their huts, and although some of them were so upset that they lay where they were all day, the majority had settled down well by the evening.

In the next few days our main problem was fighting, and in spite of all our efforts to break up the battles, two lions were killed. Then we identified the main culprit, and once we had rounded him up and taken him out, the problem receded. The greatest relief to me was the fact that, from the start, the lions did not pay the slightest attention to cars. Richard and I drove up and down the road constantly to test their reaction, but they behaved exactly as I had hoped they would, and did not seem to associate closed cars with humans – even though they very soon learned to pick out and chase the black-and-white, zebra-striped meat truck from which they were fed. I was thrilled to find many of my theories being vindicated in practice – not least that the lions did not seem to feel any threat from vehicles passing through their reserve: they had plenty of space into which they could retreat, and clearly felt no pressure from all the mechanical intruders.

Altogether, prospects looked good, both for Press Day, on 3 April, and for Opening Day on the fifth. The Press Day went off without a hitch – but only just, for that morning, not long before the reception was due to start, a serious lion hunt broke out in an area we had christened 'Born Free Valley', where three males had started stalking Atlas, a solitary old-timer who had embattled himself alone in one of the huts. The ranger who tried to break up the hunt by driving in among the predators got his tractor bogged down, and he was rescued by a Land-Rover only a few minutes before the Press party was due to come through. Yet finally all our efforts were well rewarded, for we obtained enormous coverage, not only in the national and provincial papers but also on television.

One other party of pre-viewers went through the reserve before the official opening – the Longleat estate staff, who drove through in a special convoy. Extraordinary as it must seem to the millions of sophisticated lion-fanciers who nonchalantly frequent safari parks today, those people were absolutely terrified: they sat rigidly in their vehicles, tense with fright, keeping as far from the windows as possible and scarcely daring to look to right or left until they were safely out the other end. Such was the excitement and awe that this new kind of zoo engendered when it began.

The Lions of Longleat officially opened to the public at ten a.m. on Tuesday, 5 April 1966, and Lord Bath himself took the first motorist's one-pound note, which he later had framed. Our gate that first day was a modest 164, and perhaps it was just as well that no more people came, for even with those small numbers we realised that we were seriously under-staffed, and our communication network was not yet in proper order. Nor did Wednesday and Thursday give us any inkling of what a bombshell was about to burst on us.

Then, from Good Friday, the whole place went mad. Cars came at us all day, from every direction, in a never-ending stream. The lanes leading from the main road between Warminster and Frome became jammed solid, and on Easter Sunday some drivers waited five or six hours to reach the gates of the park. Local people began ringing up the police and threatening to sue us because they could not get out of their own drives.

The radio broadcast appeals to people to stay away, as it was clear by lunch-time that the place was saturated for the day.

Inside the reserve the staff, led by Richard, fought a desperate battle to prevent the whole place seizing solid. The main trouble was that people just would not drive through, but sat there hypnotised, staring at the lions, and this natural sluggishness was made more serious by the fact that the weather was dreadfully wet. No one could drive off the road on to the grass without getting stuck, and the queue of cars which had left the reserve and were trying to drive out of the main park built right back to the reserve itself so that at one period, for about an hour, every vehicle in the place was at a standstill. Some people of course became desperate to relieve themselves, and all over the reserve women were leaping out of their cars and squatting behind trees, often dangerously close to lions. There were breakdowns by the hundred.

Richard, who went into the reserve at half-past eight in the morning and emerged, shattered, at half-past nine that evening, was shouting over his walkie-talkie radio: 'You don't know what trouble I'm in here!' but there was nothing that any of us could do to help him. By seven p.m., it was already growing dark, and cars still stretched back half a mile from the gate, waiting to come in. But the park itself was still chock-full, and since vehicles were taking about an hour to pass through, we had no alternative but to turn the rest away. Even as it was, we left our decision rather late, and by the time the last drivers emerged from the reserve they had to switch on their headlights – a move which greatly disconcerted the men on the gate, who could not be sure, in the glare of the lamps, that no lions were heading for them at the same time as the vehicles.

By the time the last car had gone we were all utterly exhausted. But we had struck gold. Some three thousand cars went through the reserve on Good Friday alone, and we calculated that during the Easter weekend about fifty thousand people must have seen the Lions of Longleat. Not that we had got by any means everything right: it was clear that we must replace the inadequate buffer-fence, and that we urgently needed more staff. We also saw that we must maintain far stricter discipline, to keep people in their cars and to stop them opening their windows, for it was only by a miracle that no one had been attacked during those first few hectic days.

Another serious omission on our part was that we had no provision for people's dogs. Lions love killing dogs, and we had not foreseen that dozens of motorists would arrive with family pets yapping in the back seat. At once we realised that it would be highly dangerous to let any dog inside the reserve, as its presence would positively invite an attack, so we instantly created a rule that all pets must be left outside, and all through the Easter weekend there were hounds of every size and shape lashed to the approach fences, yapping their heads off with frustration. Obviously we needed proper kennels – and the building of some was at once put in hand. Another essential which we had overlooked was the permanent presence of a breakdown van and mechanic, for cars expired by the dozen with boiling engines, fuel-blockages or shortages, punctures, and various kinds of electrical fault, almost all the result of poor maintenance.

All these mistakes, however, were things that could easily be put right: the main idea was undoubtedly sound, and we knew we were on to a winner. Two days after the Easter holiday, having made all the extra arrangements I thought necessary, I went off to Kenya on a previously-arranged business trip, and when I telephoned home from Nairobi I got the shock of my life, for they told me that the park was covered by six inches of snow. Now, if ever, the elements were going to test my theory that lions would not need any artificial heat to enable them to withstand the British winter. I had maintained all along that, provided they had good, draught-free houses in which they could shelter, they would be better off *without* any extra heating, but it was not very nice to be stuck five thousand miles away wondering whether I was right. In fact my theory was vindicated, even though, in the first real bite of winter that they had ever known, several of the lions insisted on remaining outside all night, and in the morning Mary found four lionesses huddled together against the perimeter wire. In spite of the severity of the weather, none of them came to any harm – and since then all our lions have adjusted themselves perfectly to the British climate, the main difference being that their coats contain more oil than those of animals which live indoors, and so presumably give them better insulation and protection against the wet.

The flow of cars into the reserve at Longleat was such that we paid off the capital cost of the installations within four months, and altogether during its first season the park attracted 106,000 private cars and nearly two thousand coaches. By the middle of the summer we had decided that the project was worth expanding, and in September we began active planning for the following year. Our first major modification had been to split the lion territory into three separate sections, the aim being to reduce the number of fights, by which we were still plagued. But by the autumn I was looking for altogether new attractions, and one day while I was in America an idea struck me – that it would be a marvellous spectacle to have sea-lions in the lake. I love water, because it is hardly ever static, and gives a sense of movement. But the way to create *more* movement, I thought, would be to have sea-lions; and furthermore, on the island in the lake, we could have chimpanzees. Chimps have an inbred fear of water, and would never dream of trying to cross a lake, so that the island would make a perfect natural reserve for them, and would need no fences or disfiguring barriers.

At once I rang up Lord Bath and told him what had occurred to me, but at first he was not at all keen. I decided not to bother with the plan, and did nothing until I saw him again in England a month later. Then he asked what was happening about the sea-lions, and I said: 'Nothing: I thought you didn't like the idea,' to which he replied: 'Oh, no – I liked it. It's just that I take a few minutes to get used to all these new schemes of yours.'

So we went ahead and installed chimps and sea-lions, and in our second season the boat-trips on the lake proved a big attraction. The third year we opened a new section for giraffes, zebras and antelopes, and the fourth a monkey jungle, inhabited by baboons, which we more or less managed to control by running a four-foot-deep strip of slippery plastic material round the upper half of their fence. This last proved the most popular of all our innovations, and all the surveys we have taken (by asking visitors to fill up questionnaires) show that it is the monkeys that people most enjoy. Although they come in the first place to see the lions – still lured by the thought that the big cats are killers – when they arrive it is the baboons that delight them most – even though they play havoc with cars, ripping off radio-aerials, lamps and bits of chrome-plated trim. It is extraordinary what insults a family man will sit and happily watch his car undergo; nor does anyone seem embarrassed when sex breaks out uninhibitedly on the bonnet, right in front of the family's eyes.

As soon as the idea of a European game reserve was seen to be viable, there came on the scene an extraordinary number of people who had precisely the same idea as I had, but had been prevented from translating it into reality by some unforeseen mischance. One after another they came and told me that they, too, had been about to build a park, but that some piece of frightful bad luck had prevented them: either they couldn't find a site, or they couldn't get permission, or they couldn't raise the money. The height of hypocrisy was reached at a conference in Seattle about Zoos of the Future at which I had agreed to give a paper. Up came a man who said – surprise, surprise – that he had planned a park himself, and indeed had a model of it. Yet, in spite of all the work he claimed to have done, he still seemed to need an awful lot of information, and was constantly asking me questions about how we did this or that. All the time he was trying to pretend that he knew the answers before I told him them, but in the end he was properly caught out: in the course of my talk it became clear that we had monkeys at Longleat, as well as all the other animals. This was too much for the other man. 'Monkeys?' he asked in amazement. 'How on earth do you keep them in?' 'It's no problem,' I told him. 'You go and look on your model, and you'll find out.'

Not only was there a sudden rush of experts on safari parks: we were also bombarded by requests to instal parks in other places, many of them from the owners of run-down stately homes who wanted to rejuvenate their estates. But the place we chose for our second venture was not in the slightest run-down: far from it – it was one of the most splendid houses and estates in the country: Woburn Abbey, in Bedfordshire. After Longleat had established itself, Lord Bath and I were invited to lunch by the Duke and Duchess of Bedford, whom I had met once or twice before. The meal was a pleasant enough occasion, although it was obvious that a fly was being thrown over me. The Duke asked, for instance, why I had done a park with Lord Bath, rather than with him, and I just said that Longleat was a lovely place to have animals in. But the whole conversation was on this level, light and flippant, and no serious proposition was put forward. It was perfectly clear, however, that the Duke intended to have a park himself, and after lunch I asked Lord Bath whether he would mind if I did one at Woburn too. His reply was characteristic: he would far rather I did it than anyone else, he said. And so, when in due course the Duke asked me if I would build him a park as well, I readily agreed.

We formed the same sort of partnership as at Longleat, sharing the expenses and profits fifty-fifty, and the agreement included the same clause as I had had before, laying down that the landowner would not interfere with the management of the animals – a limitation demanded by my insurance company. In many ways Woburn was an even better site than Longleat: the park was perhaps not quite so spectacular, but the hills were gentler and the land drier, and the place was within easy reach of London and the Midlands. Besides, the house already attracted a far higher number of people than Longleat – nearly half a million a year, as opposed to only 130,000. These various factors led us to plan the safari park on a much more ambitious scale, and the initial capital cost came to much more than £400,000.

The fences and roads were laid out by Richard, who had an excellent eye for country, and no particular problems presented themselves. Nor, this time, did anyone make the slightest fuss: already Longleat had made the practice of driving about among lions so widely accepted that the idea of a protest movement or campaign against the new park seemed utterly ridiculous. The worst problem was the price of the animals. The success of Longleat had prompted other operators to enter the field, principally the Smarts (another former circus family) who opened their highly successful safari park at Windsor, and my brother Dicky, who installed a lion park for Lord Gretton at Melton Mowbray. The result of this sudden expansion was that the price of lions rocketed: from being available at ten pounds apiece, they suddenly shot up to two hundred and fifty pounds.

At Woburn everything seemed set for a repeat of our hit at Longleat: a perfect site, a famous house, and a beautiful piece of land for the park. And yet, when we opened at Easter 1968, we got a nasty shock: instead of doing record business, we went off to a very slow start. We had expected to be absolutely packed, but in fact relatively few cars appeared. Longleat, meanwhile, still *was* packed, although much further from large centres of population: we could not make out what had gone wrong. In an attempt to find out, we sent a man on the road, touring all the factories with instructions to book up coach parties. Back he came with a gloomy report: he could get as many parties as he liked for Longleat, but practically none for Woburn. The people he had talked to seemed to think that Woburn was some sort of gimmick, infested by nudists, and nobody wanted to be bothered with it (in fact the Duke *had* allowed a nudist camp to be held in the park, but only for one day).

Whitsun came and went, and we were still in serious trouble: the flow of cars was nothing like what we had hoped. Then, in desperation, we decided to bring forward all the television advertising we had planned for the rest of the summer and to fire the whole lot off in two weeks. In the first week we spent about six thousand pounds, and we were relieved to find that our takings went up by thirty per cent. In the second week we spent the same amount again; but before we could assess the effect of the second heavy dose, there occurred an event which blew all our agitated calculations to the winds: our first serious accident.

In a Mini, driving through the lion reserve, was a family which persistently defied the ranger's orders to keep the car's windows closed. Twice the man told the people to shut the windows, and twice they opened them again – and then, by extraordinary negligence, the mother allowed her little girl to wriggle about so much that her behind stuck out of the open window. In a flash a lioness called Twiggy (named after the model, because she was so thin) dashed at the car and took a swipe with her paw at the wriggling target. The incident was over in a few seconds, for the ranger saw what was happening, drove his Land-Rover at the lioness and pushed her away. But the girl was seriously mauled, and afterwards had to spend a year in hospital receiving skin grafts.

By no stretch of the imagination could the accident be said to have been our fault. The reserve was plastered with notices telling motorists that they must keep their windows shut, and that the lions were dangerous. Even so, next day we made headline news in all the national newspapers. Had something like this occurred during the first few weeks at Longleat, when opinion was still hostile, it might have been a disaster for us and led to the closure of the park; but now, at Woburn, the effect was miraculous.

Twiggy, by that one swipe of her paw, did more than any amount of advertising could have done: she put the place on the map, and suddenly, instead of waiting anxiously for customers, the park was over-run. My theory about danger attracting people was strikingly borne out, for almost everyone who came demanded to see the lion who had injured the child; but in fact we had already taken Twiggy out of the reserve and moved her elsewhere – not because she was any more aggressive than the rest of the lions, but because I did not want to be accused of deliberately keeping a dangerous animal for profit.

Twiggy, in fact, had done what any normal lion would have done: as I have said, the animal's perception is amazingly keen, and it has nothing to do all day but watch for any small variation from its normal routine. For the lions in Woburn the normal routine is to see streams of closed tin boxes rolling past them – and of this they take no notice at all. But if a crack appears in one of those boxes, the temptation to have a go at it is irresistible.

After the accident, Woburn never looked back, and the park now gets some 350,000 cars a year. Its proximity to London Zoo's offshoot at Whipsnade inevitably gave further impetus to the controversy about ways of keeping animals, and the zoo establishment maintained its studied hostility towards us. Its members were too crafty to become involved in open argument about what we were doing (several newspapers tried in vain to draw them out), but they maintained a steady dribble of negative criticism. Every time we tried something new, like putting the sea-lions or the hippos into the lakes at Longleat and Woburn, we were told that the animals would die of cold. Then, when the animals did not die of cold, we were told that, even though they might survive, they could not possibly breed in that kind of temperature. Only when both sea-lions and hippos bred successfully did the carping finally cease.

Another cause of annoyance to old-fashioned zoos was the fact that many people, having seen lions, giraffes, elephants, and the other species at large in the parks, began to complain that it was cruel to confine animals of this kind in small cages. As I have explained before, I do not entirely agree with this view, for I believe that most animals can live contentedly in a small area provided they are well looked after. At the same time, once one has seen a herd of fifteen giraffes cantering freely around in a fifty-acre stretch of parkland, one does not enjoy seeing four or five pacing slowly up and down a few square yards of gravel in Regent's Park. From the ordinary visitor's point of view, the old-fashioned zoos compare poorly with the new ones, and the sheer volume of traffic at Woburn proved conclusively that there was a strong public demand for zoos designed specifically for the motor-car age. Oddly enough, the enormous volume of business that we began doing at Woburn did not have too bad an effect on the numbers at Whipsnade, only a few miles away. Indeed, after the first novelty of Woburn had worn off, we seemed to have the opposite effect – of increasing interest in animals generally and attracting people to both places.

Not that this stopped us having a number of bitter arguments with zoo people. Their main criticism has always been that I use animals for commercial purposes – a practice which, they imply, is somehow morally reprehensible. I *do* use the animals for commercial purposes, it is perfectly true: the parks are commercial enterprises, designed to make a profit. But what is wrong with that? Only a hypocrite – it seems to me – or a person with very muddled ideas can believe that using animals is a crime.

If one considers all the other animals that humans exploit without worrying, the absurdity of the argument quickly becomes apparent. Sheep and cattle are the most obvious examples: we rear millions of them with the express intention of slaughtering them as soon as they are old enough to provide good meat – yet no one except a relatively small vegetarian minority considers this a criminal practice. I have no intention of slaughtering any of my lions or giraffes: far from it – by aim is to cosset them and give them the best possible life. But a still better example is that of horses: thousands of horses are bred and trained for racing or show-jumping – yet how many people consider the practice morally reprehensible? What difference is there, morally, between keeping a racehorse in the hope of it making money and keeping lions in a park? The one difference I can see is that the lions are under far less strain.

The racehorse, in fact, is a particularly good case to think about, for it offers living proof of how confused our ideas about animals can become. Another complaint which people sometimes make against the parks is that it is cruel and unnatural to keep animals like giraffes in an alien environment. Giraffes, they say, belong in Africa, not in England, and it cannot be right to make them live here. Yet consider the racehorse, and reflect for a moment on the fact that it is *not an indigenous animal*. Where did it come from? Africa. The whole foundation of our present blood-stock was a series of stallions and mares imported from North Africa – animals no more British than a lion or a tiger. They were *relations* of our own horses, it is true, just as the wolf is a relation of the dog, but they were originally one hundred per cent foreign. In this respect I do not see that there is any difference between a horse and a giraffe: it is simply a matter of time, and of our having grown used to the fact of having African-type horses about. A hundred years from now no one will think it odd to see giraffes about in British parks, for by then they will be thoroughly used to the idea, and a good British strain of giraffe will have developed.

CHAPTER TWELVE

Branching Out

WITH Woburn well established, offers of further sites came in from all over the country, but in the end it was we who found a suitable place and suggested ourselves to the owner. Our choice was Knowsley, Lord Derby's house and park on the outskirts of Liverpool. We had been thinking about the north-west for some time, since for one thing it was well away from our other two parks and for another it was one of the most densely-populated areas in the whole country. Then I heard that Knowsley might be suitable, so I drove in one day to have a look at it.

That was an astonishing experience. The middle of Liverpool was only eight miles away, and the teeming houses seemed to have flooded outwards from the city centre right up to the smoke-blackened sandstone wall of the park. But inside the wall was a three-thousand-acre oasis of silent greenery, absolutely deserted. I drove about the estate roads for a bit, then parked the car and went for a walk; after a while I got lost, and the only people I could find to help direct me in the whole of that huge open space were two men digging a hole. Nobody asked me who I was or what I was doing: nobody except those two diggers even *saw* me, for the place was as empty as a desert – an extraordinary contrast with the overcrowded world immediately outside.

I saw at once that this would make a perfect site for us – masses of space, and millions of customers right on the doorstep. So I approached Lord Derby through his estate agent, and presently heard that Lord Derby was keen to go ahead. But for some reason the agent seemed extremely reluctant to let us meet Lord Derby face to face, and for months he prevaricated, saying that he did not think the time was quite ripe, and making similar excuses. When at last we did meet Lord Derby himself, he could not make out why we hadn't come to him weeks before.

Again we formed a partnership, sharing the costs and profits on our normal fifty-fifty basis. But this time I made a serious mistake in accepting the piece of land that Lord Derby first offered us for the park: I could see that it was wet, and might need draining, but I did not realise soon enough quite how much of a bog it was: in the winter, as soon as the bracken went down, the place became a black quagmire, and we had to spend an immense amount of extra money on drains. Reckoning that the potential of the place would never be quite so big as Woburn's, we planned at first to spend about £350,000; but then we found that several of the enclosures got into such a filthy mess that we had to lay out a further £80,000 on drainage. Only now, five years later, is the whole of the park beginning to look as it should.

Another major snag cropped up with the roads. Against my better judgement I agreed with Lord Derby that we would use rubble from one of his own quarries as a foundation. I was afraid that the stone might not be hard enough, but in order to humour the owner of the land I agreed to use his home product. This proved a thoroughly bad idea, for the rubble contained far too much earth, the roads sank, and we had to build the whole lot again at enormous extra cost.

The error highlighted one of the main difficulties we experienced in setting up the parks. In all the early ones the pattern was the same: the owner and his family had lived in the place for generations and were used to running it their way. In we came, commercial men with a lot of ideas of our own about how to run things – and inevitably many of the ideas were different from the ones that had prevailed before. At Longleat our project had caused much resentment among the estate workers, who naturally did not like having their established habits knocked for six, and did not appreciate our arrival until they saw how much extra money they could earn from it.

But I think the invasion was worst of all for the owners, since it meant such a drastic change in the appearance of a piece of land to which they were deeply attached, and I always went out of my way to accommodate any of the proprietor's ideas that seemed possible, so as to give him the feeling that he had at least contributed to the new system and had not had it thrust upon him wholesale by insensitive outsiders. The last thing I want is for the owner to feel that he has been steam-rollered, for the place is his home, and he is going to have to live with it. At Knowsley, however,

I went too far in this humane direction over the roads – and a very expensive error it proved.

Apart from that – and from the wetness of some of the land – we had little trouble in building the park. The police kept telling me that, no matter where I might have opened a park before, this one was going to be the worst by miles so far as vandalism went. Everything would be smashed or stolen while we were building, they told me, and even when the park opened we should want to count our lions pretty carefully, or else we should find that they were being stolen too. In fact we never had the slightest bit of trouble, either before or after the opening, apart from one or two youths who got boisterous, just as they might anywhere else. Lord Derby himself took a close practical interest in everything we did, and it was pleasant both for him and for us to reflect that this was not the first zoo that his family had built. Just as the earlier Dukes of Bedford had kept giraffes in stables behind the Abbey at Woburn during the nineteenth century, so Lord Derby's ancestors had formed a private collection of birds and animals, including kangaroos, in the park at Knowsley, and among the jumble in one of the outbuildings we found some lovely Victorian cast-iron birdcages.

The opening of Knowsley was by no means an unqualified success, for the lion sections quickly became a hideous black morass, creating a most unfavourable impression and bringing us a lot of complaints. The lions, however, evidently suffered less than anyone else, for even though most of their enclosure was boggy, they had plenty of dry places to which they could resort if they wanted, and as it was they spent a lot of time racing about in the water, which they obviously loved. That made them look even worse, of course, for they were usually covered in mud, but none of them took any harm from it – we did not have a single case of pneumonia or even a cold.

Another serious set-back occurred when some of the lions pushed their way under the dividing fence between their own enclosure and that of the cheetahs early one morning. There was no danger to the public, for the animals were still within the main fence; but there was mortal danger to the cheetahs, since most of them were too stupid to run away, and the lions killed three of them before the alarm was raised. I do not think the lions were particularly vicious characters: it was just that they saw the cheetahs and fancied a chase at them. But to us the accident was something of a disaster, for we had lost three animals worth twelve hundred pounds apiece, and – even worse – we had wasted a great deal of effort in keeping them in quarantine and fitting them into a compatible group. Of course the set-back also gave our critics fresh ammunition – and from the way they carried on you would assume that we had put the lions at the cheetahs on purpose! In a way it *was* our fault, as we had decided that it would be safe to leave the cheetahs out at night – but one can only learn from experience.

Once Knowsley shook off its early difficulties, it did better and better. In 1973 we added a large new section (on a perfect piece of parkland) for elephants and tigers; we have drained the original lion enclosures and killed the bracken, and now the park is attracting some eighty-five thousand cars a year, besides some thousand coaches, which alone bring in some two hundred thousand visitors.

Our first park in Scotland, Blair Drummond, also turned out a success, although on a more modest scale. Here again we formed a partnership with the owner, Sir John Muir, and built the reserve on a piece of flat land overlooked by his Gothic castle of a house, perched on the side of the hill. Lying almost equidistant from Glasgow and Edinburgh, the park was nicely placed to catch both local and tourist traffic, and did well from the start. The only creatures which appeared not to like the site were the sea-lions, which escaped from the lake so persistently that in the end we had to give up trying to keep any there. One was found galumphing across country several miles from the park, and another was spotted by a fisherman splashing about the river some fifteen miles downstream. We never discovered what it was that drove them away: the temperature of the water was no lower than that of other lakes in which they lived happily, and although we had tests made we could not find anything in the water that seemed likely to upset them. All the other animals did well, and the fact that they were so far north seemed to make no difference.

Our second Scottish venture – the Loch Lomond Bear Park – was the first in which we came seriously unstuck. It was my fault entirely, for I allowed myself to be talked into it by the owner of the place, Patrick Telfer-Smollett. So enthusiastic was he about going ahead that in the end, after holding out for several months, I agreed. There was no denying that he had a most beautiful piece of land – a steep, undulating hillside, thickly wooded, rising straight from the north shore of Loch Lomond – and one could hardly imagine a more splendid place in which to see wild animals at large. The trouble was that, first, the site was too small for a full-scale wildlife park, and that, second, it was uncomfortably close to Blair Drummond, which was already well established as Scotland's Safari Park. My instincts told me that this was not the sort of place with which we should become involved – yet I was won over by the owner's enthusiasm and by the natural beauty of the estate.

We decided to go ahead on a limited scale, and devoted most of the space available to bears. They made a marvellous spectacle, especially in winter when they frolicked in the snow, and altogether their behaviour was most rewarding to watch: when they dug tunnels into the hill-side, for instance, they used a highly-organised system of communal effort, some of them mining at the face of the hole while others pushed the dirt back up to the entrance, and still others spread it about. Later we added a section of Siberian tigers, and they too made a lovely sight, particularly when they forged through the pond which we built in their enclosure. Quite soon, however, it became clear to us that the place was not going to make the sort of profit we needed; it was also clear that Mr Telfer-Smollett really wanted to run it himself, and so, early in 1974, we sold him our interest in the park.

Another park which we built but have since handed over entirely to the landowner is Lambton, on Lord Lambton's estate south of Newcastle. The trouble there is not shortage of land, but more a shortage of people: although close to the densely-populated areas of Tees-side, Lambton is rather far from other sources of visitors, and the number of customers has never reached the level for which we hoped. Another factor that works against the park is its name: by calling it 'Lambton Lion Park', we inadvertently gave the impression that it contained lions only, whereas in fact it has as many varieties of animal as any of our reserves. Yet there seems no reason why, in time, it should not do really well: the site is spacious and attractive, and all kinds of animals breed well there.

Our last British park – Bewdley, near Kidderminster – came to us in a peculiar way. One day an estate agent rang up to say that he had what sounded like an ideal property for us: a place called Spring Grove – 270 acres of park and farm land, with one large mansion, farm buildings, and planning permission for a wildlife reserve. He sent us the brochure, and after a few days thinking it over I decided to buy the place. So I took the brochure with me, drove up to Kidderminster, met the agent, and found that the ground did indeed seem perfect – a very attractive piece of land, with small but pleasant hills, right in the middle of a heavily-populated area and only twenty miles from the centre of Birmingham. I said I would buy it – provided that the council and the planning authority really wanted a wildlife park on that site – for I had no intention of getting involved in another Longleat-type row. As a next step I met the owners of the property, together with representatives of the planning committee, and again everyone seemed to be agreed: they felt it was important (they said) to preserve the place as an open space with recreational facilities, and they definitely did not want it built up.

Imagine my surprise, then – and my annoyance – when, a few days later, I heard that the place had been sold *to a developer*. I sent the agent a rude message, saying I was furious, but did not suppose there was much I could do about it, and more or less forgot the matter. Then, after another week, the telephone rang late one evening, and a man whose voice I had never heard before asked if I was still interested in Spring Grove. I said, 'No – not if it's already sold.' 'Well,' said the man, 'do you still want to buy it?' Thereafter he became more and more mysterious, refusing to say who he was, except that he was a lawyer and represented a client who was interested in railways. 'What's that got to do with it?' I asked. 'Never mind,' he said. And so it went on. But the conversation finished by him saying that if I arrived at Spring Grove armed with a cheque-book by eleven o'clock the next morning, I would be able to buy the place.

Up I went, and sure enough, I was offered the place again, and bought it – although the price had jumped twenty thousand pounds since I had last been involved. The man said to be connected with the railways was present at the meeting, but still he did not make his role in the proceedings at all clear, and when, several weeks later, he rang demanding a commission on the deal, I told him to get lost. We never discovered quite what happened, but presumed that someone had bought the place expecting he would get permission to build houses, and then, finding that no permission would be forthcoming, had got rid of it again. In any case, we were left with 270 acres of park and a fine early-nineteenth-century mansion.

Since we had already made a major capital outlay, we built this park under a different system, selling a lease of the site to an American company called Hardwick, with whom we were already doing business in other countries. The site still belongs to us, and we excluded from the contract the farm buildings, which Mary uses as a training centre; but the Americans rented the wildlife park itself, and we supplied the animals and the management.

The West Midland Safari Park opened in the spring of 1973, and in its first year did not do particularly well; but its relatively poor performance was due – we felt certain – to the fact that the Americans had insisted on charging visitors per head, instead of per car, as we had done in all the other parks. From a family's point of view the great value of a park has always been that a considerable number of people can be packed into one vehicle, and that they can all gain entry for a single fee (I have seen nine in one medium-sized car). It soon became clear that people greatly resented being charged individually, especially as Longleat, Woburn, and all the other parks were still on the old system. So in our second year at Spring Grove we established single charges there also – and business shot up immediately.

In all the parks I have gradually elaborated and augmented the original idea which we pioneered at Longleat. From showing just a single species – the lions – we have built up the variety of animals until each park has twenty or so species on display, mainly in large groups. But at the same time we have tried to provide enough extra attractions to give a family an entire day's entertainment. A thrifty car-load need not spend any extra money at all: if they simply drive into the park, see the animals and have a picnic (which we encourage) they spend only one pound fifty pence between them. But for those who *do* want them, we have laid on pets' corners, gardening centres, boating lakes, amusement areas and, in the case of Woburn, a cable railway which runs down to the lake and out over the water. Quite early on it struck me that one cannot expect children to sit in a car all day: they must have places to run about and ways of letting off steam, and it was with this in mind that I installed Astroglides – a form of giant slide which I first saw in America. Although they were horribly expensive, costing over ten thousand pounds each, they proved a good investment, for children of all ages took to them with tremendous enthusiasm. Nor, among adults, is it only parents who go sliding: members of the Liverpool police force have been known to disport themselves on the Astroglide at Knowsley.

As we built up our chain of British parks, the idea began to spread all over the world, and we, the pioneers, were called upon again and again either to give advice or to set up parks overseas in conjunction with local enthusiasts. The first foreign approach came from Holland, when representatives of the town council of Tilburg came over with a Dutch zoo director to ask if they might look at Longleat and copy what we had done. My reply was: 'By all means copy it – but watch out, because this isn't as simple as it looks, and it would be easy to get someone killed.' So the Dutch delegation came, and we entertained them at Longleat, where they professed themselves most enthusiastic. But later they wrote to say that, after seeing the scale of the precautions we had taken, and having thought the matter over, they were too nervous to build a park themselves, especially as they were a public body and could not afford to have an accident. What they would much prefer, they said, was that I should go out and build the park for them.

So I went and looked at the site, and found a stretch of land that seemed to me ideal. It was entirely different from the green hills of Longleat or Woburn, being almost completely flat and with only sparse vegetation and a few pine trees growing in the sandy soil. But the ground was bone-dry and looked far more like a bit of Africa than anything we had in England. Besides, the aim was to make the park part of a full-scale leisure complex, of which a large boating lake and swimming pool were already in operation. So we formed another company, fifty per cent owned by us and fifty per cent by the Dutch, and built fences and reserves very much on the British pattern. But the Dutch – who are much better at mass-catering than anyone in England – also built a typically smart and expensive restaurant on the edge of the lion reserve, so that people eating could look out through a glass wall and see lions prowling right beneath them.

Right from its inception the park was commercially successful, but after the first year an unpleasant row developed, when the Dutch council suddenly announced that my lawyer had made a fundamental mistake in drawing up our original contract, as this laid down that I owned fifty per cent of the park, and it was illegal for any private individual to own public land in Holland. We tried to explain that I had never claimed to own fifty per cent of the *land* – only fifty per cent of the company running the park, which was an entirely different matter. But it did appear that a mistake had been made, and the Corporation of Tilburg seemed delighted that they had scored off me. I, in turn, was not very pleased with my own lawyer, because by then he should have known the system backwards.

In any case, I took him over to Holland, and luckily, searching through the small print of the contract, I found a clause laying down that the council was not allowed to enlarge the park unless I consented. As we had already agreed that expansion was essential, I realised I had them over a barrel: if I refused, the enterprise would be crippled. And so, threatening them with this possibility, I got a new contract drawn up whereby ownership of the company passed entirely to the council, but they agreed to pay me a royalty on the gate-money (not the profits). Furthermore, they agreed to backdate the contract, so that I was paid a royalty for the first year as well. Today the park is running extremely well, with the council owning it entirely, but with us providing the animals and the management. I have never had another disagreement with the Dutch, whom I very much like and respect.

Our second foreign venture was in Canada, where we went into partnership with an Englishman who had settled out there, Colonel Dailley, and built a park at Rockton, not far from the Niagara Falls. This, too, went well, but we were not involved with it for long, because when a second Canadian park was projected, near Montreal, we had begun doing business with Hardwick, the American company, and it suited us to sell our interest in the first park to Dailley, and to let the Americans build the second. Now we supply both parks with animals, and get a small percentage of the profit, but are not otherwise involved.

In Europe we next went into France, where, at St Vrain, some twenty miles south of Paris, we found an establishment very like those at Long-

leat or Woburn – a *château* owned by a noble family and set in a lovely park, graced by an exceptional amount of water. There, as later in Spain and Germany, we built the wildlife park in conjunction with the Americans.

But of all these places none – not even Longleat – got off to such a phenomenal start as did the German park, at Hogenhagen, some fifty miles north-east of Hanover. Its building had been bedevilled by an enormous number of difficulties, not least the stringency of the German planning relations, which caused repeated delays. Another set-back was that the heavily wooded site was hit by a tornado not long before we began working on it, and hundreds of shattered pine trees had to be cleared away. So thick were the woods that several hundred sound trees had to be felled as well, for I insisted that there must be no square yard of ground which a Land-Rover could not reach in an emergency: otherwise, I foresaw, if a lion attacked someone it might drag the person off into an impenetrable thicket and kill him before help could arrive. The result of this terrific surplus of timber was, first, that we built an artificial hill out of the thousands of roots that had been dragged out and, second, that we used a huge number of pine trunks for making the heavy barriers, and the whole place has an agreeably rustic and natural look about it. Eventually all the delays and frustrations proved worthwhile, for when the park opened – the first on that scale in Germany – it was absolutely deluged with cars and people: six hundred thousand visitors went through it in the first three months alone.

I do not think it is any exaggeration to say that my original idea has gone all the way round the world, for, apart from the parks which I have already mentioned, we are building one in Japan, where the tops are having to be cut off two mountains to give us a big enough site, and planning another near Singapore. A Lebanese businessman has invited us to install one near Beirut, and we have had other inquiries from both South and North America. More than thirty-five million people have been through the parks in all countries, and I think we can fairly claim to have brought about a revolution in people's ideas on how large animals should be kept.

CHAPTER THIRTEEN

Animal Facts and Figures

FROM the human point of view the parks have undoubtedly proved a success, but even more important to me is the fact that the animals have benefited no less strikingly. Before we opened Longleat everybody prophesied doom: the lions will escape or kill each other or die, they said – or, if they survive, they will certainly not breed. Well, the lions confounded the critics, as did every other kind of animal which we let loose. Of all the species in the parks, the only two which have not yet bred are elephants and white rhinos, and the only reason these have not produced is that the animals are immature. All the rest – lions, tigers, cheetahs, eland, wildebeeste, giraffe, zebras, camels, hippos, chimpanzees, sea-lions, wolves, bears and baboons among them – have mated and bred freely.

The lions, in fact, have proved so prolific that we have now been able to start selective breeding, just as one would with domestic animals or cattle. At first we had several cases of the lionesses abandoning their cubs, or of the cubs being eaten by jealous mothers or even by young males, but we found that with better management we could eliminate most of the losses, and the Dutch park alone has produced more than 400 cubs in the first seven years of its existence. The rapid expansion of the parks has brought a tremendous demand for lions, but so well have our original stocks bred that the idea of importing lions from Africa (which we had to do for Longleat) quickly became obsolete. There must now be more lions in England than at any period since prehistoric times: I suppose there are at least a thousand in the country, as well as several hundred in Europe.

Since my original aim was to establish large breeding groups, I am particularly glad about this success; and still, to my mind, there is nothing to beat the spectacle of a large group of lions in the open. We put fifty into the German park for its opening, and a magnificent sight they made. We have now reached the stage at which we have to be careful about numbers, otherwise we shall have far more than we need; but in fact the lion population can easily be controlled by sensible management, including (we hope) the spaying of lionesses, with which we are now experimenting.

Anyone who considers this cruel or unnatural might compare the situation with that of dogs or cats: most people accept the need to control the dog and cat population, either by neutering the animals or simply by keeping them under control at critical times. If pets were more efficiently and humanely controlled, it would not be necessary for the R.S.P.C.A. and independent veterinary surgeons to put down some five hundred thousand dogs every year (which they do), besides an untold but larger number of cats. Our lions, I hope, are a great deal better managed than domestic pets, and suffer less accordingly.

Another small success is that we have almost entirely eliminated the disease known as 'star-gazing', in which a lion would keep looking up in the air, turning round in small circles, and falling to the ground. This used to be endemic in circus lions, but now, with good feeding and selective breeding, it has almost disappeared.

Our animals have put paid to many of the myths which used to shroud the business of reproduction in mystery. Many zoos, for instance, failed to breed chimpanzees, and the idea got about that chimps had to be shown what to do before they would mate properly. No greater piece of nonsense has ever been believed, as was demonstrated by Charles, a tame chimpanzee whom we had reared in our house and put on to the island in the lake at Longleat.

He first distinguished himself by rowing off, on his own, in the boat belonging to two of the park staff who had come to visit his island, leaving them stranded. But his real triumph was that he immediately mated with the wife we had given him – a chimp who had lived in a zoo and was altogether different from him in temperament, having never been close to humans. According to traditional theories, they were as unlikely to produce a baby as any pair we could have devised, yet they managed it. The only unhappy consequence was that when Charles's wife did give birth, she abandoned the baby, probably because she had no milk. Mary rescued the infant, christened him Fred, and brought him up on the bottle – since when the mother has become pregnant again.

We, too, brought up a chimp which had been born in one of the parks. Ours, which we called Simone, was the daughter of Alby and Mona, two very old animals whom we installed on the island at Blair Drummond. Mona has astonishingly strong maternal instincts, for although she never had any milk she carried her infants about clutched to her chest for months after they had died. For six months, in one case, she clutched the pathetic little black, dehydrated stick to her – a heart-rending sight. Five babies were born and died like this, and we kept hoping that a miracle would occur and her milk would come; but when the sixth arrived we could not bear to watch the tragedy happen again, so we anaesthetised the mother with a dart, took the baby away, and reared it at home. Oddly enough (for both her parents were hideous) Simone turned out very pretty, and altogether is a charming animal. She naturally became devoted to Rosie, but in an attempt to avoid the kind of mistake we had made with James, we put her into the zoo much earlier, hoping that by doing so we would help her to associate more easily with others of her own kind.

Another myth which we scotched was that hippos would never breed in a cold climate. Our first hippo, Arnold, took to the lake at Longleat as though he had known it all his life, and thought nothing of breaking the ice in the winter; nor did the cold in any way hamper his sex-life – he began mating when we thought he was still much too young. Unfortunately, although a highly attentive husband, he proved a disastrous father, for no sooner was his first baby born than he attacked and killed it. Since then he and his mate have produced two more offspring, and in both cases we have had to remove the baby and rear it by hand to prevent a repetition of the infanticide. As far as we can tell, it is jealousy of the third party that makes Arnold so vicious, but we have found no way yet of curing it.

Altogether he and his mate gave us a considerable amount of trouble. At first they were fenced into a small enclosure on the bank of the lake, but Lord Bath became keener and keener to let them out, and I decided it would be all right to do so, thinking that they would not wander far, even though the lake as a whole was not fenced. I proved entirely wrong, for they began wandering miles in the night, just as hippos do in Africa, and Roger, at the park office, kept getting agonised telephone calls at all hours. Sometimes it was the gardeners from Longleat House, complaining that the hippos had been through the rose-beds again, and sometimes it was customers at the Bath Arms, a mile up the road, saying that even though they admitted that they had had one or two, they still thought we ought to know that a hippo had just sauntered past the window. The animals – and their tracks – were so enormous that when damage was done there was never any point in trying to pretend that some other creature had been guilty. Eventually we decided that there was no alternative but to fence the entire lake.

Over the years the parks have given us many fascinating insights into animal behaviour. The lions, for instance, soon realised that although the grassland of the park was their territory, the roads belonged to the cars. As long as the cars stay on the roads, no lion takes the slightest notice of them – as anyone who has driven through one of the reserves will testify. But let a strange car go a few yards off the tarmac, and immediately some of the lions attack it, chasing it, biting at the tyres and striking out at the mudguards.

I had noticed this already in the south, before we opened at Blair Drummond, but the truth of the observation was brought home to me when Princess Anne visited the Scottish park. I drove her round in a brand-new Land-Rover, and to give her a close-up view of a lion I went on to the grass, towards where a group were lying. At once they leapt up, regarding us as an intruder, and one charged up against the front of the vehicle with a thump. The Princess was never in any danger, but the incident certainly livened up her morning.

One fact about the lions which is far from obvious is that they are much wilder now than when they went out in the first place. They *look* completely tame, I know, especially on warm days when they lie dozing in the sun; but their appearance is dangerously deceptive, for in fact they are not tame at all. When the parks opened, most of the lions were used to close association with humans, having lived in zoos or circuses; but now, not having been directly involved with people at all, they have reverted to a much wilder state, and we find that if we have to tranquillise one, to move it to another park, it is liable to go berserk when it regains consciousness inside its travelling-box, because it cannot stand the close proximity of humans.

I have always had a great fear that someone, failing to realise this, will get out of his car, with fatal results, and it was in an attempt to keep the danger firmly in the public eye that during the second summer at Long-leat we took some pictures to show what might happen if a person appeared on foot in the lion enclosure. A B.B.C. camera crew were making a film in the park, and they had brought some tailors' dummies with them, so one day we took a couple of these into the reserve, stood them round an old car which we had towed in, and withdrew out of the way. The result was spectacular. The leading males instantly sprang at the dummies and ripped them to pieces, dragging bits of them off into the trees and uttering growls of excitement. In a few seconds there was nothing left except debris, and the lions had also smashed to pieces some dummy luggage which we had stacked on the car's roof. Their reaction would have been the same – I am certain – if real human beings had stood there: they would have attacked out of sheer inquisitiveness and irritation at the presence of alien figures, rather than because they thought the humans consisted of meat walking about. Only when a lion bites into a human and tastes blood does it realise that here is a potential meal.

In any case, the pictures taken of the incident were first-class: appearing on television and in many of the newspapers, they did a great deal to keep the public aware of the facts of leonine life. Later, the accident to the girl at Woburn gave people another salutary shock; but always, as time passes, there is the risk that somebody new will come along who thinks he knows best.

Only last year one of the staff at Longleat was seized by the arm when he carelessly stuck his elbow out of the window of his Land-Rover.

A striking difference has become apparent between the attitude of the carnivores towards their keepers and that of the hay-eaters, like giraffes and antelopes. Whereas the lions and tigers regard their keeper with respect, and accept him as the boss – just as they would in a circus – the hay-eaters are definitely jealous of the people who look after them. The one fatal accident which has happened in any of the parks occurred at Woburn when a bull eland gored his keeper as the man was trying to herd him in for the night. The eland had no intention of leaving his females, and when the keeper tried to move him on by flapping his jacket, the animal darted at him and with one thrust of his horns flicked him up in the air. Although the man managed to get back to his vehicle, he died inside it, gored all through the middle. That animal had never given trouble before; but, like any bull, he was touchy about his females, and his attitude (I am sure) was very much like that of a farm bull, who can often be more of a menace to the farmer who looks after him than to anyone else. Like the bull, an eland or giraffe develops a particular jealousy of his keeper, and is irritated by the fact that the man is always loitering about, moving him on and challenging him (as he sees it) for the supremacy of the herd.

I am certain that after a while he begins to say to himself: 'Why's this person always hanging around? Why doesn't he (or she) go away?' The result is that whereas in the lion and tiger sections the main threat would be to the members of the public if they got out of their vehicles, in the antelope and giraffe sections the public are perfectly safe to mingle with the animals, and it is the keepers who are at risk.

The behaviour of the giraffes at Longleat has demonstrated this perfectly. Several of the females have given birth in the middle of hundreds of visitors, taking not the slightest notice of all the spectators. But one bull giraffe, who ignores the public entirely, has several times chased his keepers with vicious intent. Once he went for the girl looking after him and chased her round and round a tree, trying to knock her down, until she was forced to call for help on the radio. The moment she was picked up and taken off in a vehicle, the animal calmed down and returned to his grazing among all the picnickers. Again, I have seen visitors in several of the parks taking pictures of each other with their arms round the neck of one of the Ankole bulls – huge creatures with enormous horns nearly five feet across. The animals do not seem to mind in the least. Yet if their keepers tried to take any such liberty, they would knock them down in a flash.

Altogether, the giraffes have given us surprisingly little trouble, and now they are breeding well. But it cost us thousands of pounds to establish good breeding groups, for many of the animals with which we started were unsuitable. A big factor in our success has been the skill of one of our vets, Gerard Bembo, who has made himself a master of the difficult art of anaesthetising giraffes reliably. Until he devised a safe method (which includes sliding a long tube down the animal's throat, to stop it regurgitating and choking itself), to tranquillise a giraffe was to put its life in jeopardy. Now we can do it as a matter of routine, and one star patient (which injured its foot and had to have an operation) has been successfully anaesthetised four times. On another occasion Bembo flew to Spain and put a stainless steel plate into the jaw of a giraffe that had swung its head sideways against the door of its travelling box and had broken a bone.

All this seems to me further confirmation of the fact that there is nothing intrinsically odd or difficult about African animals: they *look* strange to us – certainly – and that is a large part of their attraction; but as soon as you gain a thorough knowledge of them, you can manage them as efficiently as sheep or cattle. All our giraffes, for instance, are checked regularly for diseases like brucellosis to which ordinary cattle are also prone, and at Longleat the giraffe-keeper, Alec Long, has learned his new skill entirely by practical experience, having previously been a farm worker on the estate. Now he is a considerable expert on giraffes, knowing the character and individual quirks of every animal in his herd.

I think that the giraffes have benefited more than any other species from the space of the parks: their size and height alone demand a great deal of room, and there is no doubt that the freedom of being in large reserves has contributed to the success of their breeding. With wildlife parks starting to open in America, they have become one of our most valuable animals, for the United States quarantine laws forbid the importation of giraffes direct from Africa except to a few specially-licensed zoos, with the result that a giraffe born in this country (and therefore exempt from the quarantine regulations) is worth £4,500. Even in Europe they are worth two thousand pounds apiece.

In getting the various species to breed, we have had most trouble with the cheetah. Apart from the three killed by the lion at Knowsley, we lost four at Woburn, all of which died from a liver disease which they had brought into the country with them. People began to say that cheetahs could not live in the British climate, but I myself am sure that the temperature has nothing to do with their health. Post-mortem examinations showed that the casualties at Woburn were all due to this imported disease, and the fact is that most of the cheetahs exported from Africa are in very poor condition as a result of over-population.

Many people are under the impression that the cheetah is in danger of extinction, like the tiger, but this is certainly not so in South-West Africa, where the farmers shoot the animals as vermin or trap them for sale to dealers, so thick are they on the ground. I know of one dealer in South-West Africa who has thirty or forty cheetahs for sale at any given moment. Yet only now, after several years of good feeding and careful management, are we starting to establish healthy breeding groups in Europe. One difficulty is that very few people have had any experience of cheetahs' mating habits, and theories vary widely about what (if anything) one can do to stimulate them.

Some people, for instance, believe that it is best to keep males and females apart for most of the time, others that the sexes should live together permanently. Nor is anyone certain what the proportion of males to females should be. Yet, in spite of these uncertainties, we have bred cubs in Holland and at Longleat.

Breeding apart, no animals have given us so much trouble as the baboons. For one thing they proved infinitely more destructive than I had expected, wrecking the trees in their monkey jungles and stripping a great variety of objects off passing cars, from windscreen wipers and radio aerials to spot-lamp covers, pieces of chrome trim, and even whole plastic roof-covers. At one stage, in fact, their depredations became so vicious that several coach firms refused to allow their vehicles through the monkey jungles any more. An even more tiresome trait, however, is that after a relatively quiet start many of the monkeys became incurable escapers, and no fence that we could devise would keep them in. Not even when we reinforced the smooth, vertical sheets that run round the upper half of the fence with electrified wires did we manage to stop them going over the top. Almost always, we found, one ring-leader would show the others the way: he alone would practise for hours, trying out every form of run-and-jump technique, while the rest sat round watching him. Then, as soon as the pioneer had perfected a method of scaling the barrier, the others would copy exactly what he had done and follow him over.

At Blair Drummond the monkeys established an absolute ritual, whereby they made a mass exodus from the park every evening, spent the night in the surrounding woods, fields, and gardens, and returned in time for breakfast, clocking in, as if for work, just as the postman delivered the morning mail. At first their antics were regarded as a joke, but they became less amusing when they repeatedly ate everything in Sir John Muir's garden, and their popularity reached an all-time low when, just as a funeral was about to take place in the local church, the graveyard was found to be full of monkeys, all sitting about on the tombstones. Reluctantly – for in many ways they are highly amusing characters – we decided that the baboons must go, and in most of the parks we have now replaced them with smaller and less destructive rhesus monkeys.

There has been a good deal of talk about the role which the parks can play in conservation. On the whole I think this has been exaggerated, for most of the animals which we own do not belong to endangered species. What I *do* think is important, however, is that we have shown that it is perfectly possible to keep large breeding groups of animals in parks, and reserves of this kind, it is already clear, could well be used as reservoirs from which to restock wild areas in which the natural population is dwindling. I do not believe that, as yet, there is any case for exporting lions to Africa and turning them loose there: there are still plenty of wild lions left – probably too many for the shrinking space available. With tigers, however, the situation is quite different: already wild stocks have reached a dangerously low level, and somebody should surely be considering the possibility of replenishing them with animals bred in captivity.

A great deal of nonsense is talked about tigers, not least about how difficult it is to get them to breed. Tame tigers, it is said, will never reproduce. This is rubbish: given the right conditions, they breed easily, and we have had cubs in Southampton and Plymouth. Nor is there such a shortage as many people make out. There must be at least five hundred tigers in Europe. We ourselves own two hundred, and I could go out tomorrow and buy fifty with no trouble at all.

It seems to me that Operation Tiger, the World Wildlife Fund's million-dollar scheme for saving the tiger, has been launched on entirely the wrong lines. Instead of setting up a series of reserves in which the animals will be protected, a far more effective plan would be to build one or two

large enclosed parks in India, on the lines of the ones in Europe, and in
them to breed tigers intensively so that a certain number could be released
into the wild every year. It seems to me essential that some positive means
like this should be devised of replenishing the wild stocks, for it is useless
merely to rely on trying to protect the animals that are left. As in Africa,
the pressures that force penniless and starving people into becoming
poachers are too strong.

It may be that at some time in the future the parks we have created will
enable a threatened species to survive, just as Père David's deer was saved
by the preservation of a herd at Woburn. If a rare antelope, for example,
were endangered, we would have the capacity to build up a herd several
hundred strong. In the nearer future, I hope that our elephants will start
to breed in three or four years' time. Until now scarcely any work has
been done on elephant-breeding in this country, mainly because bulls are
liable to be dangerous when in must, or on heat. But our experience
suggests that provided an elephant is tame – that is, provided he is handled
and worked regularly from childhood – he presents much less of a
problem. In the zoo in Hanover there is at this moment a mature bull
elephant which can be handled perfectly well. When our own elephants
grow to maturity we shall have to modify their reserves to keep them safe
for cars. We shall probably put the roads up on steep-sided causeways,
protected on either side by strips of rough gravel, which have the same
effect as cattle-grids since they are uncomfortable to elephants' feet.
Instead of simple perimeter fences, we shall have to use a combination of
fences, banks and ditches. We have already experimented with barriers
of this kind, and our ultimate ambition is to do away with the fences
altogether, or at least to sink them into moats below ground-level, so
that the illusion of total freedom is enhanced.

I do not think there is room for any more full-scale parks in Britain,
but there is certainly space in Europe – for instance in south Germany,
near Munich, and also in Switzerland – even though land there is
fiendishly expensive and hard to come by. In America, too, more parks
will undoubtedly be built.

One strange but pleasant fact about all this expansion is that the parks
seem to have taken little if any custom away from conventional zoos. Far
from sating the public appetite for looking at animals, we seem to have

stimulated it – and this of course pleases me very much, for animals have always been the main interest of my life, and I am delighted that so many people have shared my enthusiasm for them.

Seeing the public response to the parks, I have become increasingly convinced of the need to provide people with things to do and places to visit in their spare time. As working hours decrease and the amount of leisure grows, it is going to become more and more essential to channel the great mobility that the motor car has brought: otherwise, only chaos and the ruination of our few remaining open spaces can ensue.

It would be hypocritical of me to pretend that I saw this need clearly when I conceived the idea of Longleat. At that time my aim was simply to release the animals and to make money. It was only when I saw Knowsley that the realities of the situation came home to me. There lay this huge park, three thousand acres of it, quite empty, and just over the wall were the multitudes of Liverpool. The contrast made me realise that open spaces of this kind cannot remain closed to the public indefinitely. Sooner or later, I believe, every landowner with a thousand or more acres of ground not used for agriculture will be compelled to open it to public access, either by Government regulations or by simple financial pressure. Further, I believe that even the big open areas like Dartmoor and Exmoor will have to be brought under active management, either by the State or by commercial firms: unless proper facilities like camping sites, restaurants and lavatories are provided, the places will be wrecked by sheer weight of numbers – by people lighting fires, scattering litter, destroying trees and shrubs, and generally maltreating the environment.

What we have shown in the parks is that with good organisation relatively small areas of land can handle enormous numbers of people and, far from being ruined, positively benefit from the traffic. At Longleat, for example, more than a million people go through the park in a year, but because we provide them with plenty of interest and plenty to do, they create very little damage indeed. The income they generate not only keeps the park itself in good order, but also contributes substantially to the upkeep of the estate as a whole. It is no exaggeration to claim that the land at Longleat is in better heart now, with a million people enjoying a part of it every year, than it was before the park opened. There is no reason why the same sort of management should not be extended to places like Dartmoor: obviously one does not want to start fencing the moor in, or to regiment people more than is necessary, but I am convinced that a certain minimum of basic organisation will soon become indispensable.

I am always trying to think of new ways of entertaining large numbers of people on the land, and one idea on which we are now working is for a farm open to the public. Not only will people be able to come and see a farm in action, and to watch the various operations like ploughing, sowing and harvesting; the place will also be a kind of living museum. There will be as many types of pure-bred horse and cattle as possible – Shire horses and old-fashioned breeds which one sees less and less today. Also, I hope to have craftsmen like potters and wood-turners working on the premises as a continuous practical display, with their products on sale, and also to organise permanent practical exhibitions of agriculture through the ages, having some plots worked with stone-age tools, others with medieval and eighteenth-century implements, and others again with more modern equipments, right up to the present.

Such a farm, I believe, would be of interest to enormous numbers of town-dwellers, for we have often noticed that in the pets' corners of our parks the animals which cause children the greatest excitement are ordinary calves and pigs – creatures which people brought up in urban environments hardly ever come across.

CHAPTER FOURTEEN

A Family Business

In April 1975, when this book was all but finished, Richard was killed in a car crash in Uganda. For us, his family, his death was a shattering blow. Not only did it eliminate at one stroke the best animal-catcher in the world: far worse, it removed the whole point of our being in business at all. As I have said earlier, the essential fact about us is that we work as a family, and it was precisely because the family's endeavours seemed to be going forward so well that we had all been enjoying ourselves so much. But then, with the spearhead of the next generation suddenly gone, there seemed no point in carrying on any more.

By any standards Richard was an exceptional person. Tall, slender but powerfully built, outstandingly good-looking, always deeply tanned by the African sun, he had a devastating effect on girls of every kind. He was extremely versatile: a brilliant organiser, a good businessman, a first-class mechanic, he was also a talented artist and a bit of a poet. But the most remarkable thing about him was his energy: into his thirty-three years he packed the action and experience of a man of seventy. He was the hardest worker I have ever known.

It was he who laid out most of our game parks in England, on the Continent and in America: he had a natural eye for country and by his own efforts became an excellent landscape architect. Yet it was in Africa that he really found his vocation. He adored Africa, and Uganda particularly. That huge country, he thought, was the loveliest on earth. Although fully aware of the political uncertainties which beset the place, he ran our animal-catching safaris so skilfully and straightforwardly that we have always enjoyed the fullest possible co-operation from the Government.

Richard was marvellous at working with Africans. He spoke Swahili so fluently that he could joke with the men and tease them, and they in turn worshipped him as if he were a god. They thought he could do anything, and believed he had superhuman powers – which, in their terms, he had. For one thing he was absolutely fearless and cool in dangerous situations. If elephants were threatening, for instance, and all the Africans were shouting and rushing about, he would just stand there, ice-cold, and say in a quiet voice: 'I think this one's going to charge us in a moment.' Also, he was phenomenally strong. I have seen the Africans panic and run off, leaving him holding a young elephant single-handed; and once, as a crated elephant was being hoisted on to the lorry, he was similarly abandoned, whereupon he supported his end of the box with the elephant in it entirely on his own.

He made himself master of the art of catching all kinds of animals, but it was catching elephants that he most enjoyed. The risks undoubtedly contributed to the excitement: it amused him to see everyone else so terrified by the size and weight of the animals. Yet what he really relished was the technical mastery he had achieved of a difficult and dangerous operation. He knew elephants so well that he could read the character of every new captive, and predict how it would behave, within a minute or two of its coming to a halt.

A brief description of one day during his last safari will show the pace at which he lived and worked. Mary and I had gone out to join him, about three weeks before he was killed. Mary was determined to catch an elephant with him, and because there were none in the immediate area of the camp he decided that we would drive some hundred and sixty miles to a place where he could be certain of finding one.

We set out at five a.m. After a while a track-rod broke in the Humber lorry. Richard welded the ends together, and we went on. Having descended a hair-raising precipice into our chosen area, we caught two elephants in about twenty minutes. Mary was thrilled and immediately claimed one of them (a female whom she named Rosie) for her own. We loaded the animals up and started for camp, being delayed by one argument with some game guards and another at a petrol station.

For nearly a hundred miles we kept in convoy with the elephant truck. Then we pressed on ahead to camp, arriving about nine at night. By eleven the other vehicle had still not come in, so Richard went back in search of it – and discovered it seventy miles away, broken down, with a big end gone. He towed it the whole way back with his Range Rover, arrived at three a.m., decided to see if he could repair the engine there and then, dropped the sump, fitted a new big end, and eventually went to bed at five. Next morning he was up and about in perfectly normal form.

That was typical of him: he never slowed down. I knew, of course, that his work involved a high degree of risk, but it was pointless to tell him to ease up, for he absolutely loved what he was doing. He often said to me that there was no one else in the world with whom he would willingly change places.

Oddly enough, he rarely got hurt. Once he injured his knee in a struggle with an elephant, and on another occasion he was bitten by a hippo, which charged him when he was stuck in the mud and against which he could defend himself only by shoving his arm down its throat. Only a week before his death he had an extraordinary escape when the elephant-catching lorry turned over, pinning him (and an elephant) to the ground, with petrol running over him. By a miracle neither was his leg severed nor did the lorry catch fire: his luck seemed impregnable.

And yet, a few days later, it suddenly gave out, and he was killed when his Range Rover crashed at night on the three-hundred-mile drive back to camp from Kampala. Then, as never before, we saw the esteem in which the Ugandans held him. President Amin sent his personal helicopter to recover his body, and the police, army and medical authorities did everything that anyone could possibly have done. Richard was flown to Europe in the charter aircraft that brought back the elephants he had caught, and he was buried in the tiny churchyard at Wishford, only fifty yards from where he had been born in the wagon, and alongside my own father and our first son Jimmy.

Looking back, I realise what wonderful freedom he had. He had travelled the world over – to America, to Japan, to the Falkland Islands, to Africa more times than he could count. He could go wherever he wanted or buy whatever he needed. The organisation of the catching trips was entirely his.

And yet, when he was dead, we found that he owned practically nothing. Apart from a few suits, he had hardly any personal possessions.

He had never wanted money or had the slightest personal ambition: everything he had done, he had done for the family – for his mother and for me.

The shock of losing him was so great that at first I felt we could not go ahead with the business to which he had given his life. But then I realised that to throw away everything we had worked for would be the last thing he would have wanted. Had *I* been killed instead, he himself would have been all for pressing on with the things he knew I had planned and wanted done. So we decided, as the shock wore off, that somehow we must keep going.

We have come a long way since we went back on the road that dark November evening in 1922. In those days we owned nothing but the old traction engine and the living wagon with dart-boards fitted to its sides; if we took a couple of pounds in the day, we thought we were doing well. Today we run a business with a turnover of several million pounds a year. We manage five wildlife parks in Britain, owning half-shares in four of them; we run three parks in Europe, have interests in one in America and two in Canada, and are building in Japan. We run two zoos – in Southampton and Plymouth – and we have become the biggest animal dealers in the world, with an annual turnover of more than five hundred thousand pounds.

Yet I do not think that all this expansion has changed us very much. To me – at sixty-three – the most important thing is that we have remained a closely united family, bound together by exactly the same kind of loyalty that fired my father and his generation. As in his day, there are no such words within the family as 'mine' and 'yours': everything is ours, and we work together as a unit in almost everything we do.

We now have a comfortable house on the outskirts of Southampton. To us, born in wagons and used to living in very small areas, it seems a spacious home, but other people would not think it of more than moderate size. Certainly it is not at all ostentatious, even though we have improved it in various ways, not least by building a swimming-pool and sauna bath in the garden. We can – and do – easily revert to living in wagons, and Rosie and I keep a big modern trailer for holidays or for staying with my brother Dicky when his circus is on tour. At home we eat simply and drink very little; nor are we great ones for parties. On the whole I have very few indulgences – although I do admit to a passion for cameras, which I buy and collect insatiably.

As a family our one real extravagance is our transport. We all have powerful cars, and I have a Piper Navajo eight-seater aircraft with my own pilot. We do not positively need such expensive cars, but the aircraft *is* essential, for without it I could not possibly cover the distances which I need to travel in order to manage our businesses as I want them run.

The truth is that although I now live in one place, I am still a travelling man. I suppose the habit has been bred into me over generations, and although my reasons for travelling are now rather different from those of the old days, they are still sound commercial ones. I suppose I must cover several hundred thousand miles a year, constantly visiting our parks, looking at possible new sites or buying animals; but it is not just restlessness or wanderlust that keeps me on the move. Rather, the reason is that our business depends very much on the close personal touch of the family. We employ altogether some five hundred people, but I never like to think of them working *for* us: I would rather say they work *with* us, and I hope that our family atmosphere extends outwards into the business as a whole, so that everybody feels that he or she is working with *people*, rather than for some faceless organisation. Everyone knows me as 'Mr Jim', or 'Mr Chip', and they know that they can come to me with any problems they may have. The result is tremendous loyalty, which sometimes becomes so strong as to be embarrassing: in the park in New Jersey, for instance, the head animal man is someone who has been with us since he was a boy, and his motto is that he does not take orders from any man except me. Not surprisingly, the Americans do not much care for this attitude, but since he is one of the best animal men in the world, they feel bound to put up with it.

I hope I have not made us sound a dour family. In fact we are anything but that. We are not frivolous – and I am glad of that; on the contrary, my mother's energy and my father's appetite for work have been passed on through me to our next generation. Mary, for instance, could live a life of luxury if she wanted: she could have anything she wished, if she just asked for it. But instead of that she works like a beaver, training animals all day for circus acts of her own and in her spare time bringing up the constant stream of orphaned lion cubs, infant hippopotamuses or baby chimpanzees which pass through the Pheasantry at Longleat. John is no less industrious. He copes with a hundred different aspects of the business and runs a photographic firm in Southampton. It was a great joy to us when he married Ghislaine Bennett, a girl whom we could not like more. Only Margaret, our younger daughter, has gone out of the family business, having married a hairdresser.

In all our ups and downs of fortune, Rosie has been the perfect anchor for me, running our home with unfailing cheerfulness and backing me up in whatever I have chosen to do. It seems a cruel reward for someone who has shown such devotion that fate should deal her no fewer than three savage blows. To lose your father and two of your sons in accidents is a terribly unfair ration of bad luck.

I hope that Richard's death will not change us. The family has survived drastic setbacks before, and somehow it must again. One of Richard's less obvious characteristics was a liking for poetry, and he and I often used to discuss Kipling's poem 'If', which he particularly admired. He was fascinated by the fact that several of the verses might almost have been written about *us*, so closely did they describe our own experience, and while he was in Africa he wrote down some of the lines from memory in his pocket book. He loved the verse:

> If you can make one heap of all your winnings
>   And risk it on one turn of pitch-and-toss,
> And lose, and start again at your beginnings
>   And never breathe a word about your loss

for that was exactly what we had done twice in my lifetime. He also loved the line 'Or walk with Kings – nor lose the common touch' for that we had done as well. But most of all he loved the final verse, on which, without deliberately trying to, he found he had modelled his own short life:

> If you can fill the unforgiving minute
>   With sixty seconds' worth of distance run,
> Yours is the Earth and everything that's in it,
>   And – which is more – you'll be a Man, my son!

Index

acrobatics, 39, 66, 80
Adamson, Joy, 167
African Queen, The (film), 133
Alf's Button Afloat (film), 127
alligators, 130
Amesbury, 19, 22, 23–4, 25, 27
Amin, Idi, 209
Anne, Princess, 198
antelope, 138, 152, 153, 178
Arnold, 197
Arnold, Tom, 104–5, 116
Ashford, 94
Astroglides, 192
Atlas, 175
Attwooll, Hugh, 127
Auguste, *see* clowning

Babington-Smith, 'Babs', 95
baboons, 10, 78
badgers, 130
Barcelona, 169
Bari, Prince, 90
Barney, 33
Barnstaple, 50
Basingstoke, 36
Bath, 104
Bath, Marquis of, 159–79, 197. *See also*
    safari parks: Longleat
bawdy, 33–4, 117–18
Beachcomber (film), 127
bears, 66–70, 190; performing, 10, 69–
    70; wrestling, 13, 66–8, 77, 78–80
Bedford, Duke and Duchess of, 179–83.
    See also safari parks: Woburn
Beirut, *see* safari parks

Belfast, 115
Belgium, 111, 128
Belloc, Hilaire, 167
Bembo, Gerard, 200–1
Bennett, Ghislaine, *see* Chipperfield,
    Ghislaine
Bewdley, 189–91
Birmingham, 112, 189–91
Black, George, 78
Black Harold, 36
Black Spangle, 32–3, 35, 44, 47
Blackie, Ronnie, 104
Blair Drummond, *see* safari parks
Booth-Jones, David, 158–9
Born Free (film), 166–7, 169, 173, 175
Brighton, 71–2, 93
Bristol, 16, 165. *See also* fairs
Bruni, 66–9, 77, 78–80
buffalo, 132, 148
Bulford army camp, 20, 82–3

camels, 107
cats, Siamese, 130–1
Cawley, Mary, 88, 110–11, 158, 191,
    197, 211; animal training, 124–6;
    High Endeavour, 127; film work,
    127–31, 162; marriage, 169; Longleat,
    174, 177
Cawley, Roger, *son-in-law*, 169, 198
Ceylon, 103, 105
Chamberlain, Neville, 81
Charles, 196
cheetahs, 187–8
Chessington Zoo, 148
Chester Zoo, 170

Chevalier, Maurice, 127
Chico, 128
chimpanzees, 141–6
Chipperfield, Ghislaine, *daughter-in-law*, 212
Chipperfield, Mr (*fl.* 1684), 10
Chipperfield, James (b. 1824), *great-grandfather*, 9, 10
Chipperfield, James, *uncle*, 17
Chipperfield, James (1935–41), *son*: birth, 75; death, 88–9, 110
Chipperfield, James Francis, *grandfather*, 9, 10, 11, 65
CHIPPERFIELD, JAMES SEATON METHUEN (b. 1912)
　Family life: background, 9–19; birth, 9; £100 offered for, 9; childhood, 19–24; poverty, 20–4; lack of formal education, 25–6, 80, 83; 'soft and useless', 27; made to work hard, 27–8; travelling with family show, 25–29; in car factory, 29; 'telling the tale', 29–30; first meets Rosie Purchase, 49; elopes, 74–5; first son born, 75; son dies, 88–9, 110; Rosie injured, 89; takes prince home to tea, 90–1; son John born, 110; and Margaret, 110; Richard, 110; Mary, 110–11; death of father, 126; school trouble with Richard, 131–2; son John ill, 146; death of Richard, 207.
　Early circus career: conjurer's assistant, 30–1; stage collapses, 31; learns to walk wire, 31–2; runaway lorry, 36–7; clowning, 37–40; acrobatics, 38, 66, 81; troublesome elephant, 38–47; first works wild animal, 50–1; begins lifetime's work with lions, 53; one-day tenting, 62–73; hit by flagpole, 64; wrestles with bear, 66–8, 75, 77, 78–80; injured by bear, 67, 79–80; Teddy Bears' Picnic, 69–70, 75; Hastings zoo, 70–3; trouble with emu, 71–2; 'Circus Scot', 77; at Palladium, 78–80; works trapeze, 80; runs show during father's illness, 81

　War service: fails to join Army and Navy, 83; determines to join R.A.F., 83; lack of maths, 83, 84–5; sends photos to Air Ministry, 84; passed fit for service, 84; first interview, 84–5; goes back to school, 85–6; *High Endeavour*, 85; second interview, 86; accepted for training, 86; fails to arrange call-up, 86; called up anyway, 87; learns to fly, 87; passes out at Cranwell, 89, 91; cabaret, 90; flying fighter-bombers, 91–92; 85 Squadron, 92–9; talent for getting lost, 93–4; intercepting Doodle-bugs, 95; 'intruder', 95–7; eye trouble, 98; applies for quick release, 100.
　Post-war circus career: returns to circus, 100; buys tent, 101; clowning, 101, 103; builds up Big Show, 101–122; buys elephants, 103, 105; tent-master, 103; work for Tom Arnold, 104–5; gives up ringwork for management, 105; 'biggest show in England', 105–22; family farm, 109–10; transport, 111, 211; search for new acts, 111–12; decides to branch out on his own, 121–2; farming, 123; horse-shows, 123–4; Lydd zoo, 124; Carl Purchase Circus, 124; manages Fossett circus, 124; trains Taurus, 125–6; film work, 127–31, 162; first visits Africa, 132–3; eventful flight home, 133–5; travels with Tuareg, 136–40; embarrassment of goats, 137; tries to catch ostrich, 139; Southampton Zoo, 140–5; troublesome chimp, 141–5; Plymouth Zoo, 146–7; sells farm, 146; catching animals, 147, 148–56.
　Safari parks: idea born, 157; approaches David Booth-Jones, 158–9; then Marquis of Bath, 159; negotiations, 160, 161, 162; Longleat preparations, 163–75; opposition, 165–71; buys *Born Free* lions, 166; release day, 172–4; opening day, 175; more animals added, 178–9; Woburn, 179–83; Knowsley, 185–8; Blair Drummond,

188, 189; Loch Lomond, 188–9; Lambton, 189; West Midland, 189–191; foreign ventures, 192–4, 210; Princess Anne's visit, 198; farm project, 206. *See also* safari parks

Character and opinions: on cruelty, 57–8, 138, 165, 182, 196; kindness, 73; punctuality, 105, 121; on 'animal cranks', 119; ambition, 121; dogmatic, ruthless, single-minded, 121; love for Africa, 132–3, 153; on zoos, 153, 182–183, 196; abrupt and direct, 161; on safari parks, 195–206; on leisure, 205–206; passion for cameras, 211; loyalty to, 211

Chipperfield, James William, *great-great-grandfather*, 9

Chipperfield, John, *brother*, 17, 36, 100, 103, 121; works dogs, 75; drives horses home, 81

Chipperfield, John, *son*, 110, 143–4, 146, 212

Chipperfield, Margaret, *daughter*, 110

Chipperfield, Marjorie, *sister, see* Stockley, Marjorie

Chipperfield, Mary, *daughter, see* Cawley, Mary

Chipperfield, Maud, *mother*, 9, 97; marriage, 15–16; character, 26; Jimmy's elopement, 74–5; prince comes to tea, 90–1; children's success, 119

Chipperfield, Maud, *sister, see* Fossett, Maud

Chipperfield, Myrtle, *sister-in-law*, 121

Chipperfield, Richard (1874–1959), *father*, 9, 109, 211; character, 9, 14, 15, 17, 22, 27, 28, 63–4, 75–6; excellent clown, 14, 37–9; childhood, 14; command of audience, 14–15; painter, 15, 17–18, 19, 22, 25; 'Nothing that growls', 15; marriage, 15–16; goldfishes, 18; bear cubs, 18; buys cinema, 18–24; traction engine, 18; land and bungalows, 19; motoring accident, 20; poverty, 20–4; sells bungalows, 23; goes back on road, 24; buys horse, 32;

jack donkey, 33; lorry, 34; its brakes fail, 36; second lorry, 36; Shetland ponies, 36–7; elephant, 40–1; joins forces with Purchases, 48; sells elephant and ponies, 62; buys tent, 62; one-day tenting, 62–73; buys bear, 66; Hastings zoo, 70–3; Jimmy's elopement, 74–5; permanent winter quarters, 76; circuses in department stores, 76; 'Circus Scot', 77–8; stroke, 80–1; prince comes to tea, 90–1; children's success, 119; death, 126

Chipperfield, Richard (b. 1904), *brother*, 16, 50–1, 52, 74, 75, 100, 109, 121, 122, 210; flair for handling animals, 29, 37, 47, 75, 101; conjurer, 30–1; stage collapses, 31; hopeless as clown, 38; troublesome elephant, 40–7; takes over Purchase lions and tigers, 52–3; Untameable Lion, 58–61; thrown by bear, 68; terrible driver, 71; Hastings zoo, 70–3; trouble with emu, 71–3; ringmaster, 76; runs show during father's illness, 81; Home Guard, 89; buys tent, 101; builds up Big Show, 101–22; to Ceylon for elephants, 103; works horses, 103; 'biggest show in England', 105–22; family farm, 109–110; tiger riding elephant, 116; character, 121; trip to Africa, 135–6; Melton Mowbray, 180

Chipperfield, Richard, *nephew*, 54, 110

Chipperfield, Richard (1941–75), *son*, 88, 111; farming, 123–4; no enthusiasm for working animals, 124; school trouble, 131–2; travels with Tuareg, 136–40; Southampton Zoo, 140–5; Plymouth Zoo, 146–7; animal catching, 147, 148–56, 208–9; Longleat, 165, 169, 172, 173, 174, 176; Woburn, 180; death, 207; character, 207–8

Chipperfield, Rosie, *wife*, 51, 61, 90, 102, 121, 210; first meets Jimmy, 49; dances in lions' cage, 49, 51; elopes, 74–5; first son born, 75; son dies, 88–89, 110; accident, 89; works bears,

100; to Ceylon for elephants, 105; son John born, 110; and Margaret, 110; Richard and Mary, 110–11; Carl Purchase Circus, 124; troublesome chimp, 141–5

Chipperfield, Thomas, *brother*, 16

Christchurch, 101–2

cinema, 17, 18–20, 25, 125, 127–30; effect on circus, 17

Clark, Mr and Mrs Thomas, 15–16, 17–18

clowning, 9, 10, 11–12, 13, 18, 33–4, 37–40, 65, 75, 103, 104, 117–18; Auguste, 12, 38, 39, 40; White Clown, 12, 39, 40, 90; bawdy, 33–4, 117–18. *See also* entrées

Coed Porth, 43–4

condor, 128–9

conjuring, 10, 30–1, 32, 39

Corsham, 9

Coventry, 29, 41, 42

Cranwell: R.A.F. College, 89–91

Crazy Gang, 78–9, 127

crocodiles, 29–30, 128

Crossman, Richard, 168

Croydon, 49

cruelty, 57–8, 138, 165, 182, 196

Cunningham, 'Cat's Eyes', 92–4

Dailley, Col., 194

Daily Express, 167, 174

Dar es Salaam, 132

dart stalls, 25, 26

Dartmouth, 74

Denmark, 169

Derby, Lord, 185–8

Disney, Walt, 127–31

dogs, 10, 108, 177

donkeys, 10, 33; Man-Eating, 13. *See also* horses; mules; ponies

Dring, Rodney, 141

Duck Race, 13–14, 39

Edinburgh, 91, 189

El Al, 133–5

elephants, 40–7, 103, 104–5, 107, 120, 130, 153, 154, 156, 162, 182, 188; tug-of-war, 12; tiger rides, 116; catching, 148–51

emu, 71–2

Entebbe, 148

entrées, 12, 39–40, 104; egg, 12, 39, 90. *See also* clowning

Exeter, 105–6

fairs, 16, 18, 74; Bristol, 18; Burbage, 25; Mitcham, 49; Monmouth, 42; Nuneaton, 34; Oxford, 33, 50; Shrewton, 32; Southampton, 101; Weyhill, 25

Falkland Islands, 155–6

Fiery Jack, 118–19

film, *see* cinema

Fort Portugal, 148

Fossett, Maud, 17, 49; works pythons, 29; marriage, 48

Fossett family, 48, 49, 124

foxes, 140

France, 111; Foreign Legion, 137

Fred, 198

Frome, 167, 168, 175

Germany, 111, 118

giraffe, 153, 154, 178, 182, 184, 187; catching, 151–2

Glasgow, 188

goldfishes, 18

Grantham, 91

Gretton, Lord, 180

Grimsby, 122

Hagenbeck, 163, 171

Hale, 80

Hale House, 158–9

Hamburg, 163

Hanover, 169, 194, 204

Hardwick, 191, 193, 194

Hastings, 70, 72–3

Hatfield, 87

Heidelberg, 111

high-wire acts, 10, 31–2, 75, 106, 113

hippopotamuses, 132, 182

Hogenhagen, *see* safari parks
Holland, 111, 169, 192–3
Holloway, Stanley, 167
hoop-la, 18, 26
Horsemasters, The (film), 127
horses, 10, 15–16, 100, 107, 116–117, 128, 183–4; Talking, 33; *haute école*, 116; chariot race, 116; Roman riding 116. *See also* donkeys; mules; ponies
Houghton, George, 93, 146
Human Cannonball, 114–16
Hyde-White, Wilfrid, 127
hypnotist, 124

In Search of the Castaways (film), 127–129, 148
India, 161–2, 204
Ireland, 48, 67; Easter Rebellion (1916), 20
Israel, 133–5, 164

James, 141–6
Japan, *see* safari parks
Jerusalem, 169
Johannesburg, 133, 134
juggling, 10, 18

kangaroos, 71, 187
Kano, 140
Kenya, 132, 148, 164, 177
Khartoum, 134
Kidderminster, 189–91
King brothers, 162
Kipling, Rudyard, 212
Knowsley, *see* safari parks
Königsberg, 133
Kruger National Park, 168

ladder act, 31, 32
Lambton, Lord, 189
Lambton Lion Park, *see* safari parks
Leeuwarden, 97
Leicester, 124
leopards, 128
Lewis, John, 100

lions, 49–56, 57, 68, 71, 76–7, 100, 120, 130, 141, 157–85, 187–8, 191, 194; Untameable, 58–61
Liverpool, 185–8, 192, 205
llamas, 107
Llewellyn, Harry, 158
Loch Lomond Bear Park, *see* safari parks
London: Blitz, 95; Bush House, 84; Haringay, 104–5; Palladium, 78–9; Piccadilly Hotel, 44–7; Shepherd's Bush, 45, 127; Zoo, 168, 182–4
Long, Alec, 202
Longleat, *see* safari parks
Lydd, 124
Lyndhurst, 101–2

McKenna, Virginia, 167
magic, *see* conjuring
Manchester, 50–2, 76, 111; Eaton Park, 87
Mann, Tom, 148
Marlborough, 21; College, 110, 131–2
Marquis, 146
Marseilles, 136
Marsh Court School, 110
Martin, Millicent, 127
Maya the Magnificent (film), 156, 161, 162
Melton Mowbray, *see* safari parks
Methuen, Lord, 9
Mills, Hayley, 128
Mills brothers, 103, 105–6, 169
monkeys, 178, 179
Montevideo, 155
Montreal, *see* safari parks
Mottishead, George, 170
Mozambique, 132
Muir, Sir John, 188, 189, 203
mules, 128. *See also* donkeys; horses; ponies
Mysore, 162

Nairobi, 132, 164, 166, 177
New Jersey, *see* safari parks
Newbury, 25
Newcastle, 189

Nile, River, 135
Norwich, 10
Nottingham, 41

Operation Tiger, 203–4
Oran, 136
ostriches, 139
Oxford, 84, 86. *See also* fairs

Paignton, 87
Paris, 193
Parker, Jack, 92
patter, 11, 12, 39
penguins, king, 155
Penrose, 101
Penzance, 80
Peterborough, 15
pigs, 10–11; Fortune-Telling, 125
Pinewood Studios, 127, 142
Plymouth, 74, 75, 76, 81, 105–6; Zoo,
    146–7, 169, 203, 210
poachers, 153–4, 204
Pond, Lyn, 123
ponies: Fortune-Telling, 11, 33; Count-
    ing and Time-Telling, 11; trotters, 16;
    Shetland, 36–7; Joey, 65. *See also*
    donkeys; horses; mules
Poop, Flight-Lt, 84
Portsdown Hill, 36
Purchase, Andrew, 60–1
Purchase, Rosie *see* Chipperfield, Rosie
Purchase, 'Captain' Tom, *father-in-law*,
    49, 51, 212; joins with Chipperfields,
    50; killed by lion, 51–2, 111; Un-
    tameable Lion, 58–61
Purchase, Tom, *brother-in-law*, 68, 136–
    140
Purchase, Mrs Tom, *mother-in-law*, 143

Raluy, 114–15
Ransome, Mr, 126
ringmasters, 12, 13, 38, 39, 40, 65, 66,
    76
Rockton, *see* safari parks
rolling the globe, 18, 77
Rosaire family, 48

Rosie, 40–7, 49
Royal Society for the Prevention of
    Cruelty to Animals, 196
Ruhe, Hermann, 163

safari parks, 56, 157–206, 210; Beirut,
    194; Blair Drummond, 188, 189, 197,
    198, 202–3; Hogenhagen, 194, 196;
    Japan, 196, 210; Knowsley, 185–8,
    192, 201, 205; Lambton Lion Park,
    189; Loch Lomond Bear Park, 188–
    189; Longleat, 159–79, 180, 181, 182,
    186, 191, 192, 193–4, 195, 196, 197,
    198, 199, 200–1, 202, 205, 211;
    Melton Mowbray, 180; Montreal, 193,
    210; New Jersey, 211; Rockton, 193,
    210; St Vrain, 193; Singapore, 194,
    210; Tilburg, 192–3, 195, 202; West
    Midland, 189–91; Woburn, 144, 178–
    183, 185, 187, 191, 193–4, 199, 201,
    204. *See also* Windsor
St Vrain, *see* safari parks
Sahara Desert, 135–40
Salisbury, 20, 22
Sandy Down, 100
Sanger family, 48, 49
sea-elephants, 155
sea-lions, 108, 178, 182, 188
Seago, Edward: *High Endeavour*, 85,
    127
Seaton, George, *grandfather*, 15–16
Seaton, Mrs George, *grandmother*, 16
Seaton, Maud, *see* Chipperfield, Maud
Seaton, Uncle, 16
Seattle, 179
Sileby, 14
Singapore, *see* safari parks
slapstick, 12, 39–40. *See also* entrées
Smart family, 180
snakes, 29, 71, 130
South Georgia, 155
Southampton, 26, 76, 212; Zoo, 140–7,
    148, 162, 169, 203, 210. *See also*
    fairs
Spain, 111, 112, 118
Spring Grove, 189–91

Stockbridge, 76, 81, 85, 88, 90, 92, 98, 100, 109
Stockholm, 77
Stockley, Jimmy, *brother-in-law*, 94, 97
Stockley, Marjorie, 17, 94, 103, 121; ladder act, 31; works horses, 75, 103; marriage, 94
Stratford-upon-Avon, 50
Stromeier, 106
Sweden, 77–8
Switzerland, 111

Tahoua, 137, 139–40
Taurus, 125–6, 142
Tel Aviv, 134
television: effect on circus, 17
Telfer-Smollett, Patrick, 188–9
Tennant, Lawrence, 148
tents and tenting, 12, 62–73, 76, 77, 101–2, 108–9, 121
Tetbury, 75
Thames, River: freezes over (1684), 10
Thompson, Mr, 18
Three Lives of Thomasina, The (film), 130–1
tigers, 52, 56–8, 76–7, 100, 120, 130, 162, 188; riding elephant, 116; Siberian, 190
Tilburg, *see* safari parks
Times, The, 167–8
Totton, 101
tranquillisers, 56, 143–4, 153, 198–9, 202
trapeze, 80, 116

Trimmer, Bombo, 148
Truro, 101
Tuareg, 136–40, 162
tumblers, 10
Turrell, Frank, 67, 71–3, 79, 80
Twiggy, 181

Uganda, 133, 148–55, 207, 209

Varanand, Prince, 90–1
Victoria, Queen, 11
Vixen (Vic), 58–61

Walker, Clint, 162
Warminster, 175
West Malling, 92, 93
West Midland Safari Park, *see* safari parks
Weymouth, Viscount, 159
Whipsnade Zoo, 167, 168, 182–3
White Clown, *see* clowning
Wilson, John and Muriel, 85–6
Windsor Safari Park (Smarts'), 180
Wishford, 88, 90, 97, 125, 126
Woburn Abbey, *see* safari parks
Wodehouse, P. G., 168
Wolverhampton, 87–9
Woolston, 26
World War: First, 19, 76; Second, 26, 41, 48, 81, 82–99
World Wildlife Fund, 203–4
Wrexham, 43

zebra, 132, 178